F. W. DILLISTONE

THE POWER OF SYMBOLS

SCM PRESS LTD

334 02261 4

First published 1986
by SCM Press Ltd
26–30 Tottenham Road, London N1 4BZ.

Typeset at The Spartan Press Ltd,
Lymington, Hants
and printed in Great Britain by
The Camelot Press Ltd,
Southampton

Contents

To live symbolically spells true freedom
(Thomas Mann)

It seems clear to me that we cannot distinguish reality from our symbolization of it. Being human, we can only think in symbols, only make sense of any experience in symbols.
(Robert Bellah)

Man's simian chatter becomes noble as it becomes symbolic. Facts of existence are simply facts, no more than 'cacklings' of an inexhaustible garrulity until they become symbols.
(George Santayana)

CHAPTER ONE

Introduction

I

Why did you ever get so interested in symbols? This question from an enquirer set me thinking. *Christianity and Symbolism* first appeared in 1955, not long after I had ceased to give regular lectures on the doctrine of the sacraments. In preparing those lectures it had, I suppose, become clear to me that the Christian sacraments were not just isolated ceremonies unrelated to other forms of symbolic behaviour. What then were the connections? What in any case is the function of a symbol in human life and experience?

Just before writing these sentences, I was arrested by a phrase in a political commentary. Writing critically about Mrs Thatcher's Government, Edward Pearce described one episode, and then: 'That episode illustrates the way in which this Government functions. It is too slow on its feet to make obvious and advantageous gestures; it is hideously legalistic about technicalities; it has too little flair to understand the enormous importance of symbolic acts.'

The enormous importance of symbols. In a curious way this seems to be widely recognized today. Yet there is great uncertainty about how symbols come into being, how they exercise their power, and how they often fade away into insignificance. Can we agree about what a symbol is, and how it functions? The word is so frequently and so casually used that at times it is no more than a cliché. Can we be more precise?

II

Thinking back to my own teachers, it was in 1937 that I first heard a lecture by Paul Tillich, and I have been reading his writings and studying books about him ever since. The going is never easy but there is no possibility of escaping from his central concern. No theologian-philosopher of the twentieth century made the symbol so central for his whole interpretation of God-in-relation-to-the-world-and-mankind. A symbol was for him the supreme means by which humans could speak of God and of his actions. Any loose remark such as 'Oh! That's merely a symbol' was sure to rouse his ire.

Then I was fortunate enough (I do not remember how) to become acquainted with Professor Suzanne Langer's book *Philosophy in a New Key*. Not only did this book reveal to me the essential place of symbolic forms in all artistic disciplines, but it also introduced me to another of the great German exiles, professor Ernst Cassirer, whose whole interpretation of culture is built upon his recognition of man as the *'animal symbolicum'*. Only by using symbols can humans rise to their potential destiny.

Cassirer's magnificent set of three volumes, *The Philosophy of Symbolic Forms*, is enough in itself to show the 'enormous importance' of symbols, but it gains extended illustration through the works of Suzanne Langer, in which she wrote with great sensitivity about symbols in the world of the arts. By the time I read her works I was already becoming aware of the importance of certain leading symbols in poetry, drama and literature. With her help, the connection between feeling and form (and this meant symbolic form) became increasingly obvious, and the study of symbols a central concern.

III

This process was undoubtedly furthered by the appearance at that time of the successive parts of T. S. Eliot's *Four Quartets*. The complete poem, supplemented by experiences gained through visiting the rugged shoreline in Gloucester, Massachusetts, through standing beside the mighty Mississippi and through spending part of an unforgettable December afternoon in Little Gidding, has been one of the chief means by which I have apprehended the power of symbols. In addition, my move to Liverpool as Dean of the Anglican cathedral meant that for some eight years I was virtually inside one of the greatest symbolic structures of modern times (however its symbolism is interpreted). Moreover, the late 1950s was a period of marked developments in the theatre, and in particular the plays of Arthur Miller (rich in symbolic significance) made a profound impression on me.

In the world of literature, it was my discovery of Patrick White's novels which extended my sense of the importance of symbolism still further. The symbols of the vast Australian desert and of the virgin soil of the outback were impressive enough, but no symbol that I have encountered in modern novels has seemed so powerful to the imagination and so wide-ranging in its implications as the chariot in *Riders in the Chariot*. This is one of the oldest of religious symbols (Elijah, Ezekiel), deeply revered in the traditions of Judaism and at the same time capable, in White's novel, of pointing towards the mysterious and the infinite, both in Nazi-oppressed Germany and in the newly-mechanized industrial plants of Australia.

IV

I may mention one other aspect of earlier experience. In 1931 I went to India to engage in theological education (this project had to be abandoned owing to my wife's ill health). I tried to learn a little Sanskrit and spent a long time with Urdu, but I am a poor linguist, and consequently my knowledge of other religions and other cultures has had to be gained at second hand. Nevertheless I have tried to gain some acquaintance with the symbolic forms of adherents of non-Christian faiths, and have valued in particular the writings of Gerardus Van der Leeuw and Mircea Eliade. Their massive researches into the history of religions have produced a wealth of material, and this has been supplemented by innumerable investigations of individual tribes by leading social anthropologists. It would be an oversimplification (but not too far from the truth) to say that historians of religion and social anthropologists (and many sociologists too) have, over the past half-century, been mainly concerned with the interpretation of symbols. At least symbolic forms have been at the centre of their interest, and I have followed some of their investigations with admiration and profit.

Other explorations of the ways in which cultures have, as it were, expressed themselves remain in the memory. Erwin Goodenough's splendid series of volumes *Jewish Symbols in the Graeco-Roman Period* seems to me to constitute one of the major achievements of twentieth-century scholarship. I also greatly admired Helen Dunbar's *Symbolism in Mediaeval Thought*, showing how the whole outlook of mediaeval Christianity was governed by the interpretation of symbolic forms. I felt the impact of Marshall McLuhan as he tried to estimate the effects of Gutenberg on cultural expressions. However, one memory in particular I gratefully recall. I was invited in 1960 to take part in a symposium at Bristol in the Colston Series. The chosen theme was 'Metaphor and Symbol', and the organizers drew together such experts in various disciplines as Philip Wheelwright and H. D. Lewis (philosophy), Muriel Bradbrook and Lionel Knights (literature), and George Wingfield Digby (the visual arts). It was a most stimulating occasion, the addresses there delivered being subsequently published. It left me in no doubt that whether in philosophy or art, in social psychology or religion, there is a common interest in the symbol and in its 'enormous importance' for all human living. I went on collecting material from one source and another with the hope perhaps that I could some day gather it up into a series of reflections.

V

In this review of my growing awareness of the importance accorded to symbolism in various human disciplines, however, there is one obvious omission. I have not mentioned the theories of psychologists, partly because I have found no general agreement amongst them and partly because the theories which seem most prominent appear to me to be highly speculative.

I confess that at a certain period of my investigations I was greatly attracted by Jung's theorizing, and in particular by his notion of the collective unconscious. This seemed to offer a plausible explanation of the recurrence in myths, dreams, and rituals of what could be called universal symbolic forms. But I have become less certain about this. That the same symbol operates powerfully and effectively in widely-separated contexts seems to be well-established. But that the interpretation is uniform, or that a symbol springing from the unconscious (remembered for example by its having formed a vivid constituent of a dream) has a universal significance are doubtful propositions.

I am prepared to believe that there are collective unconsciousnesses, that is, that a society, clan or tribe, inhabiting a particular area and relating itself to the conditions of its environment, will possess a common consciousness in which shapes, patterns, or even discrete phenomena, which are experienced in the regular life of the community, gain a more-than-ordinary significance and take on a quasi-mystical or religious importance. There is, it seems evident, a certain inheritance of symbols, a kind of gene pool of forms which can exercise a powerful influence on human psyches. This need not imply, however, that there are universal archetypes waiting to be projected upwards when some critical event in individual or social life occurs.

The inner consciousness or the subconscious of individuals and collectives is never open to inspection. We know that symbolic forms appear in the human consciousness; sometimes, it would appear, spontaneously. Yet we can only study these forms in their open and reported context. All theorizing about their origin and manner of projection cannot be other than hypothetical, and cannot, I believe, lead us to any firm conclusions about individual or social anthropology in general.

In this book I have tried to show how, in every department of human life, symbolic expression is the way to creative freedom. I do not underestimate the importance of ordered structures or of signs which carry a uniform interpretation to all the members of a particular society. But human experience has shown that there is always the danger that a system of order, a framework of unambiguous signs, will become ends in themselves to be rigidly imposed and preserved from any possible deviation. In contrast to all forms of totalitarianism, the symbol stands for openness, for pointing towards alternative possibilities, for readiness to experiment in the hope of gaining a fuller understanding of reality. All this is summed up for me in the quotation from Thomas Mann which I have chosen as the epigram for this book: 'To live symbolically spells true freedom'.

I owe a long-standing debt to Mrs May Davis of Liverpool who has never failed to send back my written manuscripts excellently typed. And when it was temporarily difficult for me to check library references here in Oxford Mrs Cathy Wilson came to my rescue and enabled me to supply what is I hope an accurate list of publishers and dates.

CHAPTER TWO

What is a Symbol?

I

Amidst all the varied subjects which occupy thinkers and writers today, one seems to command almost universal agreement: it is that symbols have been and still are of outstanding importance in human affairs. Thus a distinguished sociologist wrote:

> The unity of a group, like all its cultural values, must find symbolic expression . . . The symbol is at once a definite focus of interest, a means of communication and a common ground of understanding . . . All communication, whether through language or other means, makes use of symbols. Society could scarcely exist without them.[1]

More recently, in his book *Culture and Communication*, Edmund Leach[2] included signs and signals as operators in the process of communication, all three being 'expressive actions' which 'either simply say something about the order of the world as it is or else purport to alter it by metaphysical means'. Operators such as signals, signs and symbols are, in his judgment, either descriptive or transformational.

In addition there are the familiar terms image, index, icon, simile. How can all of these be classified? I suggest that whereas symbol stands somewhat apart, index and sign are primarily applicable to the world as it is. They operate in a relatively static environment in which familiar words or gestures are employed to describe some object or event. There is usually a straightforward, one-to-one correspondence; the task of decoding, when giver and receiver belong to the same stable community, presents few difficulties.

The situation is different, however, with the word *signal*. It suggests a call to attention or action such as will in some way *transform* an existing state of affairs. It is used appropriately in military and commercial contexts and in modern relaying of messages by electronic means. These enable a signal to be sharp in character, precise and instantaneously transmitted.

All these are at least intended to operate in a *direct* way. An index has a single, direct referent, as do signs and signals. As far as possible, ambiguity is avoided. In any process of communication between human beings there can never be an altogether exact correspondence between activator and receptor: this can only be achieved impersonally and mechanically. Nevertheless, in a vast number of cases, whether in description or in transformative action, communication is intended to achieve a single, direct result by using the sign or signal which belongs to the common terminology of a particular cultural system.

A far more complex situation arises when the language of *symbol* and *symbolism* is employed. 'Symbol' and 'symbolic' have become terms so frequently and almost casually used in advertisements, news-reporting, political speeches, weather-charting and economic analysis as well as in more serious writing that a precise meaning for them is far from easy to establish. I give a few examples:

The main value of the 1975 rendez-vous and docking of Apollo and Soyuz must be in its *symbolic* aspects.
(New Scientist, 20 July 1972)

They spoke little to each other. For both, to be able to see a snow leopard was a kind of *symbol* of achievement.
(Matthiessen and Scholler crossing an 18,000 ft pass in the Himalayas in October weather as reported in a *Listener* review)

'Refugee' is the *symbolic* word of the generation.
(A report on East Africa, the Somalis in particular)

In the programme *Any Questions* the issue was raised of making accusations against a citizen under Parliamentary immunity. Mr Michael Foot affirmed that McCarthy became the *symbol* of that kind of action in the America of twenty years ago.

The whole book (Moby Dick) is a rhapsody. The very theme is a rhapsody: the mad, implacable quest of Captain Ahab for the whale that took off his leg is certainly about more than a man who seeks revenge for an injury and the whale itself, perhaps the most gigantic *symbol* in all literature (it is a white whale, remember) no less certainly represents something greater than the greatest of the sea-beasts. Probably Moby Dick meant to Melville what the Hound of Heaven meant to Francis Thompson – I fled Him, down the nights and down the days – for surely the whale is pursuing Ahab even as Ahab is pursuing the whale.

(Bernard Levin, *The Listener*, 12 August 1982, p.15)

He (Jonathan Dimbleby in West Berlin) looked at the concrete *symbol* of an ideological barrier, the Berlin Wall, and popped over to the Eastern side to Weimar to explore, telling us he would be followed wherever he went.

(*The Times*, 7 September 1982, p.9)

The Double Helix
The mighty *symbol* that has replaced the cross as the signature of the biological analphabet.

(*Perspectives in Biological Medicine*, Vol. 19, p.289)

Crossroads shanty town outside Cape Town, housing some 70,000 people.
Crossroads has become a *symbol* of the right of Africans and their families to settle and work where they can best earn a living.

(*The Times*, 1984)

Of all recent examples of the use of the vocabulary of symbolism that I have noted, none has seemed to me more far-reaching in its implications than the article entitled 'Symbols of Life' which appeared in *The Listener* (4 April 1985) just before Easter. It recalled the symbolism of the traditional Easter celebration but suggested that this was being expressed in a

new, and perhaps more powerful way, by the celebrations and
demonstrations being enacted by devotees in different parts of
the world on behalf of peace. Instead of the cross, the CND
semaphore might prove to be the rallying symbol in the world
today. The article concludes in this way:

> This century has seen a retreat from religious symbolism.
> We exist within the narrow confines of an urban, secular
> world: mechanistic, technological and rationalistic. Conse-
> quent spiritual disintegration has all but destroyed our
> ability to respond to ancient symbols. But they will not go
> away. We are witnessing a resurgence, and most of all within
> the peace movements of both East and West. There, a use of
> symbolism which outsiders find laughable, confusing or
> threatening, sets itself in direct opposition to the formulaic
> acronyms and euphemisms of war – MIRV, MAD, strategic
> defence, flexible response, and so on.
>
> So at Greenham they wove webs of wool on the wire, and
> pinned up baby clothes so that even the soldiers would be left
> in no doubt about the future generations under threat. In
> East Germany peace campaigners act symbolic dramas
> within churches. And at Molesworth this weekend
> thousands of men, women and children will be carrying
> objects which ring (bells, tambourines, triangles) as they
> move to make a symbolic ring around the base. Then they
> will plant banners bearing the names of those they love,
> decorated with rainbow ribbons – the hope after the storm.
>
> And all those symbols will reach out and touch the rest of
> us, who stay at home eating chocolate eggs – the new life.
> Putting Easter bunnies on the table – the fertility. Reading
> our books – the 'lilacs out of the dead land'. Or going to the
> flower-decked church on Easter Sunday to celebrate – just as
> irrationally – resurrection.

I have recorded a few examples of the use of the terms *symbol*
or *symbolic* in our contemporary world. These might have been
multiplied almost indefinitely, for it is now a commonplace to
refer to something as being simply *symbolic* or as being a *symbol*
of something else. Yet, on a more sophisticated level, the term

symbol has become of major importance in philosophy, in sociology, in psychology and in art. Is it possible to discern any basic meaning of the term which is applicable to every kind of usage, whether in popular speech or in intellectual disciplines?

A few years ago, having been invited to give a series of lectures on symbolism, I decided to ask the members of the class (mainly university graduates) to take paper and pencil and write down their understanding of the word symbol. Only a b ief period was given for thought: the object was to find out what came spontaneously to mind out of ordinary experience. The result was illuminating. Perhaps the simplest answer was: 'A word or object which represents or calls to mind a larger entity.' This provided a threefold pattern which I propose to test by comparing the reactions of the students with more formal definitions given by writers in various fields.

One of the most famous definitions of modern times was given by A. N. Whitehead in his book *Symbolism*. He wrote:

> The human mind is functioning symbolically when some components of its experience elicit consciousness, beliefs, emotions and images respecting other components of its experience. The former set of components are the 'symbols' and the latter set constitute the 'meaning' of the symbols. The organic functioning whereby there is transition from the symbol to the meaning will be called reference.[3]

More than a century earlier, Goethe had affirmed that 'in true symbolism, the particular represents the universal not as a dream or shadow, but as a living, momentary revelation of the unfathomable', while Coleridge insisted that a symbol actually 'partakes of the reality which it renders intelligible'. This 'participation' was described later in the nineteenth century in terms of 'substance' as, for example, by George MacDonald, whose son, writing about his father's 'symbolic utterance', said: 'To him a symbol was far more than an arbitrary outward and visible sign of an abstract conception: its high virtue lay in a common *substance* with the idea presented.' As Louis Macneice has pointed out, this means that a symbol was, in a degree, for him a 'signature of God's immanence'.[4]

These more mystical or spiritual conceptions are discounted by Arnold Toynbee, who concentrates his attention on the world of the intellect.

A symbol is not identical or co-extensive with the object that it symbolizes. If it were this, it would be, not a symbol of the thing, but the thing itself. It would be an error to suppose that a symbol is intended to be a reproduction of the thing that it is really intended, not to reproduce, but to illuminate. The test by which a symbol stands or falls is not whether it does or does not faithfully reproduce the object to which it points; the test is whether it throws light on that object or obscures our understanding of it. The effective symbol is the illuminating one, and effective symbols are an indispensable part of our intellectual apparatus. If a symbol is to work effectively as an instrument for intellectual action – that is to say, as a 'model' – it has to be simplified and sharpened to a degree that reduces it to something like a sketch-map of the piece of reality to which it is intended to serve as a guide – a sketch – map, not a photograph taken from a U-2 aeroplane.[5]

In contrast Erwin Goodenough in his massive exploration of *Jewish Symbols in the Craeco-Roman Period* defines a symbol in this way: 'A symbol is an object or pattern which, whatever the reason may be, operates upon men, and causes effects in them, beyond mere recognition of what is literally presented in the given form.' He goes on to distinguish between language which is *denotative*, i.e. precise, scientific, literal, and that which is *connotative*, i.e. associative, imprecise, giving scope for varieties of interpretation, the symbol belonging to the latter category. 'The symbol carries its own meaning or value and with this its own power to move us.' In short, the purely intellectual reference is discounted. Instead the emotive, stirring to action power of symbols, is regarded as their essential characteristic.[6]

As far as the dictionary definitions are concerned there seems to be general agreement that a symbol does not attempt to express exact resemblance or to document an exact situation. Rather, its function is to stimulate the imagination, by means of suggestion, association, and relation. Perhaps the most vivid description that I have encountered of the function of symbols in contrast to that of precise scientific formulations was contained in a review by Peter Brown in the *New York Review of Books* (15 April 1976, p.15). Discussing the views of certain theologians in Western Christendom, he wrote: 'They were the self-confident heirs of Aristotelian logic whose scholastic method sought to strip from the Godhead the rustling, shimmering, shot-silk veils of symbols. In the fourth century these men were the Arian heretics in Edessa. A long tradition of scholastic thought in Western Christianity has made their like, until quite recently, the official spokesmen of orthodoxy.'

Taking these various writers together, we find widespread agreement that the symbol is a powerful instrument to extend our vision, to stimulate our imagination and to deepen our understanding. For Whitehead the symbol refers to meaning; for Goethe it represents the universal; for Coleridge it participates in reality; for Toynbee it illuminates reality; for Goodenough it effects a transformation of the literal and commonplace; for Brown it veils the Godhead. For each of these writers there is a threefold pattern of relationship which I propose to expand as follows. A symbol can be regarded as

1. A word or object or thing or action or event or pattern or person or concrete particular

2. Representing or suggesting or signifying or veiling or communicating or eliciting or expressing or recalling or pointing to or standing in place of or typifying or denoting or relating to or corresponding to or illuminating or referring to or participating in or re-enacting or associated with

3. Something greater or transcendent or ultimate: a meaning, a reality, an ideal, a value, an achievement, a belief, a community, a concept, an institution, a state of affairs.

This pattern reveals that 1. is more visible, more audible, more tangible, more proximate, more concrete than 3. The function of a symbol, according to these definitions, is to bridge the gulf between the world of 1. and the world of 3., this being supremely important for the proper functioning of the life of any particular society.

Whatever variations may appear in these definitions, there is a general recognition that a symbol somehow *connects* two entities. The nature of this connection is complex and needs further consideration. But it is of interest to note that this focussing of attention on *connection* agrees with the original use of the root verb *symbollein* in Greek. This is how a recent book on symbols describes its significance:

> When two people in ancient Greece made an agreement, they often sealed it by breaking something – a tablet, a ring, a piece of pottery – into two pieces and keeping one half each. If one of the contracting parties later wanted the bargain honoured, he or his representative would identify himself by fitting his part of the broken object into the others.
>
> To 'match' was in Greek *symbollein* and the two pieces were called *symbola*. The word gradually came to mean 'recognition sign' in a wider sense, e.g. for members of a secret society or persecuted minority . . . A symbol was originally a thing, a sign or a word, used for mutual recognition and with an understood 'meaning'.[7]

A symbol therefore connects or brings together. Whereas, however, in the earliest use of *symbollein*, the two connected parts were of the same substance and often virtually replicas of one another, in developed usage the primary component could often be very dissimilar in appearance to, and of a different substance from, yet in some way capable of representing or calling up or pointing to that which it symbolized.

II

It will be convenient to designate 1. in our basic pattern as the symbol, 3. as the *referent*. If we enquire which comes first we find ourselves in the egg-and-chicken situation. Each depends upon the other, and although it may be urged that the symbol is a word or an image or a construct which is public and apprehensible by the senses, it is equally true that the referent is there already and waiting, as it were, to be connected in an open way to an appropriate *symbol*. This connecting process is the distinguishing achievement of the human species. The inter-play between symbol and referent constitutes the excitement and the never ending interest of human existence. Amongst animals there is a rhythmic movement between instinctual drives and outward gestures (signs, signals), either bodily or tonal. But there is little or no evidence to suggest that animals can develop symbol-systems which can be consciously con-structed and revised and extended and transformed.

However, although the human species has developed this distinctive and potentially transforming capacity to create and contemplate and communicate symbols and thereby to gain an ascendancy over animals, it is clear that humans never escape the nostalgic desire for the apparent simplicity of the direct, the immediate and the exact equivalent. If there is a one-to-one correspondence between the 'drive' and its open representation or implementation; if, from the other angle, some open gesture or pattern of sounds denotes one thing and one thing only, life appears to be vastly simplified. All know 'where they stand'. Doubts and questions disappear. Yet the distinctive wonder of human potentialities also disappears and the glory of symbol-systems (which only retain their glory as they continue to incorporate new observations and experiments) fades away.

The most obvious examples of supremely important symbol systems are the *languages* of mankind. But the labours of social anthropologists have taught us that all kinds of bodily gestures and activities also possess symbolic significance. The slaying of an animal, the offering of a gift, the process of cooking, ways of eating and drinking, dancing and play-acting can all serve as symbols. All are related to the structure of the society within which they are performed.

This reference to society leads at once to another fun-damental truth about symbols: *they are intimately related to social cohesion* and *to social transformation.* It is true that an individual may be responsible for creating novel symbolic forms and relating them to new ideas and values but unless they have *some* connection with the old they have no chance of acceptance. Every individual has been shaped within a corporate symbolic system and although his or her own contribution may modify, it will not supersede it. Symbols and society belong to one another and each influences the other.

At this stage, however, I want to claim that in the course of human evolution there have been alternate types of society, depending upon particular life-styles necessary for survival. On the one hand there have been inhabitants of the less hospitable areas of the world who have been restless, questing, mobile, in tension with their natural environment and, with their animal neighbours, compelled to hunt and kill in order to gain adequate food supplies. Their communication system was primarily that of *signalling* to one another in the course of satisfying practical needs or meeting practical emergencies and of employing *symbolic* devices either to recall past experiences of or to forecast the future realization of favourable relationships with spirits, animals and fellow human-beings. A symbol which might be a pattern of words or of images pointed dramatically to some more than ordinary experience in the past or to a desired and expected situation in the future.

On the other hand, there were the settlers, the inhabitants of more hospitable territories, where roots and fruits and grubs provided daily food, where (except in periods of severe drought) water was available, where it was possible to erect clusters of shelters and to establish a relatively ordered cycle of daily life. Here the communication system was primarily one of organizational *signs* representing tasks to be performed and assigning appropriate roles to the several members of the community in order to preserve the sources of food and drink on which the life of the community depended. *Symbols* were not unrelated to ordinary human activities and relationships but their added function was to celebrate and perpetuate the ordered life-cycle of the natural world and to strengthen the community's conformity with it.

Thus, from two distinct types of human experience and social organization, have come two distinct types of symbolic forms. This is not to deny that from the earliest times known to us each type has contained within its manifestations certain aspects of the other and that in course of time each has greatly influenced the other. Nevertheless it is my conviction that no

single and unified aetiology of symbolic forms can be propounded. Symbols have gained their form *either* in complicated
strategies of communication and competition *or* in developing
processes of production and organization which have characterized the two major types of society in human history.

There are two exceptions which could be urged to the
development of the two types of symbolism which I have
proposed. Have not air and water been *universal* requirements,
lacking which neither a society nor any single individual could
have survived? And have not spirit (breath) and water
therefore become universal symbols in the history of mankind?

An affirmative answer may be given to both of these
questions, and yet a subtle difference may still be noticed in the
way in which each social type has come to employ the symbol in
speech and ritual action. In the experience of a nomadic
community, the noteworthy, even startling phenomenon is the
coming of the wind, from the mountain, or from the sea,
whipping up the waves, bending the branches of the trees, even
stirring humans to feverish activity. The spirit comes *mightily*
upon an individual, enabling him to perform extraordinary
deeds of valour. There is a symbolic world of the wind, of the
spirit, mysterious and unpredictable in its operations, except
insofar as holy men may know its secrets. On the other hand in
the experience of the more settled community, rarely visited by
violent storms, welcoming cool breezes and freshening winds in
sultry periods, more aware, perhaps, of the dependence of life
upon steady breathing, the spirit world is more beneficent and,
as in early Christianity, the spirit becomes symbolically the
lord and giver of *life*.

Similarly with water. For the nomad the major concern is to
be in reach of an oasis or water-hole or river, seeing that for long
periods there may be no rain or, if the storm comes, the result
may be floods which bring destruction in their wake. To some
degree his situation has been eased by the discovery of the
technique of well-digging, but even then wells could be few and
far between. On the other hand, it has been normal for the
settler to live within the vicinity of a constant supply of water –
the riverside or lakeside, the spring or the communal well. Each

type of society has been deeply dependent on water but the emphasis in their respective symbol-systems has been different. In the one case, the gift of water was a special boon or a fearful judgment, a symbol of gracious beneficence or of divine displeasure. In the other case water was part of the world's regular and dependable rhythm, providing refreshment and cleansing directly for the body and symbolically for the soul. Moreover, the whole process of irrigation brought new life to the soil and confirmed confidence in the goodness of the creator of the natural order.

Thus, with differing emphases, spirit (wind, breath) and water (the rain-storm, the bubbling spring) have existed as man's outstanding universal symbols but with a clear relationship to the particular conditions of those who employed them in the process of description and transformation.

I shall return to the symbolism of air and water but have referred to them now as outstanding examples of the way in which natural phenomena may serve as important symbols universally but may, at the same time, point to different meanings or values depending on the nature of the society and its environment within which the symbol is being employed. It is of the very nature of a symbol that it is neither unitary nor univocal. A sign needs to be precise, uniform, unmistakable. A symbol opens the door into a larger world full of hitherto unknown features and even ultimately to the world of mystery, transcending all human powers of description.

CHAPTER THREE

Literal and Symbolic

I

In 1933 and 1934 Dr Edwyn Bevan delivered the Gifford Lectures in Edinburgh. These were later published in two volumes, the first of which was entitled *Symbolism and Belief*. With great learning, based on long acquaintance with the Hellenistic world and, to a less degree, the Hebraic, he focussed attention on the use of the symbolism of height, time, light, spirit, and wrath by humans who have sought to bear witness to the nature and activity of God. He then turned to a subject which has been in the forefront of theological controversy in the twentieth century: how are we to distinguish between the literal and the symbolical when we read scripture or recite creeds or make theological statements? He devoted one lecture to the examination of this question.

Let me begin by quoting its opening paragraph:

One has good ground for believing that the language which men have used, in speaking of the unseen Beings whom they worshipped, was at first meant quite literally. There is no reason to doubt that there was a time when the ancestors of the Jews thought of Jehovah as really like a magnified man in the sky or on the top of Mount Sinai, perhaps a human shape of fiery substance, with actual face and hands and feet and back-parts, which, on one great occasion, He allowed Moses to see (Ex. 33.23). Later on, it was familiar doctrine with Jews that Jehovah was a spirit without any shape of which a visible similitude could be made. Similarly in regard to Jehovah's mental characteristics there was no doubt a time when the ancient Hebrews thought of these as closely resembling those of a man – Jehovah revolved different plans and went into rages and sometimes regretted His former decisions. Before Christianity came into the world, it had come to be familiar doctrine among educated Jews that all this kind of language was figurative, poetical metaphor; that Jehovah was not like a son of man that He should repent, that His purpose was unchangeable throughout the ages and His thoughts not as men's thoughts. It is impossible to say exactly when the grosser anthropomorphic ideas gave place to more spiritual ones, because the old language continued in general use long after the ideas it covered had undergone essential change. Even to-day we commonly speak of the eyes of God or the hand of God. The ideas changed by a subtle and gradual process under the uniform language, and it is often impossible to say in regard to the documents of a particular time how far expressions relating to God or the unseen world were understood literally by those who used them, how far only as symbols.[1]

What I find striking in this section, and indeed in the whole chapter, is the fact that Dr Bevan never examines in detail the use of the word *literal*. His book as a whole is concerned with the nature of symbolism and in this chapter he actually defines two types of symbol: those behind which we can see and those behind which we cannot see. Some symbolic forms, he claims, represent ideas which can be expressed more truly in other terms. Some, on the other hand, are themselves analogical representations of divine attributes and cannot therefore be more truly represented in any other way. Whichever of these types we are examining, *every symbol has the quality of referring to that which is ultimate or ideal*. It brings together or holds together some familiar aspect of human experience with that which is beyond experience or expression. (The symbol may be a word or an action or an image or a drama.) In the most general terms, a symbol connects the human search with the larger, even the ultimate, reality.

But what is the significance of the word *literal*? Taken from the Latin, it obviously has to do with letters, with that which is expressed in written form. Of all human discoveries few, if any, have been as important as that of putting speech into *writing*. It enabled words to be exhibited as an exact record of the speech-act and, inscribed in suitable material, to be preserved for future generations.

But all human advances have involved potential dangers. That which is written down can become fixed, an end in itself, only understood by those trained in 'letters'. It is true that dialogue can still continue amongst members of élites who share a common background and common interests. But as far as the majority are concerned, they will depend upon the meaning assigned to the letters by the élite and will regard the written record as comparable to the law of the Medes and Persians which could not be changed. The written word undoubtedly promotes order and continuity: yet it can also promote dogmatism and inflexibility. Thus *literal* has its primary reference to the world of language and writing but in this it has occupied an ambiguous role. In Israel the unchanging 'literal' was constantly challenged by the voices of the prophets, proclaiming through stories and dramatic actions that God was not bound either by former manifestations or by present expectations. In Greece the 'literal' was challenged by the probings of philosophers who declared that only through the dialectic of question and answer could an approach be made to the true meaning of human experience.

The distinction between the literal and the more-than-literal was commonly made by scholars in the Middle Ages and whereas far greater emphasis was laid by the Reformers on the 'plain meaning' of the text, a division between literal and symbolic was generally accepted. However, this distinction became even more problematic when the new era of historical investigation dawned. Now attempts were increasingly made to question all written texts, to pierce behind them, to compare the testimonies of different individuals, to discern the connections between language and culture: in short to ask how far any text could be relied upon to give a true record of *fact*, an account of *what actually happened*. This quest for literal meaning was combined with a quest for *historical fact*. Could the *facts* first be exactly determined and then recorded in language exactly corresponding to them? Could the literal take on a new complexion by becoming the actual representation or even facsimile of events themselves?

An interesting example of this link between literality and historic fact may be found in the Report of the Commission on Christian Doctrine appointed by the Archbishops of the Church of England in 1922 and published in 1938. By the time of the First World War, the importance of historical criticism had gained wide recognition and the members of the Commission felt bound to examine the traditional doctrines of the Christian faith in the light of historical research. In particular, what could be affirmed about the virgin birth and the bodily resurrection of Jesus?

In the report the Chairman, William Temple, affirmed 'that I wholeheartedly accept as historical facts the Birth of our Lord from a Virgin Mother and the Resurrection of His physical body from death and the tomb'. Yet he also recognized the position of those who affirmed the reality of the incarnation without accepting these events as 'historical occurrences', 'regarding the records rather as parables than as history, a presentation of spiritual truth in narrative form'.

In the text of the report, a special section is devoted to the resurrection, with differences noted between those members of the Commission who accepted the New Testament records as belonging to the sphere of 'religious symbolism' and those who accepted them as representing 'historical fact'. Another phrase occurring in the Report is 'scientific formulation', and the general distinction which emerges (closely parallel to that made by Edwyn Bevan in the book already mentioned) is that between language which literally corresponds to events actually happening in this world of space and time and language which uses reports of events in this world to point to another world, a world in which human and earthly limitations are transcended, whose activities can never be exactly represented by ordinary human language. Thus a firm distinction is drawn between literal and factual on the one hand, symbolic and parabolic on the other. The question remains as to where the dividing line is to be drawn between the literal and the symbolic, the fact and the human testimony to the fact (which could be called either evidence or interpretation).

Bevan's treatment of the whole problem is subtle, balanced and suggestive. It seems to me that he reached the crux of the matter when, towards the end of his lecture, he made the following statement:

> For it is plain that to-day there are many Christians who, while quite convinced that they are in communication with a real unseen Person, nevertheless give only mythical or symbolical value to different elements in the story of Jesus as told in the early Christian documents – such as his birth from a Virgin and the disappearance of his dead Body from the sepulchre. On the other hand, there are many Christians who maintain that to regard these elements as not literally true would be destructive of the Christian faith. It is outside our province to discuss a controversy within the Christian Church. We can take note of it only in so far as it shows a problem which must come up in any form of religion, according to which men believe themselves to be in communication with an actual Person or actual persons. A real person can never be only a symbol; but if, at the same time, certain ideas connected with the Person are admitted to be symbolical only, it becomes a vital question what beliefs about the Person it is essential to hold as literally true.[2]

In my judgment the key sentence is the final one. What happens if we turn it around, interchanging 'symbol' and 'fact literally recorded'? 'A real person can never be only a fact literally recorded (i.e. date of conception and birth: dates of physical events in the life-story: date of death: details of anatomy; bodily ailments, measurements of height, girth), but if, at the same time, certain events connected with the Person are admitted to be literally recorded facts only, it becomes a vital question what beliefs about the Person it is essential to hold as symbolically true.'

Is not the all-important point that a real person can never be merely a biological specimen, the events of whose life-span can be tabulated and recorded with scientific precision? On the other hand can a real person be only a symbol without any necessary connection with human bodily existence? The bodily and the mental, the physical and the spiritual, the literal and the symbolical must be held together in vital dialectical relationship. No clear-cut dividing line can ever be drawn between the two.

Yet the problem refuses to go away. That which the members of the Doctrinal Commission wrestled with fifty years ago surfaced again in 1984 by reason of references to the virgin birth and bodily resurrection of Jesus made by David Jenkins after his appointment as Bishop of Durham. In public comments and criticism, the words 'literal' and 'symbolic' were often used and attempts were once more made to distinguish between the two. The defenders of orthodoxy required an unqualified affirmation regarding *historical fact*: on the other side, the whole emphasis was on *symbolic significance*. At the end of the year a lengthy apologia on behalf of the credibility of the doctrine of the virgin birth was broadcast by Professor Keith Ward: such a birth, he claimed, was a wholly appropriate expression of God's interaction in history (printed in *The Listener*, 3 January 1985).

Referring to critics of what he described as 'traditional Christian faith' (including 'many Christian theologians'), he said that 'they think (the stories) are not literally true but are fictions which have some sort of symbolic meaning'. They regard the birth stories as '"myths" with a religious not a factual meaning'. Then in what seems to be a crucial paragraph:

Of all world religions Christianity is least able to make a separation between religious and historical facts. Its dominant claim is that God acts and makes himself known in history so that historical facts can be, at the same time, religiously significant facts. Their religious significance lies precisely in the fact that they show the character and activity of God. If your religious claim is that God acts in history, it makes no sense to say that this claim can be expressed in non-historical myths. All the birth stories about Jesus may be deeply meaningful as timeless myths about motherhood, infancy, the importance of camels and so on. But if they do not say what really happened, then they cannot be saying what God did in history; they become incapable of really connecting God and history; and thus they cannot logically describe or express what the historical person of Jesus means religiously *or* why he should mean anything. Jesus himself becomes a myth, a fiction meant to symbolize an eternal God. What he cannot be is an act of God in history for human salvation – that is, the Messiah.

Later, admitting that the birth stories contain 'whole chunks of poetry', he recognized that it could be inferred that 'the whole thing is almost too perfectly symbolic to be true'. Egyptian and Hellenic myths portraying a virgin mother were undoubtedly 'emotionally powerful symbols'. But all such 'intimations and archetypes' were fulfilled and corrected in Christ and 'given a definitive historical form'.

The contrast presented in this broadcast is clear. On the one hand myth, fiction, poetry, conveying some sort of symbolic meaning (religious not factual, too perfect to be true); on the other hand fact, definitive historical form, the literal record of 'what really happened'. It is through the latter, Ward claimed, that we gain true knowledge of God and of his acts in history.

Many points were raised in the broadcast and many phrases were used which seem to me to be open to question. But it is this central contrast which deserves special consideration. Can we in speech and writing maintain a sharp distinction, even a separation, between literal, historical fact and symbolic, contextual meaning? Can truth be found by concentrating attention firmly on an isolated act rather than by holding together (as a symbol always does) two entities – the record of the act and whatever relates to that act in the wider experience of mankind?

II

The most illuminating discussion of such questions known to me is contained in the book *Metaphor and Symbol*,[3] this being the

record of the proceedings of the twelfth symposium of the
Colston Research Society held at Bristol. One of the papers
was entitled *The Meaning of the Word Literal*; its author was
Owen Barfield and in addition to the paper itself, the volume
contains the subsequent discussion by literary and philosophical participants.

Perhaps the main point emerging from the paper is the
sharp question it raises about the claim made in Edwyn
Bevan's opening paragraph (already quoted) that 'One has
good ground for believing that the language which men have
used, in speaking of the unseen Beings whom they worshipped
was at first meant quite literally' (my italics). This belief has in the
past half-century been questioned or challenged by philosophers, by social anthropologists and by linguists. And it is
this belief which Barfield examines particularly from the point
of view of what is really intended by the use of the word *literal*.

He considers the case of any noun. It has a surface appearance – we may call it vehicle or form; it has a meaning – we
may call it tenor or content. This would be generally agreed.
But then two schools of thought emerge, one claiming that it is
possible to detach the content from the form, the other
claiming that they are inseparable. Thus, according to the
first school, the meaning *could* be expressed by some other
word or set of words; according to the second, no such
separation is possible. Barfield's claim is that language was
born originally through the human experience of relationship
with the surrounding environment. (This, I assume, could
have been expressed through gestures as well as through
words.) Words so used, Barfield claims, did not immediately
express a meaning which could then be written down in a
literal fashion. Rather, the words themselves constituted the
human reflection of and relation to those other parts of the
total environment to which the person belonged. They were
symbolic (joining together), figurative, relational. Only at a
later stage were they made *literal*, that is, made the external
instruments to define what had originally not been defined but
rather expressed spontaneously and imaginatively through
symbolic speech.

The whole purpose of Barfield's paper was to urge that *literalness* is a comparatively late development in the history of language. It is the product of the craving for order and permanence which undoubtedly has a legitimate place in society and which has brought immense benefits to mankind. In human relationships with the world of nature there has been the search, still as eager as ever, for *natural laws* which can be formulated and thereby given a literal definition. The problem, however, has been that literalcy has constantly proved to be inadequate to deal with newly discovered structures and energies within this world. New symbolisms have brought about revolutions in old literal formularies: ultimate mystery, it transpires, cannot be captured within a literal box.

Similarly, in human relationships with the social environment, there has been the persistent quest for a body of *social laws* which will provide stability and give order amidst conflicting ambitions. These laws have been given *literal* expression on tablets of stone, in law books, in written constitutions and as such have proved temporarily valuable. But again the problem arises that life goes on, new discoveries are made, the media of communication affecting relationships are transformed and so the application of a set of laws *literally*, that is by exact correspondence between the written form and the particular situation, becomes increasingly problematic. The totalitarian state attempts by every possible means to impose strict conformity to its laws and to define the life-style of every individual. But there is always the possibility that the symbolical, the relationship to the undefined Beyond, will spring to new life and the old order thereby be revolutionized.

Barfield constructs an interesting framework to illustrate what he regards as a common assumption. It is widely assumed that first of all names or labels were given to material objects in a *literal* fashion; then immaterial phenomena were in turn also given names, taken out of the material context, in a *symbolic* way; thirdly, these symbolic forms came to be used with less reference to their material originals; and finally these words were applied to denote immaterial or abstract qualities in a quite literal fashion. From the literal to the symbolic and back to the literal. Such a framework, Barfield claims, is misleading. Rather, he believes, the sequence has been: symbolic to literal, and then back to symbolic. He does not claim that we can dispense with the *literal* altogether, at least not with the nearly literal. In so far as the movement towards the literal is intended to promote common understanding and relationship, it plays an indispensable role in the conduct of human affairs. But if it is once inferred that the literal is the ideal to be pursued at all costs, then that which is truly human declines in value and the Orwell image for language and society becomes a sinister possibility.

In the realm of religion, as I have noted, controversy still continues between those who give the primacy to symbolic words and images as avenues towards meaning and truth and those who strive rather to employ literal words and plain images to express the given-ness of divine truth. I do not see that there can be any final resolution of this difference. Nor would I claim that there is no necessity for plain speech and clearly expressed language. Yet to infer that this implies the possibility of reaching definitive historical fact or statements about God in history which are literally true, appears to me illusory. Such linguistic goals can be approached only by reduction and retreat and by concentration on the monolith as the ideal rather than on the creativity of inter-relationship and the expansiveness of a dialectical symbolism.

APPENDED NOTES

1. The outstanding example of pure literalcy in the world today appears in the religion of Islam. The Qur'an is regarded as recording the direct speech of Allah to Muhammad.

There revelation is understood as divine mediation of speech received verbatim, in Arabic, by the chosen and single prophet Muhammad. The text of the deliverance verbally transmitted to this mind and tongue is again orally recited to and by the faithful. Calligraphy is its utterly congenial art form, just as memorization is its due reception in piety and love, while education and law turn upon its categorical quality as guidance and reminder.[4]

2. The interesting question arises whether the interpretation of a symbolic text can be expressed *literally*. C. L. Stevenson in his book *Ethics and Language* distinguishes between metaphorical (or symbolic) language as emotive and interpretative (literal?) language as descriptive, though he insists that the distinction is not absolute; there is always interaction or interplay. He makes this comment on interpretation:

> The 'interpretation' may be defined as a sentence which is to be taken literally and which *descriptively means* what the metaphorical sentence *suggests* . . . The function of an interpretation is to reduplicate the suggestive force of the metaphor in other terms – terms which have the same effect not as a part of their suggestiveness, but as a part of their descriptive meaning, realized in the ordinary way. It must be remembered, however, that no sentence can ever descriptively mean *exactly* what another suggests. This is so, if for no other reason, because the descriptive meaning of a sentence is made definite by the operation of linguistic rules, which cause it systematically to be modified by the descriptive dispositions of many other terms in the language; whereas the suggestiveness of a sentence, going beyond any fixed rules, will be far more vague. There is no such thing as giving an exact translation of a metaphor into non-metaphorical terms. One can only give interpretations and these are always approximate. It is usually necessary to give not one interpretation but many, each of which will give, with too great a precision, a small part of what the metaphor suggests by its richly vague figure.[5]

PART ONE

Some Examples of Symbolic Forms

CHAPTER FOUR

Visual and Dramatic

(a) The body and food

I

Everywhere and at all times human beings have had as their primary concern how to stay alive. A newly-born babe struggles for breath and then almost immediately for milk from the mother's breast. From beginning to end these are the needs which must be satisfied: air to breathe, food and drink to nourish and sustain.

Yet although air and food are essential for the survival of the human body the strange thing is that they have never been regarded as providing all that was necessary for a distinctively human existence. Humans live by being related to that which transcends themselves: parents, siblings, neighbours, the natural environment, the mysterious Beyond.

This universal capacity for self-transcendence is, so far as we know, the quality which distinguishes the human from the animal creation and is that which enables humans to communicate with one another through a system of *symbols* which may be expressed either through gestures or through language. To use meaningful symbols is to be human. The symbol may point to an object, an event, or a person in the world bounded by the five senses or it may point to another world and to its imagined contents.

Thus the body as a biological phenomenon is common to humanity as a whole; similarly the body as symbol, pointing to more than biological functions, also appears to be common to all. There must, in addition, be some animating force or energy within the body which enables it to express itself and communicate with others. Yet this force is unseen and unheard, like air breathed in or like wind on the cheek. In human consciousness breath becomes a symbol pointing to a spirit within or to spirits dwelling in other natural phenomena. They too must surely be inhabited by spirit forces.

The body is a superb symbol of wholeness, of variety-in-unity, of proportion, of power in males, of beauty in females. It can indeed be degraded and become a symbol of evil: fleshly, in particular, sexual passion becomes the enemy of spirit; a defiled body becomes a symbol of pollution, a wrecked body the tomb of the soul. Yet because of the co-operation of its members one with another, the body becomes a powerful symbol to represent an ideal community in which the strong assist the weak and none seeks its own separate advantage. For the early church the body became a vivid symbol pointing to the Christ either as head of the body or as incorporating within his risen body the whole Christian community. Not to discern the body or to defile the body were grievous sins.

The impact upon the human consciousness of spirit symbolism could be readily illustrated by referring to the languages of many cultures. Most obviously in the Western tradition there is the remarkable fact that in Hebrew, Greek and Latin the same word is used for spirit as for wind or breath. The force of a strong wind, the coolness of a gentle breeze, the panting for breath when exhausted, the body ceasing to breathe in death – all are universal experiences and all lend themselves to symbolic reference when describing the activity of a divine spirit. The wind on the waters of chaos, the spirit empowering superhuman deeds physically and mentally, are examples from the Old Testament of writers bearing witness to the operation of the Spirit of God. But in the New Testament there is a chorus of wondering confessions, attributing the revelation through Jesus and the subsequent experiences of apostolic witnesses to an unprecedented outpouring of the Holy Spirit. Indeed the essence of their testimony, it could be claimed, is that the Spirit is the divine creator of symbolic forms and of symbolic insights. Words and deeds, having seemingly ordinary connotations, are taken by the Spirit and invested with their true, their symbolic reference. It is through the inspiration of the Spirit that men and women are enabled to perceive Jesus not simply as man but as Lord and Son of God. It is by the inspiration of the Spirit that his words are taken to point beyond their ordinary reference to eternal realities. It is the Holy Spirit who is the divine interpreter leading humans to apprehend saving truth.

II

A body makes its first outward appearance at birth: it must be disposed of in some way at death. Birth of the body can point symbolically to a new birth, a second birth, a birth from above and so, through the vivid language of John 3, to the possibility of being born again. Further, there is in this chapter a striking contrast between the literal and the spiritual. 'Can a man enter a second time into his mother's womb and be born?' 'Except a man be born of water and spirit he cannot enter the kingdom of God.' Literalism confines a statement to what is publicly observable or can be put into effect immediately: symbolism opens out vistas of new possibilities within another order of existence. Rebirth or regeneration were to become central concepts in Christian faith and practice, and although unhappily they could sink into designations of merely formal states effected by formal rituals, they could also open windows of the imagination to a view of life as renewed and transfigured by the spirit of God. Being born again has proved to be one of the most powerful of Christian symbols.

In general, however, humans have been more deeply concerned about *death* than about birth. Birth promises growth: it is the first link in a seemingly unending chain. But death is final, irreversible, so far as the body is concerned. The human body may be mummified or painted or sculpted and thereby made into a sign of that which should never be forgotten. But is that all that can be said or done?

One answer has affirmed that although the body had died and reverted to dust or ashes, the soul, which had dwelt in the body, would continue to live in some other state. Alternatively, that the body itself, though dead, may by divine power be reconstituted. This could come about either through a process comparable to that operating in the natural order by which a seed sown, though appearing to be dead, grows into a body belonging to its own species; or by a sudden transfiguration, comparable to that of Jesus on the mount, whereby earthly elements are converted into a body of undying splendour. In both instances, the body has been regarded symbolically as that which points to that which will be perfectly co-ordinated and fully integrated. Burial and cremation can be regarded as merely utilitarian signs of the removal of a decaying corpse. On the other hand they can be symbolic acts. Which of the two points the more adequately to the Christian hope may be open to question: the one is closely related to the slow regularities of an agrarian society, the other to the more rapid trans-formations characteristic of commercial transactions. Christian tradition does not speak with a single voice in the interpretation of symbols. The very expansiveness of a symbol allows for variations in interpretative significance depending on the cultural outlook of any particular society.

The two main sources of human food from time immemorial have been animal (including fish and birds) and vegetable (including fruit and nuts) products. In hunting societies flesh has been the major intake; in agrarian societies grain. It could perhaps be claimed that the ideal has been reached amongst pastoral peoples who have lived in 'between' areas. There they have been able to draw upon their own flocks and herds and at the same time either to grow vegetables of their own or to trade with neighbours. 'Meat and two veg' has a long and generally honourable history.

By careful observation the hunter learned the haunts and habits of wild animals and often succeeded by his own stratagems in securing food for his family. But as cave-paintings and anthropological researches reveal, the need for more-than-human skill and protection when confronting his prey led to engagement in symbolic pursuits – songs, gestures, dances, mimes, simulating in anticipation or celebrating in retrospect the achievement of his quests. These symbolic forms opened the way for all kinds of cultural as well as biological developments. Food for biological needs could symbolize food for mind and soul.

The contrast between animal and vegetable sources of food has remained dominant throughout human history and has obviously depended in part on what supplies are actually available. In agricultural areas, where animals are scarce and valued for their contribution to the economy, the diet consists largely of grain and vegetables. On the wide open plains of Texas where steers can be raised and herded a steak is a frequent constituent of a meal. This contrast has proved to be the source of a major symbolic distinction. For hunter and pastoralist alike the animal must be *killed*, either after chase in open country or within domestic surroundings; for agricultural-ist, the regular cycle of sowing, irrigating, harvesting, storing builds up a continuous supply of necessary food. A domestic animal may be slaughtered and added to the meal (just as the pastoralist may add vegetables to his or her dish) but the major distinction holds between the killing of an animal and the slow tending of a crop. The crisis of killing readily lends itself to the symbolizing of an *event*; the life-cycle of a grain of wheat lends itself to the symbolizing of a patterned *process*.

Of the former category, no symbolic form known to me of eating and drinking has retained so persistently and so poignantly the flavour of recalling a critical event as has the Jewish Passover. There is good reason to believe that its origins lie far back in the past when first hunting and then pastoral tending provided the staple structure of the economy. At springtime, when lambs were born, it was natural to slay the first to come forth from its mother's womb. That was the best available and it could be offered up in thanksgiving for the safety and welfare of the flock and in anticipation of its future preservation. Alternatively, as in the story of Esau and Jacob bringing food to the blind father, the animal might have been secured in the course of a hunting expedition. Whatever the

origins of the animal-slaying may have been, the commemorative feast took on a wholly new and dramatic character when it
became associated with the critical deliverance from the
bondage of Egypt. There the Israelite tribes would doubtless
have tried, often with difficulty, to continue the celebration of
their spring festival by the killing of an animal. But when the
actual night of slaying and eating coincided with a sudden
opportunity to flee in partial confusion towards the Red Sea, a
never-to-be-forgotten occasion had occurred, marking a crisis
of identity and freedom which could be celebrated down
through the centuries in all manner of places and circumstances. The slaying of the lamb, the structure of the meal, the
hurried Exodus could all be gathered together into a critical
symbolic festival reminding the participants of redemption and
inspiring them with hopes of freedom.

Thus the association of a common meal with a critical *event* (a
slaying, a new beginning, a dramatic deliverance) has constituted one form of food-symbolism which has captured and held
the imaginations of successive generations. Nowhere has this
been so evident as in the history of the Jewish people. Whatever
else has faded from the popular consciousness, devotion to the
Passover celebration has retained its place. It has been
essentially a household or family celebration; it has displayed
symbols of servitude and constriction in the salt water and
bitter herbs; it has sometimes allowed the lamb-slaying to be
represented only by a shank bone; it has portrayed elements of
hasty exodus visibly through unleavened bread and verbally
through commemorative recital; by keeping a door open it has
symbolized the assurance of blessing still to come. It is a
remarkable symbolic re-enactment of a unique critical event.

When Dr Israel Brodie was Chief Rabbi he commented on
the fact that not only was this event to be commemorated
through the symbolism of Passover but also that the Jew was
under obligation in his daily prayers to recall the going out from
Egypt. Would this not produce familiarity and boredom? Not
necessarily. 'Prophet and poet and sage have not wearied in its
telling nor in pointing to its inexhaustible significance; nor have
their hearers been tired by its repetition. The story is told not

only by word but by symbol, action and ceremony at the festive table of Jewish families everywhere and throughout all generations.' Then, after enumerating the details of the symbolism, he concluded: 'These and other symbols on the table underline the significance and the drama of the ancient story: its lowly beginnings, its tears and sorrows and ultimate joys emblazoned in songs of thanksgiving to the Rock of Israel and its Redeemer' (*The Listener*, 26 April 1962).

A conflict, a killing, a redemption, a setting free, a future salvation – all these have figured in the symbolism of Passover. They have also played a prominent part in the commemorations of other confined or persecuted or struggling societies, not least in Christian communities celebrating the Lord's Supper. When the focus of attention has been the critical event of Calvary, the redemption from the slavery of sin and death into a new life of freedom and meaningfulness, the celebration has been essentially one of remembrance and thanksgiving and hope. Outside the direct Passover or Easter tradition, no symbolic commemorative *event* perhaps has exercised a wider appeal than that of American Thanksgiving Day. When the lot of the early pilgrims in the new land seemed desperate they were able to gather sufficient food to sustain them through the rigours of winter. The commemorative feast celebrates deliverance, freedom and future confidence.

III

However, a society whose whole existence depends on the *land* and on the cycle of *nature*, symbolizes its getting and storing and consuming of food in a quite different way. For the ancients the slain animal could not be kept: it had to be eaten almost immediately. But grain could be stored and bread could become a regular constituent of diet. Moreover, sowing and planting and reaping were constantly repeated processes: vine culture produced annual supplies of grapes which could be made into wine for later consumption. For most of Europe rainfall was adequate and reasonably regular and in consequence an adequate supply of food was assured. The major uncertainty, even mystery, was that of *fertility*. Only by dependence upon divine resources could fertility, the secret of life, be maintained.

The organization of an agrarian society was essentially hierarchical. There were labourers in the fields whose duty it was to cultivate the land and produce the crops, not just for themselves but for the feeding of the whole society. Others were involved in ruling, defending, building and healing and this meant that the social system was integrated by regular gifts to superiors of land-products or their equivalents in some kind of value-scale. Thus the total life was sustained by gifts (or tribute) from workers on the land to other members of the society and supremely to supernatural beings who alone could guarantee fertility. Workers in turn could receive their supplies from grain which had been stored or (even more important) from divine blessings producing fertility in their crops. In this way the general conception of sacrifice was adjusted to the particular conditions of agricultural life. Produce from field and vineyard was brought and offered to the deity; portions of that which had been offered and thereby associated with the source of *life* were given back to maintain the cycle of fertility in the natural world-order.

Within such a social system it was not a particular event but particular constituents of nature itself which called for understanding and interpretation. How were the life-giving properties of nature sustained? How were gifts taken from the natural world given supernatural qualities? Within the Christian tradition bread and wine were obviously of supreme importance because of the words of Jesus at the Last Supper. Were they to be regarded as symbols of the whole process of nature? And once they had been offered and sanctified, how could the change be defined?

In many agrarian societies gifts of food and drink have been offered in the faith that thereby the blessings of fertility and maturity would be sustained. In the Christian tradition, however, because of the dominical institution of bread and wine and their association with body and blood, there has been intense questioning and theorizing about the symbolism in-

volved. Differing philosophies have yielded differing interpretations and, since the rise of modern science, with its analysis of
matter and of sources of energy, the symbolism of the
traditional actions and elements in the eucharist has gained
even wider interpretations. Is the focus of symbolization to be
the elements themselves or the actions performed with the
elements? How are the regularly recurring food-supplies of the
natural order, such as grain and wine, to be related to the
sacrifice of Christ? How can the presence of the living Christ be
mediated through certain staple products of the earth?

Until very recently, Catholic interpretations of the actions
performed in a celebration of the eucharist were based upon a
long tradition derived from the Roman economy, in which
varying forms of sacrifice were regarded as essential for the
preservation of a proper relation between mankind and divine
powers. The due ordering of society demanded a continuous
process of offering gifts and these gifts were taken from the farm
with its animals or from the fields with their crops. As
Christianity became established within this context it was only
natural that the actions of the eucharist should come to be
regarded as a similar offering of the fruits of the earth. Thus
before the end of the second century we find Irenaeus writing of
Jesus' instruction to his disciples that they should offer to God
'the first fruits of his own creation'.

> He took that bread which comes of the (material) creation
> and gave thanks saying, This is my body. And the cup
> likewise which is (taken) from created things like ourselves,
> he acknowledged for his own blood and taught the new
> oblation of the New Covenant . . . we ought to make oblation
> to God . . . offering first fruits of those things which are his
> creatures.

Oblation and sacrifice have thus been key interpretations of
the actions performed with the bread and the wine, relating
them specifically to the fruitful land from which they were
taken. But it was also believed that the gifts so taken were
transformed within the eucharistic context into the body and
blood of Christ. How could such a change be effected or

explained? Only by recourse to the teachings of Greek philosophers about the nature and structure of the material order.
All natural objects consisted of form and substance. Form
might be changed and not substance: substance might be
changed and not form. In general, it was assumed, forms could
undergo wide variations without any necessary change of
substance: many varieties of bread or wine might be offered
without impairing the identity of the substance. The substance
could be defined as the eternal, perfect content which becomes
incarnated or expressed (following the language of John 1.14–
18) in and through the bread and wine, creatures of time and
space.

In the Middle Ages the momentous theory was promulgated
that in the eucharistic context while the form remained
constant the *substance* was changed so that the bread now
became substantially the body of Christ. And so far as analysis
of the material elements was concerned, for centuries this held
the field as the official interpretation of the Roman Catholic
Church.

Until this present century these two views, which have
tended to be described as the 'symbolic' and the 'instrumental'
interpretations of the eucharist, have existed alongside one
another, with one or the other receiving major emphasis. Over
the past century however, the influence of the theory of
evolution has been increasingly felt by those seeking to
interpret the relation of humans to the material order. Human
life must be regarded as part of that order: matter, at the same
time, must be regarded as more than inanimate stuff. If an
immense process of evolution has been in process and if that
can be regarded as the means by which God has been working
out his universal purpose, what are the implications for the
interpretation of the eucharistic action and of the particular
elements used within it?

This is the central problem tackled by Arthur Peacocke in his
article entitled 'Matter in the Theological and Scientific
Perspectives: a Sacramental View'.[1] His aim is to combine
what may be termed the Platonic and Aristotelian traditions by
regarding 'the incarnate life of Christ as the supreme sacra-

ment' and by affirming that 'in this outward historic life there is both uniquely expressed and uniquely operative that purpose of goodness, which is the purpose of God himself, that all life and all nature should fulfil'. In the eucharist in particular there is expressed 'the ultimate meaning of matter' (a symbol) and the operation of God's purpose (an instrument). The concept of evolution seems to make this double interpretation viable.

The crucial difference from pre-evolutionary concepts, it seems to me, is in the new emphasis on matter as living and evolving, not as inert and totally manipulable. As Peacocke writes: 'By taking seriously the scientific perspective, we cannot avoid arriving at a view of matter which sees it as manifesting mental, personal and spiritual activities.' The human body cannot be dissociated from matter: the human mind or soul cannot be dissociated from the body: humans must ingest the world of matter in order to live: humans must find *meaning* in their activities if they are to live fully. If there is to be a total integration of meaning and purpose, then God must be viewed as expressing through the incarnate Christ, and consequently through the use of material elements in the eucharistic actions, both the significance of the created material order and the actual furtherance through it of his cosmic purpose. Peacocke does not claim that this divine expressiveness can be *deduced* from what is known of the process of evolution. He does claim that the theological and scientific perspectives of the universe are neither incompatible nor contradictory. He believes that it is possible to interpret the Christian sacraments (in particular the eucharist) within an evolutionary framework and indeed that within that framework they can be seen as powerful activators of the social uplift of mankind. The 'common meal became the symbolic meal of the new humanity stemming from Christ, one might almost say of a new level of evolution of human potentialities'. Symbolism which is dominantly mental, and teleological potentiality which is dominantly physical, are combined within a single ongoing evolutionary process.

I suggest, therefore, that the tension today is not so much that between theological and scientific perspectives as between socio-ethical and socio-biological perspectives: the former is associated with the buying and selling and distributing of food, the latter with the actual production of food and the preservation of the land. In the former the common meal can strengthen the sense of community and recalls dependence both on the labours of others and upon divine grace; in the latter, it can gather up divine-human operations in the natural order and re-affirm the feeling of corporate thanksgiving for the privilege of participating in the total ongoing life-process.

IV

The human body is an apt symbol of the co-ordination of many elements within an organic wholeness: it can also become the symbol of an intense concentration on the working out of a particular purpose. For both of these functions *energy* is required – energy supplied, as I have indicated, by air (spirit) and by food (matter). This is represented symbolically by the human receiving the spirit of life and power or the food of supernatural nourishment. Symbolisms relating to the human experiences of inspiration and ingestation are to be found wherever the dependence of the body on its natural environment is recognized.

But there is another source of body-symbolism. It is that of the *relations* between bodies, whether of man and woman or of mother and child or (in some cases) of friend and friend. Here deep feeling is involved and the representation of feeling symbolically presents greater problems. The sexual act is associated with desire, love, new creation. So-called sex symbols may be constructed merely to arouse emotions or to lead to sexual activities. On the other hand they may present the possibility of relationships characterized by self-sacrifice and self-transcendence, the qualities which the term *love* in its many linguistic forms is intended to portray.

A body in healthy relationship with its environment symbolizes the ideal of harmony, co-ordination, organic life. A conjunction of bodies in healthy social relationship symbolizes the ideal of creativity, care, mutual reciprocity. Through symbolic forms the body is elevated to its true potentialities and those have been associated not only with its primary activities of breathing, feeding and feeling but also with its consequent activities of seeing and hearing. Through them humans extend their range of symbolic responses indefinitely and thereby construct imposing cultural systems. I propose to examine some of the time-honoured symbolic forms which have come into existence as the result of the human response to things seen and heard in the natural and social environment.

(b) The land

Among peasant peoples, the world over, the *land* has been of immense symbolic significance. To possess a piece of land, however small, gives assurance of identity and security, provides an eloquent mark of continuity between past, present and future and establishes a source for food which can be relied on from year to year. It might seem that the last named is the most important but this is not necessarily so. The sense of holding on trust is one of the strongest of human feelings. 'The Lord forbid that I should give you the inheritance of my father's' was the response of Naboth to the king's offer of a far superior vineyard in place of the ancestral garden.

This attachment to the land has been linked in some agrarian societies with veneration of the earth goddess, mother earth, the generator of natural life. Or it has been derived from a whole philosophy of existence in which the human is regarded as vitally related to the land itself: the human possesses the land but, even more, the land possesses humans. Thus the land is regarded as sacred, a symbol of the ultimate fount of being. For certain tribes in the Amazon basin the earth is living, as are trees and animals and the river. To harm the earth, to divert the rivers, to destroy a tree, is to heap contempt on the creator and the creative process.

Yet even amongst roaming and nomadic tribes the land has been regarded as home, a bounded area in which the animals, essential to the maintenance of food supplies, could be found. For example a proposal by the Government to take possession of vast territories in the North-West of Canada and to pay recompense to the tribes occupying it met determined resistance. In their view the land was never intended to be exploited or developed: the land, its peoples, the caribou, and the buffalo together formed a sacred whole. 'There is more to life for them' a newspaper commented 'than five dollars a year and a lot of billets for hunting'. The 'more' – a symbol.

Similarly the 40,000 Bedouin living in the Negev, an altogether inhospitable land, might have been expected to value it less intensely and to be ready to negotiate for other places of habitation. But the reverse has been the case. Even sections of desert they regard as their inherited land. They have refused to move into industrial townships or to accept offers of newly-defined areas. So a bitter conflict has ensued. The Israelite leader of the Green Patrol, commissioned to re-settle the Bedouin whether they liked it or not, exclaimed impatiently:

> There's one thing I'll fight to the ends of the earth for. And that's that this land remains ours, Jewish. The Arabs have so much land and all we have is this little state. Why can't they leave us in peace with it? Land that we bought in the Negev with blood and money is ours. It was the Bedouins' before? Fine. It's ours now.
>
> (*New York Review of Books* 19 May 1980).

Here is an apparently irreconcilable conflict. Land which is a heritage, a trust, a home, a source of livelihood however slender, a sacred area: land which like other commodities is disposable at a price, to be used, subdivided, exploited, transformed. In the former view land is a precious symbol, in the latter an instrument, a tool. This is a burning issue on every continent, but nowhere more so than in Africa.

Here a tribe's devotion to its own particular land-area is intense. Colonizers from Europe were slow to realize the depth of this feeling and imagined that waste land, uncultivated areas could be taken over and made the source of fruitful production. Or from the political point of view the advantages of grouping areas together to form a single state seemed obvious. But Africans did not see it that way. The situation, highlighted over the past twenty years in Zimbabwe, is of even longer standing and is typical of Africa below the Sahara.

Sanctions, wars, elections may come and go but the one fundamental unchanging issue of Rhodesia then (i.e. in 1923) and of Zimbabwe now is land.

It could hardly have been otherwise. Land to any African – regardless of whether or not it is cultivated – has an historical, cultural, almost spiritual quality which seems incomprehensible to European minds long distanced from their peasant predecessors. To be deprived of land was bad enough; what was worse was that the original purpose of the division of land – segregation of the races – was vitiated immediately by the inequitable distribution of acreage so that a class of landless Africans was created who became permanently urbanized in their search for work (*The Times*, 13 April 1980).

Yet the world today is such that land, however important symbolically, cannot be isolated from the wider economic scene. There was a time when populations were relatively small, when vast areas of land were still uncultivated and when peasants could be self-sufficient in food supplies and at the same time able to sell surpluses to town dwellers. But with constantly growing populations and constantly developing networks of inter-communication, land cannot be allowed to render minimal returns through the retention of traditional practices. Will the land and its resources come to be regarded simply as part of a huge economic complex, no longer to be cherished by any social group as the sacred organism through which the blood of their own veins flows, thereby maintaining its health and productivity? Will the plain requirements of ecological policy be ignored and its ethical demands scouted?

Folk culture and peasant religious forms, when Christianized, have become highly symbolic, constituting what Mircea Eliade has called 'cosmic Christianity'. The annual agricultural round appears to be unchangeable but still it needs to be constantly re-sanctified by symbolic rituals. Ploughing, sowing, irrigating, pruning, harvesting are not merely utilitarian exercises. They are something *more*. They are related to the whole life-cycle and must therefore be 'christened' symbolically. Moreover the rituals (which have their pagan origins) have been transformed by the incarnation of the Word of God so that matter itself has been potentially redeemed. It remains for the world and cosmic life to be brought into the realization of that potential by the constant repetition and re-enactment of the symbolic rituals appropriate to every phase of its wholeness. This is a religion of *transfiguration* in which the land is viewed as *more* than a means of production: it is the symbol of a total divine life-process. To pervert that process or to neglect its sanctification is to be guilty of mortal sin.

I have written so far about a devotion to the land which is common (it appears) to all peoples. Mother Earth, as the source from which the life of mankind can be sustained, is a natural conception whose consequence has been a proliferation of dramatic rituals, intended to preserve the intimate connection between the life of humans and the life pulsating within the natural order. Yet this has not, it seems, been the dominant idea motivating the devotion of Hebrews to the land of Israel. In their case, the precise boundaries of the land has remained ill-defined – it might be the territory occupied by the tribes at the end of the wilderness journeying or the land of Judah or the area occupied by the city of Jerusalem or even the site on which the Temple was built. The essential feature in relation to the land has been its complete possession by and control by Yahweh, Israel's God. It was *his* place and it was in this place that he was to be honoured and worshipped. This meant that the Law, his unique revelation, was inextricably linked to the Land. Only within the confines of the Land could the Law be perfectly obeyed without the interference of strange persons and strange customs. In a certain sense a ghetto, in an alien territory, could serve as a symbol of Yahweh's land of Israel. To fulfil the Law in all its details within the promised Land – this was the ideal and the vision of the true Jew. In other words the Land for him was a symbol, not primarily of abundant supplies of natural resources, but rather as a place of unrestricted obediance to Yahweh's commands. Away from the land of Israel, the Jew would always be an exile within a strange land, lacking the freedom to live according to God's law. Only within the land of promise could he establish his own identity and fulfil his destiny by living in perfect obedience to the law of his God.

It is true that Jews have also accorded a traditional veneration to places where special revelations have occurred but this has been secondary to their concentration upon Yahweh's land and their responsibilities towards that land. Within Christendom there have been wide variations, some campaigning to rescue the 'holy' land from pagan occupation, some devoting themselves to the preservation of sacred places associated with events in the life and passion of Jesus, some guarding the sanctity of places reserved for the worship of God and for receiving his continuing gifts of sacramental grace. In general terms the land has figured less as a symbol in Christian theory and practice than has been the case in other religions. The *person* has been central and determinative and the person transcends all times and places. Nevertheless a place (which must be related to the land) can possess a profound symbolic significance, pointing to that spiritual presence which employs things of the earth to reveal the realities of heaven.

(c) Clothes

Why take ye thought for raiment? Consider the lilies of the field how they grow. They toil not, neither do they spin. And yet I say unto you that even Solomon in all his glory was not arrayed like one of these. Wherefore if God so clothe the grass of the field, which today is and tomorrow is cast into the oven, shall he not much more clothe you, O ye of little faith?

Few of Jesus' recorded sayings have evoked such a cordial response or been more often quoted than these. They contain yet another example of the 'much more' or 'how much more' which so characterized his exhortations. Instead of Wordsworth's sad comment 'It was nothing more', Jesus delighted in raising his hearer's sights above the ordinary and apparently unalterable to higher and richer possibilities and this is surely the very essence of symbolism. There are indeed the regularities of earthly existence – we depend upon them. But in order to live according to God's design, there are higher stages in a cultural hierarchy or more exciting experiences in the march into the future and these must be represented symbolically rather than by a simple repetition of things as they are.

In every culture clothes or dress have assumed particular significance. The altogether sinister group is that which is completely uniform in its dress. Black shirts, jack-boots, brown leather jackets imply a ruthless dedication to a single aim which is usually to remake society in its own stark image. On the other hand, complete indifference to what is worn seems to imply anarchy: the view that no order in society is possible or even desirable.

Apart from these abnormalities, the history of clothes, with their symbolic meanings, is a fascinating one. Dress has been intimately associated with national identity, with class structure, with professional qualifications, with the conventions of a particular period, with stages of growth and aging, with artistic performances and celebrations. In no department of life, however, has distinctiveness of clothing been more obviously symbolic than in the sphere of religion. The man or woman set apart, either to live a religious life or to perform religious functions, is almost always clad in distinctive dress. The one whose duty it is either to stand before God representing his or her fellow human beings or to come from the presence of God to declare his message to them, such a one must be clothed appropriately to indicate set-apartness for the work of ministry.

Symbols of national identity, often remaining virtually unchanged for centuries, have become widely recognized through the vast increases in travel and in information gained through television during the past fifty years. The drab jackets of the Chinese, the brilliant saris of Indian women, the head-dress of the Sikhs, the flowing robes of Arabs and of African dignitaries, have become easily identifiable as marks of place of origin. Advances in photographic techniques have similarly revealed intimate connections between class and clothes. Whereas class fashions seem to be in constant process of change, those symbolic of professional status have scarcely altered at all – the wig for the law, the gown for the academic, the uniform for the armed services and for the police, the white coat or apron for surgeon and nurse, the formal attire for special festal occasions. Within the terminology that I have adopted I am bound to describe most of these configurations as *signs*. They are not simply functional, clothing the individual appropriately for the performance of a particular task. They signify divine choice (the sovereign), the majesty of law (judges), respect for learning (academics), the distinctiveness of scientific skills (doctors especially), but they do it with little change or development. Even in societies rapidly changing in other respects, it is somehow felt that the law, the defence of the realm, higher learning and bodily healing should retain the outward signs visible in the clothing of their representatives.

However, the question remains whether clothes serve any longer as *religious* symbols. Do they point to a supreme creator, the ultimate source of life? Or do they suggest the revelation of authoritative command and purpose? In broad terms, the former has been the symbolic aim of Catholic Christianity (as of other religions inspired by processes observable in the natural order) while the latter has been the presumption of Reformed Christianity (as of other religions claiming to be mediators of a divinely ordained law). The former has been concerned to clothe its central figure, the priest, in garments symbolizing the office which is that of elevating humans to a life of communion with God himself. The latter has been concerned to clothe its central figure, the prophet or preacher, in garments symbolizing the office of declaring that the nature of true human destiny is that of living in obedience to the will of God and in conformity with his purpose.

How, then, has this been done? Traditionally the ordinary daily habit of the priest has been black, the garment worn over it when performing the distinctively priestly functions has been white. The precise shape and additional adornments have varied from age to age and in different environments, but the pure whiteness has remained the unchanged requirement, and this has been dramatically exposed to vast numbers of viewers as the white-robed Pope has journeyed from country to country, performing in each the central priestly offering of the Mass. Other ways might be named in which he has stood out amongst his fellow human-beings symbolically, but none compares with the immaculate figure acting on behalf of all who have worshipped with him. Does the priest's black daily habit symbolize withdrawal from the pomps and ceremonies and ambitions of a sinful world? It is hardly open to question that the white robe symbolically unites him to the white-robed company in heaven and enables him to point towards that self-offering which belongs to the very nature of God himself.

Reformed Christianity has traditionally paid less attention to dress or to visible symbols. Its central concern has been to hear through chosen vessels the word of the living God and to respond to that word in faith and obedience. Visual symbolism is regarded as secondary and only to be employed in order to confirm and seal that which had been declared in words. Baptism and the Lord's Supper could be regarded as such but these did not require the presiding minister to wear special dress.

However, was dress to be of no account when solemnly declaring the word of God? Was the Bible bearing witness to that word to be the only symbolic form? In circles devoted to the pursuit of learning it had been customary for qualified teachers to wear a black gown. Would it not therefore be appropriate for the stewards of the mysteries of God, those who had been duly trained in the knowledge of God, to wear the same black gown and thereby, in the context of divine service, to become themselves symbols of the God who speaks, who declares his word through human voices?

There have been variations. In the context of ordered worship such a symbolism of dress has seemed suggestive and appropriate. But formal licences to preach and confinement to formal buildings could be inhibiting. With the great unloosing of social bonds from the eighteenth century onwards and the formation of new social groupings, there came the urge to declare the word of salvation in conventicle or in the open-air. Gowns were no longer regarded as either necessary or available. So the symbolism of the black gown faded. In the later part of the twentieth century the counterpart to the Pope on television has been Billy Graham, also appearing on the same medium while preaching in some great open-air stadium. His clothing has been that of the respectable man of the world. All the symbolism has been focussed in the Bible held firmly in the hand and used in gestures to emphasize the solemn import of the divine message. It seems more and more unlikely that Reformed Christianity will cling to or create afresh some distinctive dress for its prophets such as will effectively symbolize their function as authorized exponents of the given Word of God.

Increasing migration and travel, the break-up of communities, the influence of mass media of communication, mobility of fashion have brought about extraordinary changes in styles of clothing since World War II. In the ecclesiastical world, it has seen the virtual disappearance of apron and gaiters which, up until the 1960s, had been the hall-mark of dignitaries in the Church of England. It is true that in the case of bishops this sign or symbol has been replaced by the red (various shades) or purple vest or stock in daily life and by the mitre (worn by only a few in the first part of the century) on specifically religious occasions. The round clerical collar is far less often worn. But all these have been signs indicating degree within a particular religious community. They can hardly be regarded as symbols pointing to divine being or relationship.

In the New Testament there is no record of apostles or evangelists or presbyters or deacons wearing special clothing or marks of office. The central and oft-repeated symbolism for all Christians is that of abandoning an old garment and putting on a new. Whatever may be the changes of fashion in a country or a community, this is an aspect of human practice which does not change. A garment wears out, develops holes or tears, becomes soiled and no longer respectable. Then is the time for new creation.

This image was central in Jesus' own teaching. No patching of new cloth on old garments! It became central for those converting to the Christian faith in the Mediterranean world. Putting off and putting on. Divesting oneself of the old life, old habits, old weaknesses. Clothing oneself with new habits, new strengths and above all with Christ Himself. 'Put ye on the Lord Jesus Christ' (Rom. 13.14). In the most extensive of the New Testament passages we read (and although there is no explicit reference to baptism the putting on of new clothes as part of the ceremony seems altogether likely).

> Ye put off all these; anger, wrath, malice, blasphemy . . . and have put on the new man which is renewed in knowledge after the image of him that created him . . . Put on therefore kindness, humbleness of mind, meekness, long-suffering . . . And above all these things put on charity which is the bond of perfectness.

Outward circumstances of course may influence the retention or abandonment of certain forms of clothing. For example in the religious world a generally liberal régime will allow a wide variety of dress for ministers or members of religious orders with no pressure towards immediate identification; on the other hand a repressive régime will insist on marks of separation being readily identifiable.

> In Poland the Church is in open opposition to the political régime. Clerical dress is a symbol of that resistance and it's probably exhilarating to wear it. In the United States it has a different meaning. Here, the nun in her religious habit was regarded as the naive little girl who was not expected to understand questions of public policy. Sisters in the United States today who want to move into political ministries such as I'm involved in or press for social justice in a major way, can't afford that kind of symbolism (Sister Fiedler, *The Listener*, 3 April 1980).

It is not only the pressure from secular authorities, however, which may determine dress. In general the more authoritive an ecclesiastical régime is, the more will it insist on a clear mark of separateness being continuously observed. Blue collar and white collar is matched by Roman collar. The cassock immediately distinguishes its wearer from all other men and women. Certain garments are prescribed when the minister is performing sacramental ordinances. All such regulations are designed to emphasize *separateness* from ordinary, secular living or in some instances to denote status within a sacred hierarchy. There is perhaps no clearer indication of how authority is viewed than by an individual's dress within any particular social system.

In her valuable investigation of nineteenth-century writings on the use of the term symbol, *The Idea of the Symbol*,[2] Sr Jadwiga Swiatecka devoted one chapter to a comparison between Coleridge and Carlyle. The latter's famous book *Sartor Resartus* focusses attention on the significance of clothes, particularly as an apt symbol of the relation of the phenomenal world to God himself. She regards the following passage as central in the book, and a good summary of Carlyle's position:

> It is written, the Heaven and the Earth shall fade away like a Vesture; which indeed they are: the Time-vesture of the Eternal. Whatsoever sensibly exists, whatsoever represents Spirit to Spirit, is properly a Clothing, a suit of Raiment, put on, for a season and to be laid off. Thus in this one pregnant subject of CLOTHES, rightly understood, is included all that men have thought, dreamed, done and been: the whole External Universe and what it holds is but Clothing; and the essence of all Science lies in the PHILO-SOPHY OF CLOTHES.

Clothes symbolize a human being: the natural world is a vesture symbolizing the divine being. Therefore, in Carlyle's view, there is nothing permanent and unchanging in a symbol. It can become worn out and obsolete. It can be replaced by that which is appropriate to changing conditions. Naturally its present importance is very great (and I think immediately of an actor's costume which is of the highest significance to spectators in a play). But it does not actually partake of the being that it clothes. It is a mask, an indication of office, rank, status, role, but not an actual identification with some part of essential being. To Carlyle symbols, like clothes, were shadows calling beholders to pierce in imagination to the reality beyond. But they did not participate in that reality.

As Sr Swiatecka shows, the key-word for Coleridge was not shadow but 'embodiment'. A symbol actually participated in that which it represented and so possessed a numinous quality which set it apart. This meant, I suggest, that eucharistic vestments worn by a priest had a sacred quality: they could not be donned for secular purposes nor regarded as an arbitrary aspect of the eucharistic action. In some sense a priest in his vestments became an *embodiment* of the holy. The clothes, the symbolic garments, were part of a divine revelatory action.

As Sr Swiatecka further shows, the implications of their different understandings of the nature of the symbol were profound for Coleridge's and Carlyle's interpretation of the immanence of God. This difference comes to a focus in their assessment of the significance of the human career of Jesus of Nazareth. For Carlyle,

> the life of Jesus of Nazareth is only our 'divinest Symbol' as yet; there is nothing definitive about it; it may yet be improved upon. There is no suggestion here that Christ is a symbol of God, because he is God incarnate, God made visible to man, because he is both God and man. There is instead the contrary suggestion that his biography is the work purely of 'human thought': all idea of the 'symbol' as essentially a creation of a – hypostatic – union between God and man, something which is both of God and of man is lost.[3]

Most of the world's inhabitants are daily concerned about clothing. Are clothes merely functional or are they in some sense symbolic? If symbolic, do they indicate a status in society, a particular kind of task to be performed, a fashion for a particular period? Or are they actually part of a total relationship between human beings and the divine, a symbol which can vary in inessential details from place to place and from age to age but which in its essential form, through its relationship to the Eternal, remains constant? Questions about the symbolism of clothes have their relevance to the deepest theological questions that have engaged the human mind.

In his final speech at Encaenia in Oxford, John Wain, Professor of Poetry, linked clothes with symbolism in a memorable way. He concluded his reference to benefactions thus:

Another benefaction on an immediately perceptible human scale: the Oxford firm of Shepherd and Woodward, in their centenary year, have re-modelled the robe worn this morning by our honoured Chancellor. Four ladies, one of whom remembers working on the original garment in the 1920s, made an entirely new black gown with new lace, but carried over the virtually irreplaceable embellishments from the old one.

These ladies (who are, I understand, present with us today) have provided me, Sir, with a convenient closing symbol. To incorporate irreplaceable material from the past into brand-new present-day workmanship is to exemplify that ideal which the University has kept in mind for seven hundred years, and will surely always keep in mind: an originality grounded in tradition, a vitality continuously renewed.

(d) Light and darkness

In the whole gamut of human experiences, light and darkness, it could be claimed, are the phenomena of which we are most regularly and most consciously aware. Air to breathe is rarely unavailable and only rarely are we conscious of the process of breathing; water and food are either brought to us by other humans or we go in search of them ourselves, while in many parts of the world the same is true of supplies of heat. But the rhythm of light – dark is unique. Gradually light increases and envelops us; gradually it diminishes and we are plunged into darkness. Only recently has it been possible by artificial means to remain permanently illumined.

It is not surprising that of all natural phenomena used as symbols of a divine being and his operation none has been more widespread than light. Whether the reference has been to transcendence by reason of the light-giving properties of sun, moon and stars or whether it has been to immanence by reason of the steady, penetrating, illuminating properties of their rays within terrestrial experience, the appropriateness of light as a symbol of divinity has been unquestioned. The New Testament relates God *directly* to three human experiences: God is Spirit, God is Love, God is Light. Probably it is the last of these which has most often been employed symbolically by Christian witnesses to enable their fellows to grow in the knowledge of God.

One of the major advantages of light symbolism is that it can be used not only in verbal instruction and interpretation but also by artists using visual means to express their own insights. Light as used in a painting or as mediated through the windows of a building can produce a mysterious, strangely numinous effect. It can suggest, even point towards, a transcendent source or alternatively towards an immanent pervasiveness. And until the coming of remote and seemingly automatic methods of producing light, the candle, the torch, the lamp, the lantern have played a notable part as light-bringers and have consequently become apt symbols of divine operations in the world. It is true that the actual experience of light differs as between lands nearest to the equator and those far removed, north or south. Nowhere for instance has light symbolism been more joyfully celebrated than in the lands around the Mediter- ranean Sea. At virtually all times of the year the sun shines strongly and at night the clear skies are lit either by a brilliant moon or by myriads of stars. Egyptians, Hebrews, Greeks all associated God or the benevolent gods with light; light was a major symbol of divinity.

Sun-worship was certainly one of the living faiths of the ancient world, and it had a revival under the Roman Empire. To the naive observer, the light of the sun is both the cause of life on earth and at the same time the medium by which we became aware of phenomena. Plato gave philosophical status to this conception when he used the sun as a symbol of the Idea of the Good . . . which he identified – or at any rate was understood to identify – with the supreme God. It was mainly due to Plato, so far as I can see, that in the Hellenistic world religious thinkers of a philosophical cast generally adopted this particular kind of symbolism.

By using the symbol of light it was possible to give an account of the relation of the absolute to phenomena, of God to the universe. Light communicates itself by radiations, which are emanations (so it was supposed) of its own substance.[4]

Thus through the symbolism of light the Hellenistic world of philosophy and mysticism came very close to the Hebraic world of religion and ethic. In the Old Testament, particularly in the Psalms, light symbolism is freely used when speaking of God and his relations with mankind. In turn it is taken up by Philo and made to serve as one of the chief links between the Hebrew tradition and Greek philosophy. It appeared in the Pauline corpus but it was above all through the Johannine writings that light became one of the leading symbols for expressing and communicating the Christian faith. Life and light and knowledge were intimately linked together but of these three it was light which could most obviously be employed for symbolic development. The dramatic declaration 'I am the light of the world' has proved to be one of the most powerful of all pointers to the nature of Jesus' mission and to the continuing significance of his life, death and resurrection in relations between God and man.

In the history of Christianity the multiple qualities and gradations of light have provided material for philosophers, painters, preachers and moralists. During its first millennium Platonism and Neo-Platonism were the dominant philosophical systems to which it sought to relate itself and in these, light-symbolism was constantly encountered. The great works of Christian art made it abundantly evident that the coming of Christ had brought a new source of light into the world: unlimited variations of architectural shapes acted as silhouettes when viewed externally against the light-background, as frames when viewed internally with light streaming in; painters skilfully employed their representations of light so that a central figure might be illuminated or the theme of revelation might be symbolized. For preachers the symbol of the sun outpouring its rays was altogether the most apt for conveying to their hearers the doctrine of the Trinity. The sun itself, the emanation of its healing and life-giving rays, the actual reception on earth of light and warmth seemed to express a vivid likeness to the threefold nature of the Godhead. And finally, for the moralist, no contrast could more readily be expounded than that between good works shining as light before fellow humans and evil works clandestinely performed in some dark recess. The beacon of light and the heart of darkness were inescapable realities in every human society: the contrast had become even more stark through the Christian revelation.

Further, to hymn-writers throughout the centuries of Christian worship, the imagery of light and darkness has presented an immediate appeal. From the devout salute of Eastern Orthodoxy,

> Hail gladdening Light
> Of that pure glory poured,

to Charles Wesley's joyful acclaim,

> Christ whose glory fills the skies
> Christ the true the only light,

the symbolism has retained its power. The triumph of light over darkness is a daily earthly experience. It points to what may also be real in the realm of the spirit.

But the past two centuries have brought extraordinary developments in our understanding of the properties and processes of light and consequently in new ways of producing light. Is light any longer a natural symbol or has it become simply an amazingly useful medium within the vast technological complex? Electricity, television, lasers, information technology are all profoundly concerned with the potentialities of light artifically produced. Does the archetypal analogy between the action of physical light on the eye and that of verbal instruction on the mind still seem apt? Are flashes of insight experienced in solving mathematical or scientific problems comparable to what in Ian Ramsey's writings were described as 'cosmic disclosures'? For him a favourite symbol was the dawning of the light as a spiritual experience. Is this a meaningful symbol in a world in which human behaviour seems to be governed simply by stimulus and response?

Some of the outstanding literary works of this century have emphasized darkness rather than light as being characteristic of the spiritual condition of our time. Written just at the turn of the nineteenth century, Joseph Conrad's *Heart of Darkness* has continued to be regarded as a prophetic portrayal of the human situation. In a recent reappraisal of the book Peter Ackroyd interpreted its central significance in this way:

> He wrote it at a time when the certainties of the nineteenth century were shivered to fragments, and by chance or indirection he fashioned his narrative out of despair and inanition which followed that loss. In the process he removed the spurious prose of the world, and uncovered an authentic modern myth. If it is anything, it is the myth of emptiness; when you reach down into the heart there is simply darkness, there is no heart at all – not in man, not in Western civilization, not in religion. There is only a void.
>
> Conrad is concerned with the sudden illumination, not the protracted description, the scene and not the character, the metaphor and not the plot, images of darkness, gloom and night spread through the narrative so that it becomes itself an extended metaphor – the 'heart of darkness' is to be discerned everywhere, spreading slowly outwards like a stain (*The Times*, 25 August 1982).

T. S. Eliot in his original draft of *The Waste Land* included a passage from *The Heart of Darkness* as an epitaph. But it is in *Four Quartets* that the symbolism of darkness attains a special prominence. Between the writing of these two poems there occurred both a full commitment to Christian allegiance and the writing of *The Rock* – his contribution to the campaign for the building of new churches in London. And it is in *The Rock* that light-symbolism finds its notable expression in modern poetry.

The interpretation of history presented in *The Rock* is some-what conventional and, generally speaking, optimistic. In the beginning darkness was on the face of the deep; then divine light shone and peoples began to turn towards the light, inventing the 'higher religions'; but these became formal and lifeless and darkness returned. Then came the predestined moment when the light of the Word shone forth and it seemed as if the people must now proceed from light to light. But again selfishness and blindness caused failure in the church and the need became urgent for visible reminders of invisible light. A newly built church could be 'one more light set on a hill' and many such churches could spread the light abroad in the world.

With this prospect in view the poet concluded with his great paean in praise of the Light Invisible. All lesser lights are reminders: eastern light at sunrise, western light at sunset, moonlight and starlight, lights of altar and sanctuary, light reflected and refracted, even the little light which is dappled with shadow. All point to (in our terms are symbols of) the Light Invisible, the Light which is to be praised and worship-ped and glorified.

It seems, however, that the grim experience of the Second World War led Eliot to feel that darkness had once again enveloped the earth and that Christians were being compelled to enter into that darkness, not indeed without hope, but with the understanding that only through deep penitence and purification – the dark night of the soul – could they experi-ence moments of clear shining after rain, of brightness after shadow, of light after darkness. The Light had not been completely extinguished, but the poet could now only speak of gleams and flashes of light – on the kingfisher's wing, the sudden shaft of sunlight in the garden. Light fades on a winter afternoon or is reflected unnaturally from an icy pool or bursts out from a flaming fire. It is a dark time for all sorts and conditions of mankind. The one saving recourse at such a time is to be *still* and to let the dark come upon you: it will be the darkness of God. For in the stillness light will dawn: 'the light is still at the still point of the turning world'.

Eliot's faith had not disappeared, but it had lost the exuberant tone sounded in *The Rock*. Now the emphasis was on the moments of revelation in the stillness, on the willingness to seek a place of quiet and there to kneel in humility, waiting for the light. Through the seemingly interminable darkness of the wartime nights people yearned for the coming of the light. Will there be the same yearning for spiritual light when the physical darkness has been overcome?

In many ways light has been the supremely powerful symbol for expressing and communicating the Christian revelation. Witnesses have claimed that the man who proclaimed the Word of God and then died and rose again was the outshining of God's splendour and the light pointing the way for all men and women to find their true destiny. But will our new knowledge of the nature of light and its applications strengthen or lessen the effectiveness of this symbolism? To Eliot's moth light and glow light we now add arc-light and floodlight and searchlight and laser light – all artificially made and directed to functional purposes. We are discovering hitherto inconceivable power of light: to cut through steel and to replace wires in the conveyance of messages. But these powers scarcely direct the human imagination towards divine-human relationships. They are seen simply as further examples of the advance of high technology. Physical darkness is seldom experienced. The wonder of the coming of the light is diminished and the powerful symbolism of Epiphany is in danger of eclipse.

(e) Fire and water

Dependence on the sun and on phases of the moon was, for the earliest of earth's inhabitants, absolute. Light could come only from above or from the occasional and unpredictable forest fire. Then came the epoch-making discovery. This was the secret of the way to kindle *fire*; thereby humans gained not only comfort and convenience for themselves but also an incalculable advantage over animals. For illumination, for warmth, for protection, for cooking they now possessed an invaluable instrument. This discovery marked one of the really critical turning-points in human history.

It is small wonder that fire has become one of the most powerful and most widely applied of all symbolic forms. Fire could point to so many benefits and, to so many perils. It could never be treated lightly with impunity. Hence the cry of the man who saw it as a symbol of ultimate *catharsis*: our God is a consuming fire. Few symbols have so captured the imagination and so bonded a community as 'the bush that burned with fire and was not consumed'. Few scenes in the Old Testament are more dramatic than the descent of fire in answer to Elijah's pleading on Mount Carmel. Few sayings of Jesus are more mysterious than his declaration that he had come to cast fire on the earth.

Fire has played a major role in mythology, in legends, in poetry, in history. It functions supremely as a symbol relating to the dual character of human experience: fire warms; it also destroys.

Equally, however, fire can be a dramatic symbol of purgation. When effigies (Judas Iscariot, the Pope, Guy Fawkes) were publicly burned there came a strange satisfaction of having vicariously purged the land of evil influence emanating from some particular source. The burning of heretics and witches seemed to be a way of removing a threat of evil absolutely: a fire-drama is the most effective way of eliminating an offending element. 'No more water, the fire next time.' The burning of flags has symbolized a public protest, while a self-immolation, as in the case of Jan Palach, can arouse fierce emotions in defiance of official policies.

In the reports of rioting no metaphor has been more prominent than that of tinder only waiting for a spark to cause it to burst into flame: once the riot has begun, the throwing of petrol bombs and the burning of overturned cars seem to have provided wild emotional satisfaction as symbols of defiance and rejection. The destruction of an existing order is made dramatically visible by fire; the hope is often expressed that a new order will emerge Phoenix-like from the ashes, an ambition rarely achieved.

On the other hand fire is so clearly a source of energy that humans have craved to possess in their own beings a burning zeal, a fiery enthusiasm. No record of the experience of early

Christian witnesses has stirred later imaginations more powerfully than the reference to the 'rushing, mighty wind' and the 'cloven tongues like as of fire'. So Christians have sought to be baptized with fire, to have fire in their hearts, to glow with fire divine. This imagery captured the imagination of John Wesley, whose own heart was 'strangely warmed', and of his brother who expressed it in the notable Pentecostal hymn:

> O Thou who camest from above
> The pure celestial fire to impart,
> Kindle a flame of sacred love
> On the mean altar of my heart.
>
> There let it for thy glory burn
> With inextinguishable blaze
> And trembling to its source return
> In humble prayer and fervent praise.

The same ambivalence appears in water symbolism. Humans can be deprived of food for many days and still survive. But they cannot exist for long without *water*. Whatever other motivations and circumstances governed the wanderings of mobile tribes, the need for supplies of water was paramount: the well or the water-hole or the spring or the oasis naturally took on major significance as symbols of salvation and spiritual refreshment. An entrancing example is found in John 4. Literal and symbolic counterpoint one another. The woman clinging to the past and steeped in tradition yet wearied by her daily journey to the well; Jesus courteously requesting a drink to satisfy physical thirst but pointing beyond the well and the water to the supply of spiritual needs through responding to his words.

From another angle, however, water can be threatening and devastating. The world's literature abounds in stories of floods, typhoons, water-spouts, raging seas, rivers in spate, drownings. The story of Noah, the memory of Egyptians being swallowed up in the Red Sea, the struggles of the sailors in the ship containing Jonah were all dramatically told by Old Testament narrators. Water can be a terrifying symbol of the power either of Yahweh or of some demonic monster. One of the glories of Hebrew psalmody is the famous Psalm 107 recording the wonderful deliverances of those that go down to the sea in ships and occupy their business in great waters.

I discussed the varying symbolism associated with water-baptism in my earlier book *Christianity and Symbolism*,[5] but have since learned more about the extraordinary anxieties regarding pollution and contamination which existed in Hellenistic circles. Robert Parker's book *Miasma* shows by countless examples how widespread and continuous was the concern for cleansing and purification. To a degree this has been felt in most societies, but where daily labour with soils and fertilizers does not form a part of communal life the concern may be less obvious. In the land- and water-based economies of the Mediterranean, however, purification ceremonies were of the utmost importance religiously. There were baptismal lustrations for those being admitted as members of religious cults and further purificatory rites for those engaging in worship. It is surely significant that in the typology of the early Fathers of the church the altogether dominant themes were:

1. Baptism as entry into the new Eden of the Second Adam.

2. Baptism as rescue within the ark of the church from the waters of judgment prefigured by Noah's flood.

3. Baptism as passing safely through water as the Israelites did at the Red Sea Exodus.

4. Baptism as the crossing of Jordan into Canaan under the leadership of Joshua (Jesus).[6]

Moreover the vivid symbolism of water has been retained in the ancient prayer *Benedictio Fontis* in the Roman ritual:

O God whose Spirit in the very beginning of the world moved over the waters, that even then the nature of water might receive the virtue of sanctification: O God, who by water didst wash away the crimes of the guilty world, and by the overflowing of the deluge didst give a figure of regeneration, that one and the same element might in a mystery be the end of vice and the origin of virtue.

The descent into a place of humility, the resemblance to birth out of the water flowing from a mother's womb, the stripping from vestiges of a former life and the assumption of new clothing, all made Christian baptism a symbolically powerful ritual in which water was the central element possessing unlimited possibilities of vivid religious interpretation. As the writer of the Epistle to the Hebrews shows, there was an intimate connection between bodies washed with pure water and consciences becoming cleansed before God.

Water, then, though capable of being employed simply as a sign to attract or repel, has throughout human history been an extraordinarily powerful symbol. In his chapter on 'The Waters and Water Symbolism' in *Patterns in Comparative Religion*, Mircea Eliade leaves us in no doubt that (as he puts it) 'water symbolizes the whole of potentiality: it is the *fons et origo*, the source of all possible existence . . . water symbolizes the primal substance from which all forms come and to which they will return.'[7] He draws upon cultures of many places and many periods to show how water and its symbolism have been associated with cosmogonies, the creation of life, regeneration, epiphanies and miraculous renewals. If any element can be regarded as a universal natural symbol it is water.

(f) Blood and sacrifice

I

Of all ancient symbols apparently exercising a universal appeal none, I think, has retained or even increased its power in our contemporary world to the extent that *blood* has done. In the ancient world it seemed to be the very source and bearer of life. To share blood, as in initiation or covenant ceremonies, was to share life; to drink blood (as amongst certain Eskimo tribes) or to apply blood on the body was to promote life-giving properties; to pour blood on the ground was a way of fertilizing it to preserve the balance of life. Blood of an animal had to be shed when a son was born into the world; to lose blood was to lose life. In the more sinister context of tribal conflicts blood revenge was a terrible reality, blood for blood an unquestioned maxim. In the same context, to shed blood in an honourable cause was a way of attaining supreme merit. And this remained true in Christianity where baptism in blood was regarded as a legitimate alternative to water-baptism and where 'resisting unto blood, striving against sin' and passing through great tribulation, 'washing their robes in blood', were regarded as the marks of sainthood.

Is it possible to determine how it came about that blood and blood-symbolism have occupied so prominent a place in human cultures? In relatively settled communities deriving their food supplies from the earth and its vegetation, public contacts with blood were infrequent. Its association with birth and menstruation may have caused wonder and apprehension, and severe accidents must have caused anxiety. But it was the direct shedding of blood in conflict either between man and man or between man and animals which aroused a far deeper concern. In particular, when roving tribes came to depend on animal flesh for their own sustenance (and this could have been at a time even earlier than that of a more sedentary pattern of existence) the question of how to manipulate the blood which, as in humans, was a direct bearer of life-substance, became acute. Could blood be drunk and its life-giving properties absorbed? Could flesh from which the blood had been drained be eaten? Or should blood and the consumption of blood be taboo? Further, if blood was so precious and so powerful, might its properties be transferred to deal with human predicaments – defilement, alienation, sickness, misfortune? These anxieties could well have been accentuated as humans succeeded in taming animals and caring for them as part of the domestic unit. When animals of this kind were slain, the question of the manipulation of their blood became the more urgent.

Though countless records exist revealing attitudes to blood amongst different peoples at different times and their methods of handling it, there still remains a great deal of mystery if we try to fathom the symbolic references of blood. Clearly it was not something which could be rationally explained. Deep emotional feelings were mixed with practical necessities, and this appears to be the same today. In the context of medical care on the one side and terrorism on the other the emotional appeal of blood-symbolism seems as strong as ever.

This has become specially obvious in the vocabulary of the news media. Blood-baths, blood-revenge, 'bloody Sunday', blood-lust, reports of pouring blood on draft files as a protest against bloody warfare: such terms and incidents reveal the emotional strength of this form of imagery. Nowhere has this been more starkly manifested than in the Middle Eastern conflicts. A Lebanese paper presents a picture of Mr Begin washing his hands in blood; the Ayatollah Khomeini proclaims that Shiism is a school of blood and sword and this will remain so to the very end; most realistic of all, an American journalist is allowed to visit the Iranian martyrs' cemetery and there to see a fountain of blood. In the vast expanse of graves not only the central fountain but a number of auxiliaries spout the blood-coloured liquid 'as would an open heart'. Martyrdom is glory: to give blood is to promote the life of the whole society.

In a happier context, strenuous effort in writing, in praying, even in thinking is perhaps most vividly portrayed as an outpouring of blood. In the famous words of Milton, a book is 'the precious life-blood of a master-spirit', and for Nietzsche only what was written in blood was, in his judgment, worth reading and learning. In the Christian tradition no description of prayer is more moving than that of Gethsemane where Jesus 'prayed more earnestly: and his sweat was as it were great drops of blood falling down to the ground'. But it is perhaps through developments in medical knowledge and techniques, particularly in the twentieth century, that blood-symbolism has attained an altogether new relevance and power.

That blood circulates in the body has long been known, but I am not aware of this being applied symbolically to the life of society until recently. (Though long ago St Gregory made an interesting symbolic connection. 'A few drops of blood renew the whole world and do for all men what rennet does for milk: joining us and holding us together.') Most dramatically, it was Mrs Indira Gandhi who declared, not long before her assassination: 'Unless the blood circulates, the body dies. If I die today every drop of my blood will invigorate the nation.' More dispassionately, an article in *The Listener* (7 December 1978) stressed the connection between self-giving and true community:

> Like a hard currency, human blood now circulates not only through the individual but through the human community. This wealth is shared or, at least, it should be. What blood each of us has, we hold on trust. We are free to use it as long as we live. But since we expect to receive it when we are in need then we are honour bound to open this personal account to an infinite number of anonymous others.

The writer went on to compare the sharing of blood to the ritual of handing on cowrie shells which exists amongst the Trobriand Islanders. The shells have no intrinsic value. Yet the 'apparently useless circulation forges a chain of mutual obligation and that helps to create the Trobriand society'.

The possibility of blood transfusion has been one of the most exciting developments in medical history. There is at present no substitute for blood. Plasma is effective to a degree but, for example, in the Sicily landings during the Second World War, though plasma was readily available, the life of a commando with both legs shattered was only saved through one of the surgical team giving his own blood.

II

I have drawn upon these examples to show how powerful the appeal of blood-symbolism still is: blood, it may be affirmed, is the most vivid and dramatic connector between life and death. But it does not exist alone. It is intimately related to the symbolism of sacrifice. The history of attempts to interpret sacrifice is an extraordinary one. Effort after effort has been made to give a *single* all-inclusive interpretation and then to use it as basis for some religious dogma. Yet what is quite clear is that sacrifices were offered with *differing* intentions, that no invariant pattern of practice can be established, that writers in varying cultural contexts have advanced their own theories and that it is exceedingly easy for the modern investigator to read his or her own ideas into ancient practices.

First it is evident that sacrificial rituals existed long before the institution of organized agriculture. The new era inaugurated by the parcelling out of fields, the sowing and watering of crops and the harvesting and storing of grain brought vast changes into social life and these were reflected in attitudes to and relationships both with animals and with the gods. Animals still played an important part in farming, though now not as enemies to be hunted or as flocks to be tended but as assistants to be used in ploughing and transporting and fertilizing. They were valued as means to ends. They were no longer part of the essential provision of nature without which humans could not continue to live. Gods, too, were associated with the bestowal of conditions propitious for sowing, maturing and harvesting crops, and in this context nothing could be more appropriate than sharing the produce and offering gifts. Sacrifice came to be dominantly the oblation of fruits of the earth with accompanying supplications or thanksgivings. Blood symbolism ceased to be dominant in the sphere of ordinary life.

However, there was one sphere in which sacrificial and blood symbolism remained powerful, even in pastoral and agrarian societies: it was the sphere of *law*. The simplest rule in the whole history of tribal law is that of equivalence. An eye for an eye, a tooth for a tooth, a life for a life, blood for blood. Only a few weeks before I was writing this paragraph the newspapers contained gruesome details of justice in Iran where a wife, having blinded her husband, had her own eyes blinded. Revenge, retaliation, retribution, repayment have seemed a natural expression of justice in all types of society. The only differences have lain in the allowing of *substitute* penalties and in the determination of what those substitutes ought to be. Could the substitute be another human being or an animal? Or could the substitution be negative rather than positive – withdrawal of possessions or of personal freedom? Roman law (the word 'substitute' is taken over from the Latin) defined and formalized the concept and Tertullian, a great Roman lawyer, brought it into Christian theological interpretation. Christ came to be regarded as the substitute who died on behalf of the sinner and whose merits completely offset the demerits of sinful mankind. In far greater detail Anselm and Calvin, each schooled in legal language and procedures, devised theories of atonement in which the sacrifice of Christ was regarded either as merit or as penalty. Having been offered or endured by none other than the Son of God, the sacrifice must be viewed as a satisfying equivalence for the guilt of the whole human race.

In a context of *natural* law, sacrifice can be viewed as the way of constantly repeating and re-enacting symbolically the fundamental principle of death being the necessary prelude to new life: a cycle regularly repeated on the earth being symbolic of a heavenly process. Alternatively in the context of law established by *authority* for any particular society, sacrifice can be viewed as the method of restoring equilibrium. Deeds deserving death are paid for by inflicting death either on those responsible for the offence or on a substitute sacrificed on their behalf. These two interpretations of the meaning of sacrifice are relatively straightforward and have easily hardened into formal signs within a rigid system of inflexible law.

Yet whereas Western European and North American cultures have been deeply influenced by the heritage of Hebrew and Roman law, and while this has had a major effect on their general interpretation of sacrifice, this does not for a moment imply that theirs is the only possible interpretation or that earlier motivations or interpretations did not exist. A recent example of radical difference of opinion occurred when Sir Edmund Leach reviewed Hyam Maccoby's book *The Sacred Executioner*.[8] Maccoby's theory of sacrifice was drawn dominantly from the Hebrew tradition contained in the Old Testament and its adaptation by Christians in the course of their history. It concentrated attention on the holocaust, the whole burnt-offering, in which, in the sacrificial praxis of Israel, the body of an animal was completely consumed in the fire as an offering to God. In reply, Leach appealed specially to the classic treatment of sacrifice by Hubert and Mauss, a treatment which inferred that quite different attitudes governed sacrificial intentions. But their treatment had in fact concentrated on the dominantly agrarian context of *India*, a country where sacrificial ceremonies have been related primarily to creation and the renewal of creation, to inducing divine beings to look favourably on human efforts to maintain the regular system of life-renewal.

There seems little doubt that at a very early period of human existence the killing of animals (and sometimes of humans) and the shedding of blood were an essential part of the struggle for daily food and that this was re-enacted dramatically in some kind of sacrifice. The latter seemed to relate the actors to more than human powers. As Walter Burkert has written:

> The worshipper experienced the god most powerfully not just in pious conduct or in prayer, song and dance but in the deadly blow of the axe, the gush of blood, and the burning of thigh pieces.[9]

Such an experience, as Burkert later affirms, constituted the 'most thrilling and impressive combination' of the elements of 'terror, bliss and recognition of an absolute authority' which Otto claimed to be characteristic of every recognition of the Holy. 'Blood and fire and vapour of smoke', to use biblical terms, were all included.

My concern in all this is to stress the *multiple* meanings which have been attached to the most fearsome of all human acts – the killing of a fellow human-being, the slaughter of an animal or bird, even the cutting down of trees and grain stalks (and when carried to an extreme conclusion the extinguishing of any manifestation of *life*) – when symbolically represented in sacrificial ritual. The Book of Leviticus itself shows how widely varied were the intentions and interpretations associated with sacrifice amongst priestly writers: communion, purification, a new covenant, a fresh beginning, a winning of divine favour. In his book *The Religion of Ancient Rome*[10] Cyril Bailey drew attention to the many forms of sacrifice in Roman religion – votive, piacular, propitiatory, protective. Burkert comments similarly on the way in which in the Hellenistic world sacrifice was constantly enacted in order to 'reach a new plane',

> Whenever a new step is taken consciously and irrevocably, it is inevitably connected with sacrifice. Thus when crossing

frontiers or rivers, there are the διαβατήρια, when opening an assembly there are strange purifications, when passing into a new age group or on entering an exclusive society there will be sacrifice . . . If it is followed by a predetermined βίος or life-style, the sacrifice becomes an initiation. Those who have undergone the unspeakable are both exonerated and consecrated. Thus the new life style and the sacrifice at its inception are almost complementary: omophagy is followed by vegetarianism. Killing justifies and affirms life; it makes us conscious of the new order and brings it to power.[11]

Killing in order to continue in life: throughout human history this has constituted one of the most terrifying of all dilemmas. Must this act be committed? How can its guilt be expiated? Can it be enacted symbolically by some kind of substitution? And can purification be similarly secured? Can the act of killing be directed not towards some external rival or enemy but towards traitors in one's own camp, even in one's own self? Must the evildoer in one's own society, when guilty of killing, pay the penalty of death? Or, even in this case, can some symbolic death be dramatized? This dilemma, with its multiple variations and implications, has never ceased to trouble individuals and societies. The great decision to employ imaginative symbolism rather than grim realism has resulted in the performance of sacrifice with its multiple applications and interpretations. The one feature common to all dramas that can be called *sacrificial* is a killing (the very term decision is etymologically connected with cutting off, renouncing the old and embracing the new), regarded not necessarily as a negative ending but as in some mysterious way the dark prelude to a new and a better kind of life.

In the Christian tradition, outside the legal context, the sacrifice of Christ has been specially associated with renunciation, the blood of Christ with purification. No symbol has been more powerfully operative in the baptismal drama of initiation than that of the sacrifice of Christ through which he died to the constraints of demonic powers, to the rigidities of law, to the sinful world, and to every manifestation of evil within it before being raised again to newness of life.

Know ye not that so many of us as were baptized into Jesus Christ were baptized into his death? Therefore we are buried with him by baptism into his death: that like as Christ was raised up from the dead by the glory of the Father even so we also should walk in newness of life (Rom. 6.3f.).

Like: even so. It is the supreme symbol evoking the supreme response, from old to new, from sin to righteousness, from death to life.

Similarly no symbol has been more powerful as a spiritual cleansing agent than that of the blood of Christ. Now that most flowings of blood are hidden from public gaze in abattoirs or in hospitals, reference to the blood-symbol has been less common and has often seemed undesirable. The language of the Book of Common Prayer, 'that our sinful bodies may be made clean by his body and our souls washed in his most precious blood', or that of hymns such as 'Rock of Ages' with its reference to 'the water and the blood, from thy riven side which flowed', and, 'There is a fountain filled with blood drawn from Immanuel's veins', has seemed too realistic and at times almost magical in its implications. Yet as the testimony of the Christianity of the New Testament and of subsequent history shows, this has in fact, both in Catholic or Protestant circles, been a symbol bringing assurance of remission and release to countless souls. It may embarrass the sophisticated mind. It speaks powerfully to the popular imagination, especially perhaps when blood has become so powerful a symbol in the internecine struggles now rampant in the world.

The symbol gains one of its most powerful expressions in the lyric which forms Part IV of T. S. Eliot's poem *East Coker*. In this, Christian experience is analogically related to that mediated by what, it has been said, has replaced the church as the archetypal institution of our time, namely, the hospital. The poet does not hesitate to speak of bleeding hands and bloody flesh. These are essential inescapable consequences of the practice of the healer's art. And so we call that Friday, when the blood of the world's Saviour was made to flow, Good.

CHAPTER FIVE

Spoken and Written

No subject has gained more sustained attention in scholarly circles during the past fifty years than that of *language*. Philosophers, social anthropologists and psychologists have concerned themselves with origins, rules, grammar, and meaning: new disciplines have been created such as semantics, semiotics, psycholinguistics and sociolinguistics. If there is one feature which all peoples share in common it is spoken language. It is true that animals and birds have ways of communicating with one another and it is therefore possible to speak of animal language. But the differences from human language are radical. Whereas the non-human appears to be confined to giving signals and receiving immediate responses, human language ranges over the whole gamut of experience: the past history and future prospects of the human race, the interconnections and interrelationships of humans with their environment and the expression of those totalities which we call cultures.

How has all this been possible? What are the distinctive characteristics of human language? How does the language of one human being become intelligible to another? How can 'tradition and the individual talent' be combined? How is language learned? How is poetry distinguished from prose? These have become insistent questions in philosophical and literary circles and all are connected, in one way or another, with *symbolic* activities. Is it correct to refer to *all* words as symbols? Are *all* forms of communication symbolic? In a very general sense this may be so. If a symbol is a connector of two entities, the 'signifier' and the 'signified', then indeed it can be claimed that all words and gestures used in communication are symbols. Yet I have already made certain distinctions between signals, signs, indices and symbols. It is, I believe, necessary to preserve these distinctions in any study of language and to reserve the term 'symbol' for those forms which go beyond the direct and immediate and that which has settled firmly into the category of one-to-one correspondence.

I

Two familiar patterns of human experience have exercised a marked influence on forms of language. These are the rhythmic and recurring on the one side, the sequential and goal-seeking on the other. Within a closed circle, language ranges around familiar objects and their detailed manifestations (human, animal, vegetable, mineral). These can all be given names and their relationships defined. Quantities (size, weight, age) can be numerically indicated. Many types of events (birth, stages of growth, death) recur and these too can be represented verbally. Stable and recurring patterns constitute a system of *signs* which are relatively unambiguous: they can be deciphered by the whole community.

Yet even within such a closed circle unfamiliar objects appear, unexpected events occur. How are these to be represented linguistically? There are sicknesses and malformations in humans and animals; there are storms of wind and rain; there are accidents and failures to conform to custom: what forms of language are appropriate to describe or refer to them? Here pre-eminently is the place and function of the symbol. It must preserve some connection with that which is already familiar through regular experience. Concurrently it must also stretch out towards the unexpected which does not exactly fit the regular pattern. The symbol imaginatively describes the new phenomenon by an *analogy*; it is different from, yet proportionate to, that which has hitherto been a normal experience. Such a symbol does not attach a completely new name to the variation in social experience but tries to *extend* the original negatively or positively in such a way that it now embraces it. The symbol may be a word-form which qualifies the original by a prefix or an adjective or an adverb: alternatively it may extend the original in such a way that it retains the original structure while pointing beyond it. The crucial character of such a symbol is that it points to an expanding horizon without losing contact with the familiar and the traditional.

The supreme example of analogical symbols of this kind occurs when humans endeavour to speak of unseen and inaudible influences or operations or powers: they seem real yet cannot be included within either known patterns of human experience or customary patterns of human activity. How can these powers be described or how can relations with them be regularized? Only by extending human language forms to the limit. For stable and circumscribed social groups, God is visualized as living at the apex of a hierarchical complex. The base may be extensive in diameter; there may be many levels in the ascending analogies; but at the limit of transcendent height there is the One to whom all the symbolic forms point and whom they all celebrate.

II

Turning to the second form, linear language seeks to recall the memory of past experiences and to express the anticipation of some hoped-for future. The legacy from the past is derived from learning through successive events: of encounters with humans and animals, of experiences of natural phenomena. The prospect for the future is that of surmounting obstacles and gaining personal fulfilment. Genealogies provide significant lines of descent; roll-calls of heroes celebrate a succession of earlier exploits. What has happened in the past, it is confidently believed, will again be manifested in the future. The linear record seems to constitute a clear *sign* of some purpose being worked out on earth.

But can the course of human history be represented as one unbroken sequence like a mathematical series? Linear language may attempt to express a continuous process, but what is to be done with divergences and seeming contradictions? How can these be included within a total recall of the past or a comprehensive anticipation of the future? Can apparently antithetical elements be included and harmonized? Only by a *symbolic* leap or conjunction which holds together apparent inconsistencies and thereby gives breadth and variety to the line. It is the essential function of the paradox or the parable to hold together in creative interplay apparent anomalies and disparities and even contradictions within social experience. The linear direction is preserved, but it is seen as a road travelling over mountainous country and bridging dangerous chasms: those who travel on it are willing to accept temporary disruptions and detours rather than smooth and unhindered progress.

A study of history reveals that parabolic symbols can easily become formal, being reduced to a single interpretation. This may well be the result of expanding knowledge either of the natural world or of the history of mankind, knowledge which enables us to recognize that what had appeared to be incompatibles are vital parts of a rich texture. But when the search for metaphors and parables ceases, life becomes regimented and confined to an invariant and monotonous straight line.

III

The two leading symbolic forms used by scholars of the Middle Ages were analogy and allegory. The former was the method applied to the interpretation of nature and of human existence, seeing them as having been divinely created and capable therefore of pointing towards the divine mind and intention. The latter was the method applied to sacred texts, seeing them as coverings under which divine truths had been hidden.

In that mediaeval world, life was intimately related to the land, to its seasonal variations, to its cultivation, to its cycle of fertilization, to flocks and herds, to decay and corruption, to the miracle of growth. Communities were relatively self-contained and self-sufficient, with stipulated levels of duties to be performed and of privileges to be enjoyed. Outwardly the form of society was pyramidal: this pattern, embracing life on the home and work in the fields, was extended to interpret analogously the life of nature as observed and experienced. Objects and events were regarded not as independent or as ends in themselves. All were in some way related to the divinely created hierarchical order and were therefore to be regarded as symbols pointing beyond themselves to their divine Creator.

In such a view, the universe is a vast organism, animated by and expressive of the divine life. In agrarian situations, there are multiple evidences of life and the task of those who dwell within them is to propagate and preserve that life. Ordinary language is concerned with these living processes and is then extended by analogy to embrace the higher social necessities of organization, distribution, healing, and possession, rising ultimately to describe the world of transcendence and the activities of the living God himself. *Analogy*, the method of proportional extension in verbal form, and *synechdoche*, the method of the partial representing the whole, were normal means by which mediaeval scholars sought to bear their witness to the One who had created the whole universe and ordered the hierarchies of life upon it.

This method of analogy in theological construction is remarkably parallel to that used in the construction of sacred buildings. The glory of Catholic Christendom has been the central church building, comparatively small in the village, imposing in the market town and magnificent at the centre of the diocese or of the great city. All have been built by the same method: the foundation of durable material on solid earth, the patient placing of stone upon stone in accordance with a plan in which proportions of weight and breadth and height are strictly observed, and finally an upsoaring thrust through arch or dome or tower or spire towards the infinite. Even on a small Mediterranean island, with perhaps thirty churches erected by local builders, there is no uniformity of design. Each has its own striking features. Yet the basic method is uniform. Out from the earth, the source and guardian of *life*, appears the analogical symbol, rising by successive stages towards the transcendent. Each edifice, in its own distinctive way, is a model of that which exults in the finite but knows that it can never fully express the infinite. And no one was more conscious than Thomas Aquinas, the master of the analogical method, that his massive *Summa* could only point towards, could never completely encompass the divine Being.

David Tracy has chosen a fine title for his systematic theology: *The Analogical Imagination*.[1] Careful logical reasoning is involved, with due attention to whatever can be learned about the inter relationships and interactions of the constituent parts of our universe and its life-processes. Beyond that, however, there is still place for the intellect to ascend analogically from the known towards the unknown, from the visible to the invisible. The intellect does not attempt to grasp the ultimate in some abstract formula. Rather it grasps earthly terminology and directs it analogically towards that which is finally beyond all verbal expression.

Analogy is essentially the tool or the method of the interpreter of the natural order, the scientist, the philosopher of science, when prepared to look beyond that which can be observed immediately and represented by univocal signs to a wider and more extended context, even to some universal all-embracing reality. As Francis Bacon declared: 'The universe is not to be narrowed down to the limits of our understanding – rather our understanding must be stretched and enlarged to take in the image of the Universe as it is discovered.' And the most powerful instrument to effect such an enlargement is analogy.

To give one example from the writings of modern scientists: J. Z. Young in his Reith Lectures, *Doubt and Certainty in Science*, was at pains to emphasize the importance of using analogies in order to extend our knowledge of the universe. Only by comparing the unknown with that which is already (at least in a measure) known can we clarify our own thinking and talk about the unknown. Only by constructing analogies can we communicate information about the world in which we live.

Regarding his own work on the human brain he wrote:

From the very number of analogies I have mentioned you can see how doubtful we are in this present phase of scientific research. I have compared the brain with a government office, a calculating machine and with the waves on the surface of the water . . . This whole business of making comparisons may seem to you absurd and useless. It is, however, one of our chief aids to exploring the world . . . It is not a question of whether or not to make comparisons but of which comparison to make . . . It is by comparison . . . that each of us shapes his future. We *must* compare things because that is the way our brains are constituted.[2]

Thus the method of the scientist (as well as of the 'natural' theologian) is to compare and then to communicate his findings by means of analogies. Analogy may extend our knowledge of the natural world: it may, at the limit, increase our knowledge of God. As David Burrell has affirmed in his book *Analogy and Philosophical Language*, analogical theology 'consists of terms sufficiently empirical to be germane to our experience yet sufficiently resilient to be said of God'.[3]

In simplest terms, analogy is the supreme way by which humans refuse to be content with the limited and obvious and seek instead to rise to the '*more*'. It is surely the voice of despair which affirms that the primrose by the river's brim is *nothing more* than a yellow primrose. It was a fine tribute to the late Professor Ian Ramsey that his biographer entitled the central chapter 'The Philosophy of the More'. And amongst the recorded words of Jesus few are more appealing than those which begin with a well-known earthly relationship and then proceed to declare 'How much more' in regard to the heavenly relationship. Analogies are central in the task of communicating scientific knowledge of the natural world: they are central in the task of extending our knowledge of God by referring to phenomena in the natural world which are seen as his creation.

A recent writer has argued that it is proper and valuable to speak of the universe itself as God's body, 'understood analogously to persons and their bodies'.[4] In a Foreword, Professor John Macquarrie comments:

Much of the argument depends on an analogy between the being of a human person and the being of God. Incidentally, if there were no such analogy, how could we ever know anything of God or how could God have revealed himself in a human incarnation? In particular, there is an analogy between the human experience of existing as body and soul and the relation of the physical universe to God.[5]

Thus the value of using analogies, whether in natural science or in natural theology, is hardly open to doubt. Yet there is always a danger either of concentrating on a single analogy or of coming to infer that an analogy is to be accorded a literal or univocal interpretation. Analogy is one way, an important way, of extending our knowledge of God. It is the way of aspiration, of the human desire to ascend, of the construction of ladders and staircases, of the construction of hierarchies. But it is not the only way.

IV

The method of allegory was used to unravel the mysteries of sacred texts. One might seek to ascend towards the ultimate by first studying and then piercing beyond forms discernible in the world of nature. But a source of *revelation* was also available, Holy Scripture, which could be studied by those possessing the necessary equipment. It was, however, far from easy to interpret. Even those who could read might find little of spiritual significance in its lively narratives. It seemed essential therefore to look beyond what seemed to be the obvious meaning in ordinary discourse to the moral and mystical and spiritual truths embodied in the literal words.

By the use of allegorical interpretation mediaeval pastors sought to establish and extend the spiritual apprehensions of their flocks. The story of St Augustine, for example, depicts a learned man, patiently expounding passages from Old and New Testaments by showing how terms, drawn from ordinary human conversations, could actually refer to important spiritual realities or could summon to responsible spiritual activities. In competent hands this interpretative exercise could be stimulating and even exciting, for the hearers felt that they were sharing in the solving of puzzles and the unravelling of mysteries. Alternatively, the exercise could become a dreary recital of equivalences, established by recognized authority.

As distinct from analogy which begins with earthy foundations and seeks to build, stage by stage, an edifice of symbolic forms, allegory begins with an interpretation of Christ and his work, already accepted as authoritative within the particular Christian tradition. For centuries the critical question was the interpretation of the Old Testament. This collection of writings had been accepted as Holy Scripture by the Christian church in face of attempts to abandon it as sub-Christian or even anti-Christian. Moreover it was well-known that the Jewish interpretation of the Old Testament allowed no place for its fulfilment in Jesus the Christ, a conviction which was central in the New Testament writings.

So far as the New Testament was concerned, there was comparatively little need to seek interpretations beyond what was accepted as a reliable record of a series of events and the drawing out of the meaning of these events by inspired apostles. It was, however, a different matter with the Old Testament. Certainly in a general (and sometimes detailed) way, New Testament writers regarded the events recorded in the Gospels as having fulfilled predictions made by ancient prophets. But could this be said of the Old Testament as a whole? Did all the writings of the Old Testament, assembled within the official Jewish canon, testify to Christ? If so, how?

This matter has been discussed by Andrew Louth in his book *Discerning the Mystery*. He defends the method of allegory, first adopted by the early Fathers and subsequently continued by mediaeval theologians, mainly on two grounds. First he draws attention to poetic experience and the way it has constantly happened that an 'inspired' poet has spoken or written words possessing a range of meaning beyond that of his own consciousness or of his own time. If, then, the writers of the Old Testament were inspired, is it not readily comprehensible that their words can be interpreted as bearing witness to the mystery of Christ? Secondly, he dwells on the importance of tradition and the fact that no interpreter today can divest himself completely of the tradition of the Christian church, at least so long as he claims to be interpreting the Old Testament as a Christian.

I do not find either of these arguments convincing. There seems to me no support in the New Testament for the claim that the *whole* of the Old Testament could be allegorically applied to the mystery of Christ. Louth develops what is in many ways a striking idea that, 'The Old Testament builds up a context, a matrix, in which the mystery of Christ can be incarnated. To become man is not just a physical fact, but a cultural event: in the Old Testament the cultural matrix is developed in which this can be possible. In the New Testament there is fulfilment: the mystery becomes a fact. And the mystery become fact transforms the whole of history.'[6] This passage raises serious questions about 'culture' and 'fact' and 'history', but my chief difficulty arises from the way in which the *whole* of the Old Testament is viewed as constituting ('building up') a 'cultural matrix'.

What is the character of this cultural matrix? It is a culture dominated by the conviction that the living God has chosen a particular people, has covenanted to prosper them if they remain faithful (but to execute judgment upon them if they disobey his laws) and has promised them ultimate blessing under a righteous king. It was indeed a remarkable matrix without parallel in the ancient world and it was into this matrix that Jesus was born. In his person the election, the covenant and the promise received their symbolic fulfilment and (as with other symbolic forms) this was patient of indefinite expansion, pointing onwards to the final consummation of God's purpose.

But did this imply that *all* words written in the Old Testament were capable of prefiguring the Christ-event in its manifold detail? Or the mystery of Christ? Were all the writers so 'inspired' that their recorded words might take on meanings of which they were themselves unconscious? That *some* of the writers, the major prophets in particular, were in a real sense poets and that they expressed themselves through symbolic utterances which were destined to disclose truth to future generations I have little doubt. But that records of treks

through the desert and battles with hostile tribes, regulations
for ritual sacrifices and personal purity, can all be allegorized in
such a way as to point to the mystery of Christ I find impossible
to believe. Rather, it seems to me, the early Fathers, with their
knowledge of the method of allegory having been used to gain
edification from ancient classical texts, determined to do the
same with the Old Testament. Already an apostolic tradition
was available for use as the transforming agent by which the
sacred words could be turned into significant prefigurings. A
fixed solution was imposed upon the words rather than, in most
cases, the words pointing to an expanding solution. To value
tradition in the task of interpretation does not seem to me to
require the acceptance of the way the original tradition was
understood by a particular group of church leaders at a
particular time. The Reformers rejected the method of allegory,
regarding it as encouraging triviality and fantasy. And, even at
its best, it tends to promote a one-to-one correspondence of
dissimilars which is alien to the whole concept of creative
symbolism.

Of modern writers Coleridge was one of the most forthright
in rejecting the method of allegorical interpretation. It is of the
essence of allegory to keep apart, to hold in parallel, to say one
thing but to mean something other than what is said. The very
form of the word (Greek *allos*, other, and *agoreuein*, speak openly
in public) implies that by means of it that which is immaterial
or abstract can be represented accurately and tellingly by a
verbal structure which is normally in picture-form. In Coleridge's words, allegory is merely 'a translation of abstract
notions into a picture-language, which is itself nothing but an
abstraction from objects of the senses'. In contrast the symbol
'always partakes of the reality which it renders intelligible; and
while it enunciates the whole, abides itself as a living part in the
unity of which it is the representation'.

Thus whereas it is of the very essence of a symbol to hold two
entities together, it is of the essence of an allegory to keep things
apart. This, moreover, is not simply a matter of language.
Rather a whole world-view is involved. Are man and the world
strictly separate? Or is man at all times responsible for

establishing a vital relationship with his world? Can we by means of allegory provide a one-to-one pictorial correspondence with some super-natural, trans-mundane reality? Or do we, by means of symbols, express our relationship to and our participation in that Reality which is indeed beyond but also manifested in earthly forms? Allegory is associated with monastic and sectarian forms of religious life, withdrawing from the world; symbolism with the attempt to hold together the life of the world with divine life, the divine thereby purifying and sanctifying the earthly. If, for example, one considers Philo's enthusiasm for allegory, it is directed towards migration from Ur with Abraham, flight from the passions of Esau with Jacob and departure from the fleshpots of Egypt with Moses. By allegorization of this kind readers were exhorted to come out from the world with its vanities and bodily passions into the immaterial world of ultimate reality. Allegorization and withdrawal from the sinful world tend to go hand in hand. Through the symbol the struggle continues to change the world by relating it constantly to the divine purpose.

V

The most famous alternative to analogy, when response is being made to similars and dissimilars in life and literature, is *metaphor*. I recognize that it is no longer possible in everyday speech and writing to preserve any clear distinction between these two symbolic forms. For example, the revised *Oxford Companion to English Literature* defines metaphor as 'the transfer of a name or descriptive term to an object different from but analogous to that to which it is properly applicable', thus virtually identifying metaphor with analogy. Yet I am still persuaded that in the course of human history analogy has been the appropriate instrument to link dissimilars which yet have strong ties of similarity (in form or in substance) whereas metaphor has triumphantly bridged a gap when marks of similarity had scarcely been noticed by the ordinary observer.

The following quotation (whose origin I have been unable to trace) cogently expresses my own understanding of the distinction between analogy and metaphor:

The Unconditioned grasps us in the kairotic, surprising, unpredictable revelation. This is the nature of metaphor. A sudden revelation of meaning, power, vision, illumination. Analogies of being arise from reflection on public experiences within humanity. Relations of fatherhood, motherhood, shepherdhood, liberationhood, rulerhood, constructionhood. Analogies are of care, leadership, building, farming. But metaphor is life out of death, new creation out of equilibrium, new relation out of alienation, forgiveness out of hostility, purity out of defilement.

'Public experience' is at its maximum when a community is closely-knit within a bounded environment, rarely visited by strangers, its members working at the same tasks within a familiar and scarcely variable economy. Likenesses are readily noted and it is natural to extend them in order to include unseen spiritual powers who, it is assumed, are concerned with the fortunes of the earthly inhabitants. Thus, in speech and writing, similes and analogies gain ready acceptance in communicating 'public experiences'.

For those who go out from settled and secure homesteads into the unknown and unpredictable wilderness there comes the constant challenge to relate new experiences to what have hitherto been subjects of ordinary speech. It is not so much a matter of extending the old as of transforming or transfiguring the old, of carrying over (and this is the root meaning of metaphor) the new into the old and thereby metamorphosing it.

I have found an interesting illustration of the difference between analogy and metaphor in a poem by the Irish poet Seamus Heaney. It is entitled 'Dawn Shoot',[7] and records an instance of a quite familiar pastime in agricultural areas, especially amongst young men – the shooting of birds. Two youths prepare to go out hunting, thereby engaging in one of the oldest of all male pursuits. Heaney begins with a vivid analogy: the clouds above are running wet mortar over the sky, plastering the daybreak grey as workmen regularly do on the ceiling at home. (Later he makes the comparison even more direct when the plaster thins on the skyline as the whitewash bleaches on walls of houses.) The boys proceed along the railway lines and again a vivid analogy is applied to cows over the hedges, belching out steamy breath like that which arises from an engine's funnel. Suddenly the poet jumps to metaphor. There has recently been war. There has come a new awareness, not only amongst the participants, but also amongst those at the home base, of rifle-practice, sentry-duty, and (newest of all) the exploits of parachutists. First the poet sees the rails 'scoring a bulls-eye' in the eye of the distant bridge. Then a corncrake suddenly challenges the boys 'like a hoarse sentry' while a snipe 'rockets' away on reconnaisance. Finally the adventurers, rubber-booted and belted, 'tense as two parachutists', climb the iron gate and 'drop' down into the field of action.

The combinations of the human eye with the form of the bridge, of rails with target-shooting, of corncrake with sentry, of bird-flight with rocket, of dropping from a gate with dropping from the skies are all new and to an ordinary reader unexpected. They stimulate and excite the imagination. It appears that the poet is recalling an actual experience from boyhood days which could have been 'factually' and thereby flatly and inconsequentially described. By his richly *symbolic* language, bringing together two apparent incompatibles, two seeming unlikenesses, he arrests our attention and gives a new dimension to a pattern of human existence which had for ages been moulded in a conventional way. This process Koestler called *bisociation*. It is one of the most remarkable features of language that the bringing together of two apparently unconnected terms can produce a conjunction which ultimately gains social acceptance and becomes a creative addition to human culture.

In general (though often the distinction has been disregarded) analogical language is used by the scientist in analysing and describing man's relationship to a world which can be managed and manipulated; metaphorical language is used by poets, novelists, historians to portray man's interaction with objects and persons and events which are beyond his immediate control. Analogies abound in scientific records, metaphors in poetry and drama. It is true that a scientist may suddenly see a remarkable connection and may represent it metaphorically: similarly a poet may represent some rhythmic correspondence by an analogy. But the poet's imaginative leap or search for interactions amongst phenomena will normally lead to the construction of vivid metaphors which surprise and delight.

A man who combined scientific expertise with love of poetry to a marked degree was the late Jacob Bronowski. Writing about the link between style and content in literature he admitted that the musical cadences of words are certainly important:

> But in the end, the words are most intimately bound up with that great fund of imagery which is a poet's real way of thinking. What he does for you, what he does for us all, is always to produce a metaphor in which we suddenly see two separate parts of the world, and we say, 'My God, why did I not think that they belonged together?' . . . Why did I not think that 'When the stars threw down their spears And water'd heaven with their tears' is the right way of saying that God is full of pity – he wants to make the lamb, but in the end the instrument has to be the tiger.
>
> And it is the essence of poetry, and of painting, as of all art, to communicate that, to leap over the gulf between us – to make the metaphor suddenly speak to us, not so that we understand it, but so that we recreate it.[8]

At first sight it may seem strange that Aristotle, scientist and philosopher of science, should have written so enthusiastically about metaphor. Paul Ricoeur often quotes his words: 'the greatest thing by far is to be a master of metaphor. It is the one thing that cannot be learnt from others, and it is also a sign of genius, since a good metaphor implies an intuitive perception of the similarity in dissimilars.' It is surely significant that this comment occurs in the *Poetics* (1459a, 5–8). It was many years later that Dr Johnson in his *Lives of the Poets* (I.14) remarked that metaphor is what happens when 'the most heterogeneous ideas are yoked by violence together' and a still more modern poet (P. J. Kavanagh) speaks of 'the lightning flash of intuition as one seeks the connectedness of apparently wildly disparate things'. Richard Rorty notes that,

> Yeats asked the spirits (whom he believed were dictating *A Vision* to him through his wife's relationship) why they had come. The spirits replied: 'To bring you metaphors for poetry.' A philosopher might have expected some hard facts about what it was like on the other side but Yeats was not disappointed.[9]

Human thought as its best and ultimately most influential seeks for relations and likenesses. The exciting moment occurs when apparent dissimilars are seen by the human imagination to be open to a connection, an interaction, an association of images, a transaction between contexts (Ricoeur), which thereby transforms a whole situation. Metaphor is dynamic, promoting continuing interaction, leading in turn to ever new possibilities of meaning. *Metonymy* simply transfers a name, thereby substituting one fixed form for another. Similarly a *code* substitutes a series of ciphers, representing a one-to-one correspondence with an original message. But metaphor at its best is vibrant with new and creative possibilities by reason of the dialectical interaction which is its essential characteristic.

I have tried to indicate how important a place metaphor has occupied in the development of linguistic forms. McNeile Dixon affirmed in his Gifford Lectures that metaphor has been the most powerful force in the making of history, it being the instrument of the human imagination which rules all our lives. Yet there remains one puzzling element in the distinction which I have drawn between analogy and metaphor. Aristotle declared that metaphor must have some *structure* besides its power to delight ear and eye and this structure he defined as proportionality. The best kind of metaphor, he claimed, is the *analogous metaphor*. Would it be equally true to say that the best kind of analogy is the metaphorical analogy? There is obviously no rigid dividing line between the similar and the dissimilar. In the realm of the dominantly similar the most desirable feature is *proportionality*: in the realm of the dominantly dissimilar the most desirable feature is *beauty*. If this is so, then it seems to me to make sense to seek after beautiful proportion on the one side and proportional beauty on the other. The two are not identical. To give due place to both in our manner of using language should perhaps be our highest ambition.

VI

There is clearly a close connection between metaphor and parable. Yet whereas Greek thinkers were primarily concerned with the appropriate use of *words* in rhetoric or poetry or drama, Hebrew writers were more concerned with *stories*: records of events and movements and interrelationships. The Greek dwelt upon the significance of analogies and metaphors; the Hebrew employed records and parables. The records endeavoured to celebrate or to lament the vicissitudes of the past history of God's chosen people. The parables were normally employed to give a kind of preview of likely future happenings. Naturally there were elements of surprise in possible future developments, and this proved to be a link between metaphor and parable. Parable has been described as an extended or expanded metaphor, and while this may underplay the elements of movement and change in a parable, there are undoubtedly common features. Within Christianity the most famous of all collections of parables are those of Jesus contained in the Gospels. Some of these may more aptly be described as expanded analogies, but the larger number may rightly be categorized as metaphors.

The chief distinction which may be made when surveying Jesus' parables is between those which focus attention on natural processes and those which take as their subjects human pursuits and relations. In the case of the former, there are the obvious examples taken from sowing and reaping, the struggle with weeds, the growth of tiny seeds into large trees, the action of leaven in a bowl of meal, the culture of vines, the properties of light and bread and water and fire. Normally a basic activity in the natural world is extended to portray the larger activity of God himself in his salvific kingdom. If the order of nature is such that eminently satisfying results occur, *how much more* can it be assumed that God will bring to pass good effects in the sphere of human needs. And the analogy is made even more convincing when the context of the comparison is that of ordinary and regular human relationships: a father with a son, a shepherd with his sheep, a ruler with his servants. 'If ye being evil, know how to give good gifts unto your children, *how much more* will my Father in heaven give good gifts to those who ask him.' 'What man of you if he have a hundred sheep and lose one of them, will not leave the ninety and nine in the wilderness and go after that which is lost until he find it?' There are natural processes and natural relationships which provide analogous models for the task of bearing witness to the nature of God and his relations with mankind.

Yet the greater emphasis in Jesus' parables is on the new and the surprising, on the witness to forms of divine activity which are neither suggested by natural processes nor proclaimed within orthodox religious traditions. In simplest terms, this may be described as the activity of *grace*, the surprising transcendence of all rigid canons of exact correspondence between law-abiding conduct and reward, between law-breaking and punishment. Such parables are narrative metaphors, holding together disparate and dissimilar characters and situations, bringing them into a new symbolic relationship which can be called conjunction or conciliation.

The range of human activities appealed to by Jesus in his parables is remarkable. He is in no way confined to the social customs and limited experiences of life in a Galilean village. Instead there are travels to a far country, hazards on the robber-infested roads, festal occasions in royal courts, dealing in money and in valued goods, strategies of war and conquest: Jesus was able to bring together the unexpected with the habitual, the unfamiliar with the conventional because he was aware of the much wider world with its practices and images, ready to be transformed into symbols of the all-embracing activity of God himself. The symbol which aroused the greatest incomprehension and even hostility was that of taking up a cross, of enduring suffering, of being betrayed and condemned to a felon's death. These things were actually happening in the world of the Roman empire in first-century Palestine. Could even a cross be metaphorically transfigured and new life be created through death? This was the question which received its triumphant affirmative answer in the gospel proclaimed by witnesses to the resurrection.

Even so, as the New Testament shows and as the subsequent history of Christianity has confirmed, no single form of language has been employed in bearing this witness. There has been the form of *analogy*: taking for granted certain well-known processes observed in the world of nature and extending them to represent or describe what has actually been taking place in the world of eternal reality. In I Corinthians 15, Paul reminds his readers of that which happens year by year as crops are sown and appear to die. God gives to each particular grain a new body though it confirms to its own species. Such a process, Paul affirms, was extended analogously within humanity when Christ, being raised from the dead, became the first fruits of them that slept. The 'miracle' of the natural world, life out of apparent death, was dramatically re-enacted in the 'spiritual' world so that those who were 'in Christ' could now be confident of sharing in his immortality. The language of one section of I Corinthians, together with that of John 12.24 ('Except a corn of wheat fall into the ground and die it abideth alone') is that of *analogy*, using a process familiar in everyday life as a pointer to that which has operated and will operate with abiding efficacy in the realm of eternal reality.

Yet the witness to the resurrection was not confined to symbolic language drawn from the agrarian world of sowing and reaping. There was also the use of more dramatic *metaphors*, inspired by faith in a God who had acted in a way which, by the standards of ordinary human experience, seemed virtually impossible. Could God overcome death? Would God, in the first instance, allow his chosen representative, his Messiah, his Prince of Life to suffer and die? On the face of it this seemed incredible. Yet the inclusion of suffering and death within the messianic vocation had in fact revealed to mankind the triumph of God over every hostile force which had become an integral and institutionalized part of human history. Satan, rigid law, sin, death confronted God as enemies and in the death of Christ appeared to be victorious. The resurrection from the dead, to the contrary, showed that Christ himself was the victor and that (as in a metaphor) what appeared to be utter dissimilars had been brought together within a triumphant conjunction. This may be called the language of *paradox*, though paradox is normally confined to a combination of antithetical expressions both of which are held to be true while no further resolution is in sight. A metaphor, however, while emphasizing dissimilarity, does allow that there is a point of similarity which inspires the metaphor-maker to express his perception in the way he does. There is, he claims, a connection, a creative union, between the Jesus of Nazareth, who went about doing good and giving new life to humans, and the exalted Son who is God's vicegerent and giver of Holy Spirit. The living, reigning Son is the same person as the man who preached and healed and suffered and died. Jesus is to be acclaimed metaphorically as Son, Lord, Messiah and Saviour. This is the way the witness to the resurrection from the dead is to be proclaimed.

If this survey of language-forms is in substance correct, it means that although the second metaphorical paradigm is dominant in the New Testament literature, the first is by no means to be rejected. To use David Tracy's term, the 'analogical imagination' can draw upon multiple observations and experiences in the natural order (which must surely be regarded as *God's* order) and thereby express the faith that God raised up the 'natural' body of Jesus of Nazareth, giving it a 'spiritual' form appropriate to the extension of his earthly humanity into the 'heavenly' sphere: the mortal has put on immortality through divine action. Yet this is still only one form of human language. Another will affirm that God's chosen Messiah was subjected to death in order that the victory over all things hostile to the divine purpose might be openly displayed when he who accepted them was by the right hand of God exalted to triumph over them. No language, no symbolic forms, are adequate of themselves to bear witness to the critical divine action. Through analogy and metaphor, through parable and paradox, Christians have sought to confess that Jesus who lived in Galilee and Jerusalem and died on a cross is Son of God and Saviour of mankind.

PART TWO

Some Theories of Symbolism

CHAPTER SIX

Social Anthropologists

Only comparatively recently has social anthropology been recognized as a serious academic discipline. For centuries European scholars concentrated their attention on the literature of the ancient world contained in the Bible and in Greek and Roman classical texts. Ancient literature was scarce and that of the classical world was held in such high regard that other languages and customs were regarded as of minor relevance for the construction of theories about human nature or about patterns of human relationships. These had been authoritatively revealed through the scriptures or through the records of the great Mediterranean civilizations.

This attitude began slowly to change with the extension of horizons through pioneering travel and trade with non-European peoples. Yet it was not until the nineteenth century that the possibility arose of including the whole of humankind within a single all-embracing theory. Could not empirical investigations determine common characteristics, common habits, common means of communication, common forms of social organization? Could not a vast store of information be assembled by Western researchers spending periods of time living in the midst of tribal peoples, learning their languages, observing their habits, and trying to determine the nature of the 'primitive mind'?

The outcome has been a wealth of knowledge which can be roughly divided into two compartments though they are clearly interrelated. On the one hand there has been a vast increase in our knowledge of the human *body* – its genesis, its structure, its development, its health or disease, its physical determinants.

On the other hand there has been a similar increase in our
knowledge of what has come to be called human *culture* –
languages, oral traditions, social organization, religious ceremonies and artistic creations. It is in this latter area that the
importance of symbolism has gained recognition by virtually
all serious investigators. However widely tribes and peoples
may differ in their life-styles and social structures, they all
inhabit what may be called symbolic worlds. Eating and
drinking, cooking, cleaning, bodily functions, are all performed
within a wider context of social relationships which is expressed
in words, gestures and rituals. The 'society' includes dead
ancestors, good and evil spirits as well as kinsfolk and other
members of the tribe. By means of symbolic forms the well-
being of the tribe is maintained and the merely physical needs
of the individual are transcended.

The widespread recognition of the high importance of
symbols has not, however, resulted in a uniform pattern of
interpretation so far as the actual social activities of any
particular people is concerned. A researcher can never completely shed his or her own cultural inheritance, an inheritance in which certain symbolic forms have already assumed a
dominant role. Moreover he or she can never enter fully into
the total growth-pattern of another society, having entered it
at a certain stage of his or her own development. The task of
translation, therefore, whether of language or of art or of
customs or of religious activities, is never finished. Hitherto,
indeed, every investigation has been largely a one-way exercise with the Westerner taking the initiative and establishing
the terms of reference. It appears that dialogue is still only at a
very early stage. Yet this does not detract from the fascination
of interpreting symbolic forms. Just as the scientist pursues
the task of observing and classifying and experimenting with
and theorizing about elements and structures within the
material order, so the anthropologist pursues the task of
achieving a sympathetic relationship to the symbolic forms of
the cultures both of the wider society in which he or she lives
and, ideally, of other societies also with their own distinctive
traditions. This second task is even more complex than the

first, for the range of variation within living human communication is even greater than that which exists within inanimate systems.

(a) Raymond Firth

I propose to refer briefly to four social anthropologists who have in recent times explored and emphasized the place of symbols in social development. A full-scale treatment is provided by Raymond Firth's book *Symbols: Public and Private*,[1] based upon his own experience of living with the Tikopia people of Western Polynesia for extensive periods. Firth discusses in detail symbols associated with the body and hair, with food and flags, with giving and receiving, with status and roles. He also makes a number of affirmations about symbols in general.

'The essence of symbolism,' he writes, 'lies in the recognition of one thing as standing for (re-presenting) another, the relation between them essentially being that of concrete to abstract, particular to general. The relation is such that the symbol by itself appears capable of generating and receiving effects otherwise reserved for the object to which it refers – and such effects are often of high emotional charge.'[2] And again: 'For many of us the prime relevance of an anthropological approach to the study of symbolism is the attempt to grapple as empirically as possible with the basic human problem of what I would call "disjunction" a gap between the overt superficial statement of action and its underlying meaning.'[3] He assigns a very important role to symbols in human affairs: 'man orders and interprets his reality by his symbols and even reconstructs it'.[4] Moreover the symbol, in his view, does not only serve to establish order – a function which might be regarded as primarily intellectual. 'A symbol may succeed in concentrating upon itself all the fervour that properly belongs only to the ultimate reality it represents.'[5] In fact, according to Firth, a *symbol* may be a means either of establishing social order or of stimulating social loyalties; in addition a symbol may at times fulfil a more private and individual function, though it is hard to recognize any value in a symbol which does not have *some* reference to wider social experience.

These generalizations are based on observations and records made while living and working within a well-defined and well-ordered society. Yet they raise problems for anyone seeking to determine the nature and function of symbolism in human culture generally. Concrete and abstract, superficial statement and underlying meaning, representation and ultimate reality – these are pairs of terms which presumably illustrate the 'disjunction' which Firth regards as the basic human problem. But is not this 'disjunction' a relatively late phenomenon in human development? Does it not belong to civilizations which have made notable advances in understanding the structure of the human environment and expressing that structure in abstract terms? Or the disjunction between statement and meaning· does the user of symbols recognize any meaning other than that which he expresses through a particular statement? And is not 'reality' or 'ultimate reality' often regarded as embodied in or at least as operating through the symbolic form? It seems to me that the notion of 'disjunction' between statement (or gesture) and underlying meaning belongs to the questionings and speculations within Western culture rather than to mankind as a whole.

But there is a further difficulty regarding Firth's view of symbolization. He admits that his evidence is drawn from a relatively settled society in which symbols of status, roles and interior relations play a dominant part. In a circumscribed area, where flora and fauna are seasonally regulated and where humans can rely upon a stable means of subsistence, the all-important matter is that of social organization, how a proper order is to be maintained with each individual performing his or her responsible function for the well-being of the whole. Normally these functions are established within a hierarchical framework and this means that symbols of status are supremely important. Only when all relationships are ordered and represented within a symbolic system can the well-being of the total society be maintained.

But our knowledge of the past experiences of mankind tells us that not all societies have been static and related indefinitely to a particular land-area. There have also been dynamic, restless,

mobile societies whose manner of life and of communal organization has been very different from that of 'landed' peoples.
In societies of this kind 'status' is of far less importance. The
continuing existence of the society now depends upon
dynamic leadership, on courageous exploits, on expectation of
a goal, on perseverance through adversity, on loyalty to
fellows, often on belief in some ultimate purpose. Symbols
therefore are orientated towards persons-in-time rather than
towards persons-in-space. Not the imperial head but the
dynamic leader, not the overseer but the warrior, not the
agriculturalist but the trader. In both cases the symbol points
beyond itself to the functioning of the total social system, but
in different ways. Over thousands of years the general distinction between settled and mobile communities has persisted. It
is only within the past two centuries that boundaries of space
and time have become increasingly tenuous so that those from
settled communities can move freely around the world, those
in mobile communities can experience a relatively settled
existence. Symbol systems have undergone major adjustments: to retain or maintain a *system* becomes problematic.

The concluding chapter of Firth's book is entitled 'Symbol
and Substance'. This chapter focusses attention on the question which is fundamental to all theories of symbolism. Firth
states it bluntly: symbols of what? If in any society symbolic
forms are employed, what do they represent, what is their
function, what meaning do they encapsulate, what effect do
they actually have on the life of those who use them?

The two terms Firth uses are significant: 'symbol' denotes
the holding together of two entities; 'substance' denotes
underlying, indivisible, material. A world-view which includes symbols is binary: there is no complete coalescence of
crystallization into a solid mass but rather a constant inter-
relationship of elements with one another. A world-view
which seeks to define substances is unitary: there may be
many substances but each is atomic, independent, final. Substance then is substance only; it cannot be livingly related to
anything else and cannot therefore enter into any symbolic
relationship.

During the Presidency of Gerald Ford a proposal was made that he should meet Alexander Solzhenitsyn who was by that time a resident in the USA. The answer from the White House was that such a meeting would be pointless if it was 'merely symbolic'. What *substance* could Mr Solzhenitsyn produce? Then the White House relented. The President would be prepared to arrange such a meeting. But now it was Mr Solzhenitsyn who objected. What concrete action was the President prepared to take against the USSR? What was the point of talk (symbolic) if it did not issue in definite act (substance)? Each of the protagonists was in fact denying the fruitfulness of living in a symbolic world. What mattered was hard manipulation of substances, the defining of irreducible elements which could then be treated as impersonal *things* and moved around accordingly.

In a very interesting way Firth points up the distinction between symbol and substance by raising the question of the ethnicity of Jesus. How far is it legitimate to depict Jesus as black in any attempt to portray him visually? The earliest representations of the Redeemer were symbolic: as shepherd or as Orpheus. When paintings appeared they were of a *white* Christ, a face such as might have been seen in any country of Europe. Jewishness was certainly not emphasized, though if anything was clear about Jesus it was that he was a Jew.

Yet, as Firth points out, 'in the fifteenth-or sixteenth-century bronzes of the Crucifixion from the lower Congo, it is said that "the face of the Christ generally presents the negroid type". Pictures and carvings of the Son of Man by Indian, Chinese and African artists often show Jesus with ethnic features appropriate to the artist's own group.'[6] There have also been book-titles: *The Christ of the Indian Road, The Other Spanish Christ*; and in New York a sculpture of a female Christ recently appeared.

The motive inspiring these artistic creations is obvious. It is to represent Jesus as saviour of all mankind and therefore as capable of being identified with the humanity of all, red and yellow, black and white. But the question still arises: do not these symbolic representations make light of the witness of the

New Testament evangelists? No Galilean Jew in the first century would have been black. And there is clear evidence that the Son of Man was male and not female. Does this mean that there was no full identification with the humanity Jesus had come to save? That there were many features of human life untouched by the birth and career of Jesus?

One answer has been that we know nothing about Jesus' physical appearance and next to nothing about his human life. But it is said this need not alarm us. We know that Jesus *died* and we know that all humans must die. He was identified, therefore, with all humanity in his death and all may in turn be identified with him in his saving action. Such an answer regards symbolism as irrelevant. It is open to humans to believe that redemption from death has been performed on their behalf, whatever their race or colour or physical circumstances may be.

Equally it is possible to accept as non-symbolical but as actual divine interventions Jesus' birth of a virgin, his victories over temptations, his miraculous cures and his feedings of the multitudes, his physical resurrection and ascent into heaven. These all may be regarded as actual divine operations within a human body. Again symbolism is irrelevant. The events did not point beyond themselves: they were simply direct manifestations of divine power. As such they revealed God's saving grace being exercised for the benefit of all mankind.

To give either of these answers and to live in the light of it brings confidence to the individual and a ground for hope. But the exclusion of any symbolic reference from the Gospels involves the exclusion of any relation to the natural order and to human history. If the records of the career and teaching of Jesus are interpreted symbolically, then they must provide meaning for the worlds of nature and social history to which they are related. It becomes impossible to isolate and define substance or substances to which the symbols refer. Rather the symbolic relationship is to aspects of nature and history which have constantly to be re-interpreted in the context of new environments and new circumstances. The new environment may be China instead of England, it may be a society of blacks instead of whites. Symbolic reference is a continuing process and an unfolding of expanding meaning. Restriction to substance is to confine the activity of God within limits defined by human assumptions. The attraction of the substance, the sign, the secure is immense. Yet it is through the symbol that humans have risen above self-enclosure and self-sufficiency and have begun to experience freedom and to discern meaning.

My own comments on symbol and substance might not win Firth's assent in detail. But I think they are compatible with his main criticism and even denial. He will not allow that any symbolic form can be used to represent that which is 'uniquely real' or 'absolutely valid'.

> The primary problem for an anthropologist is not to pronounce on 'ultimate reality'. It is to examine the forms of symbolic statement, to try and understand the system of ideas they express, the order of that system and the effects associated with the use of such symbolic concepts.[7]

(b) Mary Douglas

In her book *Natural Symbols*[8] Mary Douglas entitles one chapter 'The Two Bodies'; this title aptly describes her central concern which found expression also in her earlier book *Purity and Danger*.[9] She has been deeply impressed by the intimate relationship which exists between the human body and human society, at all times and in all places. The body provides a vividly appropriate analogy to apply to society at large: the structure, the operations and the relationships between the varying parts of the body can be paralleled in the life of any closed society. Boundary maintenance in the one, for example, corresponds very closely to boundary maintenance in the other.

It is this correlation which led to the choice of the title *natural* symbols.

> Natural symbols will not be found in individual lexical items. The physical body can have universal meaning only as a system which responds to the social system, expressing it as a system. What it symbolizes naturally is the relation of parts of an organism to the whole . . . The two bodies are the self

and society: sometimes they are so near as to be almost merged: sometimes they are far apart. The tension between them allows the elaboration of meanings.[10]

Just as man tries to establish order and control in matters concerning his own body, so he seeks categories of stability for his social life. He cannot in fact grow to bodily and cultural maturity except within a coherent symbolic system. Equally, the most satisfactory symbolic system it seems is that which is structured organically and maintains an intimate relation between social and bodily expression. It is basic to the thesis of the book that human language and ritual are profoundly influenced by the structure of society and *vice versa*, that every society discovers its most authentic symbols by drawing upon the analogies offered by the patterned behaviour of a human body. Because of her deep conviction that symbols are of vital importance, not only for the ordering of society but also for the expression of its cosmology, Mary Douglas registers her feeling of strong disquiet about recent movements which reveal a contempt of ritual or are even prepared to abandon ritual. She is frankly critical of statements by certain Roman Catholic bishops, for she believes that the spiritual cannot be fostered by separating it from the formal and material. Ritual is for her the institutionalized means of establishing and preserving symbolic order.

Yet is this the only function of symbols? The author is eager to show that there are *variations* between different types of society, but her societies all exist within the general category of closedness. The closed social group is invariably concerned about status and the land and hierarchical structures. But there are also – or have been in history – open, dynamic societies, related to experiences in *time* and to creative encounter with new circumstances. They are not necessarily anti-ritual or anti-symbolic in character but are characterized by different kinds of ritual behaviour, structured by celebrations of past deliverance and future hope. The pre-eminent example of this type of society is to be found in the Old Testament records of the Hebrew tribes before the settlement in Canaan. Their symbolic forms, as described and interpreted for example by Pedersen in his book *Israel*, seem to me to represent a quite different pattern of symbolic interactions from that described by Professor Douglas. Unquestionably bodily symbols are natural and appropriate in a closed society situation. But in the prophetic legends and stories of the Old Testament the dominant symbols are those of election and destiny, of covenant and redemption. Bodily *actions* may be involved, but the stress is on openness to future blessings rather than upon unchanging patterns.

Natural Symbols gives impressive testimony to the value of a certain type of ritual forms in bringing coherence and stability to a society: position and boundaries are aptly symbolized by bodily characteristics. But symbolic forms are also needed for social experience in *time*, for change, for interaction, and these, it seems to me, have a right to be regarded not as *natural* but as *historical* symbols, as shaped, patterned, formed by critical events in social experience.

Significantly Mary Douglas's concern to safeguard the use of 'natural symbols' and of traditional ritual forms in social life finds vigorous expression in her comments on the Christian eucharist. The *New Catechism*, she declares, plays up the commemorative and communion aspects of the sacrament and plays down the doctrine of Christ's local presence and 'the transformation of the bread into divine body'. Those responsible for framing it and those who accept such a 'watered-down expression of a faith that has practically lost meaning for them' are possessors of an 'impoverished symbolic perception': 'they cannot conceive of the deity as located in any one thing or place'.

In contrast, she affirms, there are people scattered all over the globe who do not share this disability. 'By reason of their positional upbringing and social experience they are capable of responding profoundly to symbols of orientation and boundary.'[11] So, 'the drawing of symbolic lines and boundaries is a way of bringing order into experience. Such non-verbal systems are capable of creating a structure of meanings in which individuals can relate to one another and realize their own ultimate purposes.'[12]

The curious feature of these comments is the failure to take account of societies which are not closed so far as land-boundaries are concerned and are not definable by symbolic lines and boundaries. The appeal to *verbal* forms is not the only alternative to the rituals of a closed society. There are the ritual forms of wandering, mobile, eschatologically orientated societies, the outstanding example perhaps being that of the Jewish Passover. To say this is not to deny the importance of symbols of 'orientation and boundary' in the case of societies enjoying settlement in a particular land-area and needing to organize the *bodies* of all their members within a coherent, organic whole. But for migratory, eschatological communities the symbols needed are those of beginnings and endings, of retrospect and prospect, of bodily redemption and bodily transfiguration. One may agree entirely with Mary Douglas that 'it is an illusion to suppose that there can be organization without symbolic expression',[13] and still be convinced that there is more than one type or form of 'symbolic expression'.

A review of *Natural Symbols* pointed out that the book makes no mention of the Calvinist tradition. Yet this tradition has contained societies as tightly organized as could be imagined. And the symbolic expressions have not been exclusively those of the Word or of verbal forms. The sacraments of Baptism and the Lord's Supper have been celebrated with great solemnity, the sabbath rest has been strictly observed, forms of musical appropriateness have been regarded as of symbolic import-ance. Moreover, bodily abstinence from certain secular activities has often assumed a prominence comparable to the fasting of the Bog Irish, the community that figures so largely in *Natural Symbols*. Thus to the author's claim that symbols dependent upon bodily analogies are of outstanding import-ance in the organization and coherence of landed societies I am ready to assent. However, I am equally ready to affirm that there are other types of society not attached in the same way to the land or to island territories or to the regular rhythm of an argicultural economy. For these, symbols are essential if loyal co-operation is to be maintained, but they will not depend in the same way upon bodily boundaries or the enclosed system of a body. They will rather be symbolic forms of interrelationship, of mutual support and of covenant-commitment sealed by ritual bodily actions.

(c) Victor Turner

The titles of two of Turner's major books reveal at once his interest in symbolic forms. *The Forest of Symbols* and *The Ritual Process* are concerned with the function of symbols in the ordering of social life: he is keenly aware that there are *two* aspects that have to be considered: the establishment of roles and regulations making ordinary social existence possible and the emergence of communal groups, sharing common convictions and ambitions, and organizing themselves in ways different from those of the larger society. There is a dialectical interaction between society as a whole and specialist communities within it. Obviously this is only possible where totalitarianism on the one side or anarchy on the other are absent.

This duality in the ordering of social groups he finds symbolized in a significant way by the ritual practices of Ndembu tribes which carry a double meaning.

In Ndembu ritual context almost every article used, every gesture employed, every song or prayer, every unit of space and time, by convention stands for something other than itself. It is more than it seems, and often a good deal more. A ritual element or unit is called chijikijilu. Literally this word signifies a 'land mark' or 'blaze' (i.e. from blazing a trail). Chijikijilu also means a 'beacon', a conspicuous feature of the landscape, such as an ant hill . . . Thus it has two main significations. (i) As a hunter's blaze it represents an element of connection between known and unknown territory; (ii) as both blaze and beacon it conveys the notion of the structured and ordered as against the unstructured and chaotic. Its ritual use is already metaphorical: it connects the known world of sensorily perceptible phenomena with the unknown and invisible realm of the shades. It makes intelligible what is mysterious and also dangerous.[14]

If this interpretation of the term *chijikijilu* is correct it means that there is a firm desire to maintain a 'beacon' of ordered and regular life, a central sacred space, a clearing in the formless bush where symbolic persons can operate by establishing rules and maintaining a regular ritual cycle. In this way ordinary life is given a shape and any aberrations can be dealt with by prescribed remedies. Yet for this particular tribe this was not all. It was necessary for certain members to go out to the hunt in search of food supplies or sometimes to engage in warlike activities. To venture into the unknown is always dangerous. So there was also a need for the 'blaze', the symbol marking the proper trail, and this could be augmented by other symbols stimulating courageous action on the part of the hunting or warring tribesmen.

Not only for the Ndembu but for many other tribal societies this dual function of symbolic forms is necessary. On the one hand there is the symbolic representation of regular order: a sacred circle or temple, a continual observance of rites associated with birth, puberty and death or with the calendrical cycle, a celebration of the motions of the heavenly bodies. On the other hand there is a symbolic ritual to be performed when a critical event is about to take place: a voyage, a hunting expedition, an encounter with another tribe. These are critical experiences in which limited groups have to venture out into the unknown. Symbolic rites are needed to ensure a safe passage and a happy return. Thus there are on the one hand symbolic forms necessary for the maintenance of the regular health and ordered existence of the whole society. These constitute a kind of intellectual framework, subject to only minor deviations or adjustments from generation to generation. There are on the other hand forms necessary to rouse and encourage and provide a sense of purpose for those facing unknown hazards, whether in individual or community life. Such forms are more variable, more related to the emotions and dependent more upon charismatic leadership.

Turner's analysis where he distinguishes between structured social order, in which functions and roles are well defined, and 'communitas', 'visible in tribal rites of passage, in millennial movements, in monasteries, in the counter culture and on countless informal occasions,'[15] is of very wide application. No society can exist for long without some kind of established order. This may be structured either by the demands of a particular physical economy (especially agricultural) *or* by the imposition of binding laws. In either case, there is always the danger that the seemingly necessary order will become rigid and oppressive, as in totalitarian régimes. At the same time it is clear from historical records that individuals or groups have repeatedly felt compelled to separate themselves in some way from the accepted order, seeking new territory or valuable commodities or ways of organizing their religious or artistic life. The struggle for freedom has issued in some of the most creative advances in the whole story of human development. Yet there has also been a danger of dissension, fragmentation, and ultimately of disintegration and anarchy.

In 1978 Victor Turner, in collaboration with Edith Turner, published a book entitled *Image and Pilgrimage in Christian Culture: Anthropoligical Perspectives.*[16] It examined and described the social structures and processes associated with pilgrimages at different periods of history and in various countries of the world. It directed attention to the conditions motivating pilgrims, to the ritual processes involved and to the symbolic forms characterizing the shrines which were the goals of the pilgrim quests. The chief distinction which emerged was between what he called 'liminal' and 'liminoid' systems, the former remaining within the general embrace of an ordered structure (though concerned with threshold situations), the latter being open and voluntaristic, and tending to go beyond or even to break the pattern of the parent structure.

As an appendix to their book the Turners provided for their readers a series of notes on 'Processual Symbolic Analysis'. These define in a useful way the most important terms used by Turner in his books and articles – terms such as ritual, liminal, root paradigm, and *communitas*. For my own purpose the notes of special interest are those dealing with symbols and signs. They throw light on Turner's findings in the field of social anthropology.

In company with many other writers he distinguishes sharply between symbol and sign.

In symbols there is some kind of likeness (either metaphoric or metonymic) between the thing signified and its meaning: signs need bear no such likeness . . . Signs are almost always organized in 'closed' systems while symbols, particularly dominant symbols, are themselves semantically 'open'. The symbol's meaning is not absolutely fixed. New meanings may be added by collective fiat to old symbolic vehicles. Moreover, individuals may add personal meaning to a symbol's public meaning.[17]

Dominant symbols occupy an important position in any social system, for their meaning is largely unchanged from age to age and 'may be said to represent a crystallization of the flow pattern of the rituals over which it presides'.[18]

Other symbols constitute the smaller unit of ritual behaviour but they are not mere counters: they influence social systems and their meaning must be derived from the particular context in which they occur.

The distinguishing mark of Turner's writings I find in his emphasis on process and ritual and social transitions. There is a place for social stability and that, he states, is marked by *ceremonial*. But the more important feature of any society is its *ritual*, which includes its rites of passage and its relation to new situations. Basically the ritual pattern may appear to be unchanged, but if the flow of life is to continue, the symbolic forms which constitute the ritual must be open to new interpretations related to new circumstances.

At the very end of the main text Turner refers briefly to the effects of the industrial revolution and to new forms of 'pilgrimage' which have followed in its wake. These may be national or political so far as large numbers are concerned: only a comparatively small number now undertake pilgrimages of a religious kind. Can the old rituals be reinterpreted and gain meaning for those engaged in mechanical or information industries? Or can new rituals be created such as to endue with a religious significance the travel habits and possibilities of the modern age? Can traditional ritual forms still be dramatically re-enacted in such a way as to bring their participants into vital relationship with transcendent reality?

Turner's distinctive contribution to the social questions of our contemporary world seems to me to lie in his insistence that society must be regarded as a process and not as a fixture. For society to exist at all there must be *structure* yet at the same time there must be an element of anti-structure, of free expression.

There would seem to be a human need to participate in both modalities. Persons starved of one in their functional day-to-day activities seek it in ritual liminality. The structurally inferior aspire to symbolic structural superiority in ritual; the structurally superior aspire to symbolic *communitas* and undergo penance to achieve it.[19]

Formerly the 'ritual' was a dominantly religious activity, directed towards transcendent powers or possibilities: today it is more likely to be expressed in processions, protests, chantings, demonstrations, directed towards the attainment of some immediate secular advantage. In varying ways, the *ritual process* continues.

(d) Clifford Geertz

Over a number of years Geertz has made it his chief aim to interpret cultures. In an important contribution to the book *Anthropological Approaches to the Study of Religion*, edited by Michael Banton,[20] he declared that in the field of religious practices explored by social anthropologists he would be confining his own efforts to the development of 'the cultural dimension of religious analysis'. But 'culture' has in many quarters become a vague and often ambiguous term. In his own use, 'culture' denotes 'an historically transmitted pattern of meanings embodied in symbols, a system of inherited conceptions expressed in symbolic forms by means of which men communicate, perpetuate and develop their knowledge about and attitudes towards life'.[21] Thus 'meanings embodied in symbols', 'conceptions expressed in symbolic forms' are at the centre of his interest and research. Symbolic forms, in any particular social context, constitute a pattern or system which can be designated a *culture*. To interpret a culture is to interpret its system of symbolic forms and thereby to derive authentic meanings. He quotes with approval Suzanne Langer's emphasis on the dominant place that meaning and symbol hold in the philosophical disciplines of our time.

Focussing attention on religious or sacred symbols, Geertz offers this paradigm: they 'function to synthesize a people's ethos – the tone, character and quality of their life, its moral and aesthetic style and mood – and their world-view – the picture they have of the way things in sheer actuality are, their most comprehensive ideas of order'.[22] Way of life and world-view complement one another, often through a single symbolic form. This gives a picture of comprehensive order and at the same time provides a synthetic pattern of social behaviour. There is a *congruence* between life-style and universal order and this finds expression in a symbol which is related to both.

How then can a symbol be defined? Again following Langer, Geertz proposes 'any object, act, event, quality or relation which serves as a vehicle for a conception',[23] and this conception is the symbol's 'meaning'. Thus the interpretation of cultures is basically the interpretation of symbols, symbols being tangible, perceptible, public, and concrete. *Religious* symbols are those which synthesize and integrate 'the world as lived and the world as imagined'[24] and they serve to produce and strengthen religious conviction.

Holding this view, Geertz discards all theories of primitive mentality or of cultural evolution. His concern is rather to understand what symbolic actions *mean* to those who perform them, to unpack the 'conceptual structures' which ritual actions reveal. This may seem a purely relativist solution. It may seem to imply that every culture is a bounded system in which all who belong to it reveal by their actions what objects or events they regard as 'sacred' and the method by which they preserve and strengthen the sense of 'sacredness'. If this is the case, how is it ever possible for a member of a different culture to understand what is going on and to interpret the symbolic forms correctly?

When all allowances have been made for the difficulties of translation, not only of language but of other symbolic forms, from one cultural context into another, Geertz still believes that translation is, at least in a measure, possible. The major obstacle is any feeling of superiority or of adverse judgment. There are different approaches to common problems and there are lessons to be learned from the employment of symbolic forms other than one's own. But for Geertz there is no magic key to unlock the secret meaning of symbolic forms. It is the task of the anthropologist to recognize the congruence of life-style and world-view as expressed in symbolic ways and to seek by sympathetic study to interpret those forms by means of his or her own cultural apparatus.

Much of this I find persuasive. My chief difficulty arises through Geertz's restriction of the religious symbol to the expression of *totalities* whether of the life-style of a particular people or of their holistic world-view. What place does this allow for the dramatic emergence of a new symbolic form within a culture? What are the possibilities of (following Thomas Kuhn's terminology) a paradigm shift? Many cultures have been subject to re-formations or so-called 'heretical' challenges which have expressed themselves in new symbolic forms. Do not symbols of alternate life-styles appear even within a traditional culture? May not 'translation' be more possible in relation to the apparently dissident or dissonant symbols than to long-established traditional forms? We have seen many examples in this century of peoples possessing long established religious ritual forms being seized by a new nationalistic fervour expressing itself through flags, marches, celebrations symbolizing a new life-style and a new view of communal destiny. These appear to be the really powerful symbolic forms of our time and I do not find it easy to include them within Geertz's emphasis upon synthesis and compre-hensive order. Symbols, as they appear in history, seem to me to be sometimes integrative but also sometimes revolutionary. Interpretation is a double task, sensitive indeed to inherited traditions but sensitive also to the upsurge of new convictions and new demands.

CHAPTER SEVEN

Philosophers, Theologians and Historians of Religious Forms

(a) Ernst Cassirer

I

No modern philosopher has made the symbol more central in the development of his interpretation of reality than has Cassirer. He chose as the title of his major work *The Philosophy of Symbolic Forms* but insisted that this did not constitute a final system. He never ceased to be concerned with the varieties of human thought and expression and how these could be integrated within a total philosophy of culture. Yet he never regarded his own writings as constituting more than prolegomena. The most concise summary of his own contribution to philosophy is contained in the book which he wrote after leaving Germany and taking up residence at Yale: *An Essay on Man.*[1] He called this *An Introduction to a Philosophy of Human Culture*, and it is on this that I shall mainly rely in seeking to explore his definition of the place of symbolic forms in human culture.

The first chapter in *An Essay on Man* is entitled 'The Crisis in Man's Knowledge of Himself'. It is a rapid survey of the development of Western thought since the time of Socrates and Plato, the thinkers who insisted that an unexamined life is not worth living: that to be truly human is to question, to criticize, to theorize, to reason with one another about the nature and destiny of man. Over the centuries since, the debate has continued amidst major crises of thought such as came about through the theories of Copernicus and Darwin. But now, in a paradoxical way, though possessing apparently unlimited sources of information, man seems more problematic to himself than ever before. This is Cassirer's estimate of the twentieth-century crisis:

> No former age was ever in such a favourable position with regard to the sources of our knowledge of human nature. Psychology, ethology, anthropology and history have amassed an astonishingly rich and constantly increasing body of facts. Our technical instruments for observation and experimentation have been immensely improved and our analyses have become sharper and more penetrating. We appear, nevertheless, not yet to have found a method for the mastery and organization of this material. When compared with our own abundance the past may seem very poor. But our wealth of facts is not necessarily a wealth of thoughts. Unless we succeed in finding a clue of Ariadne to lead us out of this labyrinth we can have no real insight into the general character of human culture; we shall remain lost in a mass of disconnected and disintegrated data which seem to lack all conceptual unity.[2]

These words were written more than forty years ago. The mass of *data* has increased exponentially so that today we talk of data-banks and transmit data by electronic means to remote parts of the universe in a moment of time. Yet the two words used by Cassirer continue to puzzle and sometimes to alarm us: connect and integrate. How can there be real connections between peoples of different cultures? How can there be a real integration within a fragmented and multi-faceted culture?

II

Cassirer's book is concerned with getting out of the labyrinth. Is there an Ariadne thread, a clue, a means to distinguish man from all other sentient creatures? Yes, he replies:

the functional circle of man is not only quantitatively enlarged (this may be an open question: in some respects the sensitivities of animals seem to be far superior to those of humans); it has also undergone a qualitative change. Man has, as it were, discovered a new method of adapting himself to his environment. Between the receptor system and the effector system, which are to be found in all animal species, we find in man a third link which we may describe as the *symbolic* system. This new acquisition transforms the whole of human life. As compared with the other animals man lives not only in a broader reality: he lives so to speak in a new dimension of reality.[3]

This claim to the possession of a 'third link' is obviously of crucial importance. Biologically, in Cassirer's view, humans share with all other living creatures a receptor and an effector system. But humans also possess the capacity to interpose between the two a symbolizing process which can issue in cultural forms rather than direct and immediate responses to stimuli. The dividing line is not easy to universalize because humans often respond to stimuli in ways indistinguishable from those of animals. Yet in spite of all the claims of behaviourists and sociobiologists, the claim that there is a distinction (and that a fundamental one) is widely accepted. But how is that distinction revealed?

I have had no experience in controlled observation or experimentation with animals but have recently become aware of a difference between humans and cats in reacting to a TV programme. My wife, the cat and I have been on separate chairs in the room where a TV set was on. In general, the cat showed no interest. But when a nature programme came on, with the rapid movements of mice and the chirping of birds, the cat's attention was obviously aroused. It gazed at the screen, adopted a stance such as it would take when preparing to attack a living mouse, appeared uncertain when it heard the cries of birds, yet made no attempt to advance towards the screen or to take action as it normally would in the environment of the garden or the open pasture. In a certain sense the animal's

reaction was neither direct nor immediate. It did not leap at
the moving animal on the screen nor attempt to relate itself to
the bird cries. Somehow it was aware of a difference though it
had clearly been stimulated by sights and sounds. Other
senses – smell? awareness of context? the two-dimensional
character of the images? – forbade it to take action. There was
an awakening of interest, but it did not lead to action, and the
interest quickly subsided. Although it could be claimed that
the animal's response to a stimulus belonging to its own
instinctual pattern was not entirely characteristic, there was
no suggestion of the immediate experience being related to the
movements of birds and rodents on the walls of a Cotswold
village which the camera and the TV transmission was
enabling us to see. The drama, visible and audible, as
presented on the TV set, was naturally for us human viewers
linked with what had been happening at a particular time and
place. Moreover the link was not simply that of direct
reproduction. It opened up possibilities of interpreting the
living world, its ecology, its threatened stabilities, the relation
of plant and animal, the role of humans in construction and
destruction; in fact the signals which proved to be of vague
interest to the cat were transcended for humans by symbolic
forms which potentially increased knowledge and sensitivity
and could lead to creative action.

In the words of Cassirer:

> Man lives in a symbolic universe. Language, myth, art and
> religion are parts of this universe. They are the varied
> threads which weave the symbolic net, the tangled web of
> human experience. All human progress in thought and
> experience refines upon and strengthens this net . . . Instead
> of dealing with the things themselves man is in a sense
> constantly conversing with himself. He has so enveloped
> himself in linguistic forms, in artistic images, in mythical
> symbols or religious rites that he cannot see or know
> anything except by the interposition of this artificial
> medium.[4]

III

Cassirer's central theme is that of symbolic forms. I find it specially interesting that in two definitive passages which I have quoted he uses two symbols which at first sight seem to suggest very different objectives for the life of humanity. He describes the position of our contemporary world as a *labyrinth* of disconnected items of information: how can we discover the Ariadne thread which will lead us towards the exit, presumably a new integration? Yet having given as the clue the construction of symbolic forms, he then describes the new situation as that of a symbolic *net*, which is constantly being strengthened and which envelopes man in linguistic forms and artistic images. And he even speaks of this net as being *tangled*.

The juxtaposition of these two images suggests to me that the clue to the human situation is not a single one: it is more akin to the double helix or to a thread made up of two interwoven, differently coloured, cords. The Ariadne symbolism suggests a striving for disentanglement and freedom: the net or web suggests a flexible conserver of that which has proved its value. (This latter image is one of the earliest to appear in the history of mankind. The criss-crossing of threads produces strength, adaptability and beauty.)

Although the two images seem in certain respects to contradict each other, the book's conclusion reveals that Cassirer is well aware of the duality of human life and the polarity of human experience. Some symbolic forms provide security and stability; some point forward to new discoveries and free enterprise. Having surveyed at length the activities of humans as expressed in language and myth, in art and history, in science and religion, he declares:

In all human activities we find a fundamental polarity, which may be described in various ways. We may speak of a tension between stabilization (*the net?*) and evolution (*the Ariadne thread?*), between a tendency that leads to fixed and stable forms of life and another tendency to break up this rigid scheme. Man is torn between these two tendencies, one of which seeks to preserve old forms whereas the other strives to produce new ones. There is a ceaseless struggle between tradition and innovation, between reproduction and creative forces. This dualism is to be found in all the domain of cultural life. What varies is the proportion of the opposing factors. Now the one factor, now the other seems to preponderate. This preponderance to a high degree determines the character of the single forms and gives to each of them its particular physiognomy.[5]

Cassirer, having affirmed the existence of an inescapable polarity, proceeds to comment on those manifestations of human expression which have been more conservative while others have been more innovative. Myth and primitive religion, language related to social regulations, have all been conservative. Later forms of religion, science and art have all directed the imagination towards the future. This polarity must be maintained. To conceive human life as consisting solely in pursuing an Ariadne thread is to emerge finally into nothingness. To conceive it alternatively as strengthening the net until it becomes an iron cage is to embrace futility. Traditional symbols are essential for holding together successive generations and achieved values within any particular culture. Innovative symbols are essential for bringing together representatives of different cultures and for the expression of new perspectives in all cultures.

I have tried to focus attention on the central theme of Cassirer's massive exposition of man's activities in language, art, science, history and religion. He was convinced that through the use of symbolic forms man had advanced to his present eminence in the world and that only through the construction of new symbolic forms could that eminence be maintained. 'It is symbolic thought which overcomes the natural inertia of man and endows him with a new ability, the ability constantly to reshape his human universe.'[6]

(b) Paul Tillich

If symbol is the central clue in Cassirer's doctrine of man, it is equally the central category in Tillich's doctrine of God. Not surprisingly, numerous repetitions about the nature and function of symbols are to be found in Tillich's writings and, in discussions of his theology, the significance of his concentration on symbolism is frequently explored. Indeed, one of the most famous questions addressed to Tillich concerning his theology was provoked by his assertion that only one non-symbolic statement could be made about God and that was that God is Being-itself. Further, the most famous gathering of philosophers assembled to debate with him about his intellectual system chose as the focus of their questions and comments his claims concerning the meaning and truth of religious symbols. I do not know of any Protestant theologian who has made the concept of symbol so basic and so all-embracing in his system.

There are certain fundamental characteristics of a symbol to which Tillich returns again and again in his writings. First he distinguishes clearly between symbol and sign. Each points beyond itself to something else. But whereas a sign is univocal, arbitrary and replacable, having no intrinsic relationship with that to which it points, a symbol actually participates in the reality towards which it is directed and which in some degree it represents. It does this not independently but in the power of that to which it points.

This view of the symbol's function is of special importance in Tillich's discussion of the place of sacraments in Christian experience.

The sacramental material is not a sign but a symbol. As symbols the sacramental materials are intrinsically related to what they express; they have inherent qualities (water, fire, oil, bread, wine) which make them adequate to their symbolic function and irreplaceable. The Spirit 'uses' the powers of being in nature in order to 'enter' man's spirit. Again it is not the quality of the materials as such which make them media of the Spiritual Presence; rather it is their

quality as brought into sacramental union. This consideration excludes both the Catholic doctrine of transubstantia-
tion which transforms a symbol into a thing to be handled,
and the reformed doctrine of the sign character of the
sacramental symbol. A sacramental symbol is neither a
thing nor a sign. It participates in the power of what it
symbolizes, and therefore it can be a medium of the Spirit.[7]

Such a view of God's relation to the natural order and of the
Spirit's entrance into the human spirit may provoke questioning and criticism but it was reiterated frequently by Tillich
as crucial for his interpretation of the function of symbols in
mediating the spiritual presence.

The second function of a true symbol, in Tillich's view, was
to open up to humans levels of reality which could not be
apprehended otherwise. This is particularly true of artistic
symbols.

Artistic symbols – in fact, all artistic creations – open up the
human spirit to the dimension of aesthetic experience and
they open up reality to the dimension of its intrinsic
meaning. Religious symbols mediate ultimate reality
through things, persons, events which, because of their
mediating functions, receive the quality of 'holy'. In the
experience of holy places, times, books, words, images and
acts, symbols of the holy reveal something of the 'Holy-itself'
and produce the experience of holiness in persons and
groups.[8]

In other writings Tillich often refers to his own experience of
'ecstasy' when 'grasped' by a picture or other symbolic object.
Thus the symbol 'opens up' the human spirit to wider vistas
and expanding views of the 'Holy' in its transcendent dimensions.

The third function of a symbol is to unlock dimensions of the
inner spirit of the human subject so that there comes into being
a correspondence or correlation with aspects of ultimate
reality. This third characteristic can hardly be separated from
the second. It simply describes one aspect of what is bound to

be a two-way process. The symbol expands the vision of transcendent reality: concurrently it expands the human spirit to enable it to be grasped by the vision and thereby to grow in spiritual apprehension.

The fourth characteristic is the likeness to living beings: the symbol emerges from the darkness, and lives through its relationship with a particular culture. When it ceases to evoke a vital response, it dies. Tillich, who was born in 1886, became vividly aware, in the early years of this century, of the psychological investigations and theories of Freud, Jung and Adler. He recognized that dreams and myths, regarded by these men as highly significant, abounded in figures and postures and gestures which could be regarded as symbolic. These constituted part at least of the human unconscious, either of the individual or of the collective. How could a researcher describe and evaluate the process which selects a symbol, brings it into consciousness and allows it to exercise its appeal to viewers or listeners?

Tillich, I think, never felt able to answer this question. 'Symbols cannot be invented; they cannot be produced intentionally.'[9] Of course a symbol such as 'sunlight soap' can appeal to the public as can the designs of many clever advertisers. An individual may spot a need widely felt – for cleanliness, for food and drink, for travel – and may seize upon a glamorous wrapping for the product he or she wants to sell. But such fabrications belong to the realm of signs rather than of symbols. A symbol in some mysterious way emerges as a powerful agent, perhaps representing the welling up of long repressed desires, perhaps representing an archetype formed in the collective unconscious, perhaps providing a way to release from frustration and oppression. Whatever theories psychoanalysts may offer, there remains a large element of mystery surrounding the appearance of a powerful symbol and particularly of a religious symbol. Tillich was convinced that some symbols die and cannot be revived: certain of these he specified. But whether there are religious symbols which never die, having the vitality to open up constantly expanding dimensions of reality, is a question which no one can answer with certainty.

There appear to be 'constants' in nature and recurring patterns in history but it is doubtful whether even these can be given symbolic form which is in no way subject to cultural change.

I have tabulated four main characteristics which appear in substantially the same form in various of his writings. There is, however, another fourfold description of basic characteristics contained in an oft-reprinted essay by Tillich which appeared originally in 1924. In this he sets out the characteristics of all symbols in this way.

1. They are *figurative*. They are always pointing beyond themselves to something higher in rank. A supreme example:

> Devotion to the crucifix is really directed to the crucifixion on Golgotha, and devotion to the latter is in reality intended for the redemptive action of God, which is itself a symbolic expression for an experience of what concerns us ultimately.[10]

2. They are perceptible, either as objective forms or as imaginative conceptions.

3. They possess an innate power.

> This characteristic is the most important one. It gives to the symbol the reality which it has almost lost in ordinary usage.[11]

Tillich's own artistic and mystical experiences undoubtedly led him to emphasize the symbol's 'innate power'. Being 'grasped' by a great painting, being deeply moved by the sight of the ocean or of the primeval forest, were unforgettable experiences which could not be analysed or described in technical terms. What he saw or envisaged possessed the power to disclose higher or deeper realities. This power might be called magical or mystical or religious or spiritual. To him it was profoundly real.

4. They are socially rooted and socially supported. The third characteristic might seem to be of a purely individual nature. But Tillich was quick to affirm that 'if something becomes a symbol for him (i.e. for the individual) it is always so in relation to the community which in turn can recognize itself

in it'.[12] He failed to give any general definition of how the individual is related to the community: this is a problem which he considered in other contexts.

Finally, having presented these four characteristics of all symbolic forms, he gave what he regarded as the distinguishing mark of a *religious* symbol.

> Religious symbols are distinguished from others by the fact that they are a representation of that which is unconditionally beyond the conceptual sphere; they point to the ultimate reality implied in the religious act, to what concerns us ultimately.[13]

The definition of religious symbol thus depends on the definition of religion. 'That which concerns us ultimately' has become a familiar, even a famous phrase. If a symbol points to *that* it may legitimately be termed *religious*.

In 1963, near the end of his life, Tillich conducted a seminar at the University of California, Santa Barbara, and the series of questions and answers was recorded and printed under the title *Ultimate Concern*. Inevitably questions were raised about symbols and their place in his own theological system. One detects a certain wistfulness in his replies, as though the concentration on the symbol which had meant so much to him in his writing and lecturing had failed to make any marked impact on an increasingly secularized society. The immensely powerful symbols – God, sin, redemption holiness – had virtually lost their power and been rejected by the secular world.

> How this situation can be overcome without a fundamental reformation of the way in which Christianity expresses its symbols, preaches them and interprets them, I really do not know, although my whole theological work has been directed precisely to the interpretation of religious symbols in such a way that the secular man – and we are all secular – can understand and be moved by them. On this basis I believe it *may* be possible to reinterpret the great symbols of the past in a way that restores meaning to some of them.[14]

And Tillich went on to suggest ways in which the symbols applied to Jesus might be reinterpreted.

The terms 'understand' (intellectual) and 'be moved' (emotional) are significant. So often an attempted reinterpretation fails to move; an appeal to feeling is dismissed as intellectually unacceptable. This is a continuing problem. Culture itself is a mixture of the rational and the mystical, the intellectual and the imaginative, and the symbol which appeals to the one side may fail to appeal to the other. Tillich did not solve the problem and admitted at the end that his efforts were uncertain of fulfilment. Was not his great achievement that he remained *open* to further possibilities of symbolic representation? For him the highest characteristic of the symbol was to 'open up' new dimensions in Reality and in the beholding subject. In a real sense Tillich himself was a symbol who in a remarkable way succeeded in opening up new dimensions for his students and for readers of his writings.

(c) Paul Ricoeur

I

In the essay entitled 'Existence and Hermeneutics', which he regarded as an important statement of his own position, Ricoeur included a careful account of his own use and understanding of the term symbol:

> I give a narrower sense to the word 'symbol' than authors who, like Cassirer, call symbolic any apprehension of reality by means of signs, from perception, myth and art to science, but I give it a broader sense than those authors who, starting from rhetoric or the neo-Platonic tradition, reduce the symbol to analogy. I define 'symbol' as any structure of significance in which a direct, primary, literal meaning designates, in addition, another meaning which is indirect, secondary and figurative and which can be apprehended only through the first.

Armed with this definition Ricoeur tackled the immense task of interpreting texts. He defined interpretation as 'the work of thought which consists in deciphering the hidden meaning in the apparent meaning, in unfolding the levels of meaning implied in the literal meaning . . . Symbol and interpretation thus become correlative concepts.'[5]

It seems to me that by committing himself to this definition, Ricoeur confined himself to speech and language, whereas the term symbol is widely applied in the contemporary world to *visual* structures also. He is at liberty to do this but it seems to me that this is an unnecessary limitation. The visual can often be of immense help in the task of interpretation and it is even open to question whether *words* were in fact the earliest means of symbolic communication amongst humans.

Further, I find difficulty in Ricoeur's reference to reducing the symbol to *analogy*. In *The Symbolism of Evil*[16] he states quite definitely that the literal meaning effects an analogy and thereby constitutes symbolic meaning. Does this not imply that the symbol, which is the 'structure of signification', is in fact an *analogue*? How is the second meaning constituted if not by analogy? It seems that Ricoeur is endorsing the very limitation which he deprecates in other authors. I believe that a verbal *symbol* need not necessarily be an analogy, but this does not become clear when, in Ricoeur's use, symbol and analogue are so intimately related to one another.

However, the all-important matter is that in Ricoeur's philosophy symbol and interpretation are inextricably bound together. Except in strictly technical contexts words can have two or more meanings. In his view the supreme duty of the interpreter is to go beyond the literal in order to elucidate hidden meanings, secondary meanings, enriched meanings – meanings which are properly called *symbolic*. It is through the discovery of symbolic meaning that the self is opened out towards a new level or dimension of existence. To interpret symbols, to explore symbolic meaning, is to be transported into an altogether higher and fuller life.

II

What seems to me the crucial question in all considerations of

religious symbolism emerged clearly first in interchanges
between Jaspers and Bultmann on the subject of demythologization and then in a debate between Jaspers and Ricoeur on the
subject of revelation through myth and symbol. The central
issue is really one and the same in both cases. It is whether the
divine transcendent can be represented and mediated through
ciphers (Jaspers' term) or symbols, gaining expression in space
and time and thereby becoming authoritative and possessing
permanent validity; or whether every such representation must
be regarded as historically conditioned, culturally limited, and
therefore evanescent, to be accorded every respect and to be
valued for its particular contributions but never to be regarded
as final, fixed, singular or definitive. This is an issue which has
become increasingly acute through the growth in knowledge of
the non-Christian religions of the world and through philosophical critiques of religious language. It can be illustrated, I think,
by reference to Ricoeur's essay on the relation of Jaspers'
philosophy to religion, followed by Jaspers' considered reply.

Amongst twentieth-century philosophers Jaspers had the
distinction of possessing an early background of practice in
medicine and psychiatry, a comprehensive knowledge of the
history of philosophy and a profound regard for the importance
of the Judaeo-Christian tradition as contained in biblical
literature. He and his wife endured with courage the travail of
the Nazi régime, made the more poignant for them because of
his wife's Jewish ancestry; through those dark days they were
constantly sustained by the records of those who survived
comparable experiences in biblical times. Thus Jaspers was in
no way antagonistic to a *religious* interpretation of human
existence. He identified himself as primarily a philosopher but
urged that he was an ally with theologians in the struggle
against forces of waste and in opposition to rationalistic and
nihilistic ideologies. He and Ricoeur shared much in common.

In his essay Ricoeur begins by pointing out that whereas
Jaspers would regard both a mystical flight *from* the world or an
ethical immersion *in* the world as unacceptable forms of *religion*,
his real opposition was to religion as represented in human
history by any authoritarian system, defined by cultus and

dogma, 'the supreme objectivity'. The centre of his concern was always the individual in his or her unique originality, existence, responsibility and authenticity.

> The existent puts into question all universal validation and thus puts himself in question. He is the being who risks himself. Hence Karl Jaspers employs a philosophy of freedom in order to reject the certainty and security of religion.[17]

From this point onwards, Ricoeur's major concern is that of the meaning of *freedom*. It is clear in the interchange that both men were passionately determined to give full weight to what is meant by *freedom* in human existence. Can a man be free without any religious commitment? How is freedom achieved? Can freedom ever be more than a momentary experience? What in particular is the relation of freedom to the human sense of guilt and finitude?

Ricoeur outlines Jaspers' objections to revealed, cultic, dogmatic, authoritarian religion. In Jaspers' view, this kind of religion presumes to objectify and guarantee Transcendence and thereby to escape the burden of freedom. Yet while this criticism of religion is exalting human freedom in the face of objective authority or of the authoritarian objectivity of cult, prayer, revelation and church, another theme rises slowly on the horizon of the critique, the theme of a hidden divinity'.[18] So a paradox is created: for Jaspers, the striving for self-identity is the essence of human freedom; at the same time freedom is the gracious gift of the hidden divinity. In a crucial passage, quoted by Ricoeur, Jaspers states: 'The search for Transcendence lies in the existential references to this Transcendence, its *presence* lies in the cipher-script.' To read this 'cipher-script' and thereby to experience the presence of the Transcendent constitutes the paradigm of human freedom. 'Symbols (i.e. ciphers) exhibit the ontological presence of the real.' *Any* sensible reality, *any* object, may become transparent, pointing beyond itself to transcendent reality. 'No sacred book can fix them, no sacred history can contain them, no sacred Church inherit them.'[19]

The 'existent' apprehends the Presence through the cipher (or symbol) and thereby acts in *freedom*. Thus to postulate a God-man as the unique mediator of transcendence is completely antithetical to Jaspers' theory of the symbol. Incarnation at a particular time and place, and the potential encipherment of all things, are for him poles apart.

Proceeding to a critique of Jaspers' philosophical faith, Ricoeur returns to the question of the nature of freedom and with it to the concept of *guilt*. Religion, he claims, has (at least in its authentic manifestations) been concerned not to thwart or suppress freedom but to *save* it, to preserve it from vanity and nothingness. He points out that Jaspers defines four extremities to which every human being is subject – death, suffering, struggle and guilt. Thus guilt is part of the inevitable consequence of being human; it is part of human *finitude* which hampers freedom. Only by relationship to the transcendent, through the mediation of a symbol, can freedom exist.

In contrast, Ricoeur affirms, the whole Christian tradition has regarded *guilt* as in some sense a *fall*, a revolt against the divine intention. Whereas Jaspers concentrates attention on man's constitution as essentially limited and finite, Ricoeur sees man as fallen and therefore guilt-ridden. In Jaspers' philosophy the individual gains freedom in every upsurge towards the hidden transcendent through the mediation of a cipher: in Ricoeur's theology the individual is set free by the saving act of the divine redeemer mediated through the unique Christian symbols.

III

With many points in Ricoeur's essay Jaspers either found himself in broad agreement or stood ready to discuss differences caused by the possible ambiguity of terms used such as religion and mysticism. But on the basic question of the connection between guilt and freedom he was uncompromising.

> My philosophizing looks totally different . . . when the problem of guilt arises. There is no such thing in philosophizing as liberation from freedom by the grace of a divine act which

cancels guilt, an act mediated by faith in the death of Jesus on the cross as substitutionary atonement in such fashion that faith in it justifies whereas without that faith one is lost. More than that, philosophy rejects such assertions of belief outright. Only by transforming its meaning can philosophy find any possible truth acceptable which may lie hidden therein.

I cannot agree with Ricoeur, therefore, when he places the problem of guilt in the centre. Even though, in harmony with the entire philosophical tradition, I, too, connect guilt with man's finite nature, I have not the slightest inclination to veil it as unavoidable and therefore as innocent necessity. The difference begins only where forgiveness of guilt is sought and found in the religious relation to the thou of the godhead. I do not deny the possibility of this cipher, could even talk about it, but I can only say that to myself it does not speak in any essential fashion. This implies no diminution of guilt on my part. Nobody forgives guilt, I have to answer for it. This is by no means the last word but it is one which does intrude when I hear of redemption of guilt, of which redemption men, in their faith, are certain.[20]

The crucial difference then between Jaspers and Ricoeur (and it is virtually the same as that between Jaspers on the one side and Bultmann with Tillich on the other side, cf. my study of Tillich and Jaspers in my book *Religious Experience and Christian Faith*[21]) is to be found in their contradictory views concerning the nature of God's self-relevation. Jaspers cannot believe that God speaks at a privileged, definite place or that he appears at a privileged, singular period of time. Rather he holds that God speaks 'in so far as possible, everywhere, yet always indirectly and ambiguously. For God is hidden.' Thus the massive Christian symbolism representing or pointing to the birth, life, death and resurrection of Jesus cannot be accepted as central or determinative for human life. He would not, I think, have denied that it constitutes one of the most impressive clusters of symbols in human history, though, for him, probably too direct and unambiguous. Certainly he could not regard it as the essential symbol for dealing with the human extremities of suffering, death, struggle and guilt. He made a major contribution to the human understanding of *tragedy*: he could not conceive of the need for a human understanding of *atonement*.

In contrast to Jaspers, Ricoeur creates a fine symbol – 'the binding golden thread of religious conciliation'.[22] Is it not significant that the first book by which he gained the attention of English-speaking readers was entitled *The Symbolism of Evil*? No human experience, it seems, is more inescapable than that of defilement, becoming dirty through ordinary exposure to the pollution which is either from the human body or from the natural environment. To be cleansed physically is a universal human need. To speak of being stained or unclean is natural and denotes what Ricoeur calls 'a first intentionality'. But beyond this first intentionality a second intentionality emerges which, through the physically 'unclean', points to a certain situation of man in relation to the sacred which is precisely that of being defiled, impure. The literal and manifest sense, then, points beyond itself to something that is *like* a stain or spot. 'Thus the first obvious meaning points analogically to a second meaning which is not given otherwise than in it. This opacity constitutes the depth of the symbol which is inexhaustible.'[23]

Ricoeur concedes that the term symbol is employed both in the realm of formal logic and in that of allegorical interpretation. But both, he insists, reduce the symbol to the status of a definite and clearly accessible *sign*. He is concerned to give *symbol* an analogical reference; 'by living in the first meaning . . . I am led by it beyond itself; the symbolic meaning is constituted in and by the literal meaning which effects the analogy in giving the analogue.'[24]

Jaspers once portrayed his own philosophy of existence by employing a striking metaphor: 'To be on the road to the One and miss it by prematurely seizing the One as a will-of-the-wisp . . . this is to let oneself be blinded by a pretense to clarity.' The danger of *premature grasping* is obvious. Ricoeur, I think, would reply that while agreeing with Jaspers about the danger of premature grasping, he had himself, like Tillich, *been grasped* by the revelation in Jesus Christ. The symbol of cleansing exhibited through the work of Christ is not something temporary and provisional, capable of being superseded, but is rather a critical disclosure of God's remedy for human guilt, a symbol whose interpretation is never finally settled but gains ever widening meaning to successive generations of mankind.

(d) Karl Rahner

If there is one word which can be regarded as the centre around which Rahner's whole system revolves it is the word *symbol*. 'The whole of theology,' he wrote, 'is incomprehensible if it is not essentially a theology of symbols, although in general very little attention is paid, systematically and expressly, to this basic characteristic.'[25] Sometimes he uses the term *real symbol*, perhaps in order to guard against the looseness with which the word symbol is often employed. But that in his system symbolism belongs to the very nature of the Godhead can never be doubted. The supreme example of symbolic expression is God's own self-expression in the Word (Logos): 'The Logos is the symbol of the Father.'[26]

Such a theory of symbolic expression does not detract from the unity and perfection which belongs to the Godhead but rather enriches our whole conception of the Trinity in Unity.

> The symbol is the reality constituted by the thing symbolized as an inner moment of itself, which reveals and proclaims the thing symbolized and is itself full of the thing symbolized, being its concrete form of existence.[27]

With this basic interpretation of symbolization, Rahner proceeds to develop by means of it a comprehensive christological and ecclesiological system. For him it is of vital importance that the symbol shall never be regarded as *separate* from the object it symbolizes, standing over against it, pointing towards it, illustrating it. Rather, an object, a self comes to expression *in* the symbol and thereby becomes *present* in the symbol. A real symbol constitutes real presence. It 'does not divide as it mediates but unites immediately, because the true symbol is united with the thing symbolized, since the latter constitutes the former as its own self-realisation'.[28]

In Rahner's exposition of this process of symbolization, keywords are 'expression', 'pouring itself out into *the other*', 'self-realization in the other', being 'present' in the other. The Logos is the symbol of God, the human Jesus is the symbol of the Logos, the church is the symbol of the continuing gracious action of God in Christ, the sacraments are symbols of the grace poured into the church. In his summary of Rahner's teaching on the church and the sacraments, Gerald A. McCool writes:

> The Logos, the Father's real symbol, expresses himself in the Incarnation through the real symbol of his human nature . . . The Church . . . is the real symbol through which the Incarnate Word expresses himself in human history . . . The concrete individual sacramental signs are the real symbols through which the Church expresses herself as the fundamental sacrament of God's grace.[29]

The individual may refuse, reject, be guilty of wrong subjective dispositions and thereby fail to receive the grace of God. But Rahner's massive system of symbolic forms retains its 'objective' character. It represents theologically and philosophically the dictum of Maurice de la Taille: 'He placed himself in the order of signs' (symbols).

Although Rahner develops his exposition with complex philosophical argument and impressive theological learning, it is possible, I think, to discern an overall picture of a simpler kind. It is that of a seed, an embryo, a hidden potentiality, finding its true expression in and through an outward and visible manifestation. The soul through the body, the mind through the word, the father through the son, the mother through the child, all examples of a single organic, evolutionary process. Every potential within the realm of Being only finds its true expression and fulfilment by giving itself away to *the other*, by pouring itself out into the other, by drawing its energy from the other, by operating within a continuing dialectic of fulfilment through self-giving.

This is an impressive model. It epitomizes the way in which God is continuously giving himself to humans for their salvation.

God's salvific action on man, from its first foundation to its completion, always takes place in such a way that God himself is the reality of salvation because it is given to man and grasped by him in the symbol, which does not represent an absent and merely promised reality but exhibits this reality as something present by means of the symbol formed by it.[30]

(e) Bernard Lonergan

It is remarkable that the two leading philosopher-theologians of the Roman Catholic Church in the mid-twentieth century define the place and function of symbols in such different ways. Rahner's approach is philosophical, Lonergan's psychological. The former begins with man the knower, the latter with man the feeler; the former concentrates on self-expression, the latter on the self's intention. For the former the 'other' is of supreme importance, for it is in the other that the self comes to symbolic expression. For the latter the self comes to spontaneous expression in a symbolic form which needs to be interpreted. The two approaches may not be contradictory but they are certainly different.

Yet the symbol plays an equally important part in Lonergan's theology. This is his definition: 'A symbol is an image of a real or imaginary object that evokes a feeling or is evoked by a feeling. Feelings are related to objects, to one another and to their subject.'[31]

An example of the first kind of feeling is the desire to eat and drink, of the second a personal relationship, of the third a general consciousness of well-being or fear.

In another summary description of the function of symbols in human life Lonergan refers to,

the *elan vital* that, as it guides biological growth and evolution, so too takes the lead in human development and expresses its intimations through the stories it inspires. Symbols . . . are a more elementary type of story: they are inner or outer events, or a combination of both, that intimate to us at once the kind of being that we are to be and the kind of world in which we become our true selves.

Later in his essay the author refers again to the advance from biological evolution to cultural.

> The spontaneity that has been observed in the humming bird for the first time building a nest also has its counterpart in us. But to us that counterpart is complemented, transposed, extended by the symbols and stories that mediate between our vital energies and our intelligent, reasonable, responsible lives.[32]

Lonergan insists that the symbol itself precedes any interpretation or explanation. It is intentionality which is of fundamental importance. The subject feels drawn towards or repelled from an object: responds spontaneously (thereby expressing intentionality) in symbolic form. 'It is through symbols that mind and body, mind and heart, heart and body communicate.'[33] But such a communication is not easy to interpret, for a true symbol has a wealth of possible meanings. It can express tensions, conflicts, struggles, even contradictions. It is able to do what logic and dialectic cannot do, especially as its normal form is that of the image rather than that of the statement or proposition. In Lonergan's view the symbol is the supreme expression of or recorder of *feeling*. The task of interpretation is never complete.

This task of interpreting symbols is one which has gained special prominence in the twentieth century because of its centrality in the systems of the great psychologists, particularly Freud and Jung. The psychoanalyst seeks to relate the imagery of dreams or of free association or of obsession to repressed feelings and unconscious desires. Lonergan views the scope of interpretation much more widely and describes the *meaning* to be extracted from symbols in this way:

> It is a meaning that fulfils its function in the imagining or perceiving subject as his conscious intentionality develops or goes astray or both, as he takes his stance to nature, with his fellow men and before God. It is a meaning that has its proper context in the process of internal communications in which it occurs and it is to that context with its associated

images and feelings, memories and tendencies that the interpreter has to appeal if he would explain the symbol.

To explain the symbol . . . is to go beyond the symbol. It is to effect the transition from an elemental meaning in an image or precept to a linguistic meaning. Moreoever it is to use the context of the linguistic meaning as an arsenal of possible relations, clues, suggestions in the construction of the elemental context of the symbol. However, such interpretive contexts are many and perhaps this multiplicity only reflects the many ways in which human beings can develop and suffer deviation.[34]

The distinction between 'elemental meaning' and 'linguistic meaning' is not easy to apprehend. One can conceive a subject expressing an intention by means of a symbol. But does that symbol already possess 'elemental meaning'? If so, how can we become aware of it? Does not the interpreter seek to express it linguistically but with the knowledge that he or she can never be certain that it represents the 'elemental meaning' which its originator intended to express through the symbol? It seems to me unnecessary to use the phrase 'elemental meaning', for this is something which we can never be sure of. We have the symbol itself. We know that it represents an intended communication. The only possibility open to us is to seek to interpret it linguistically by investigating in every way possible the context out of which it came. Such interpretative contexts, as Lonergan affirms, are many. There can never, it seems to me be any possibility of ascertaining 'elemental meaning'.

(f) Austin Farrer

Farrer was both philosopher and poet. As philosopher he regarded it as his vocation to construct a *natural* theology; as poet he tried ever to be open to new revelation which could be incorporated into *revealed* theology. The category which bound together these two enterprises was the *image* but it was a *verbal* image rather than a visual. It is true that Farrer was always looking for images in the natural world which could be transcribed in spoken or written language. At the same time, when in his writings he referred to images, it was normally to that which could be expressed verbally and could therefore be employed by both philosopher and poet in their respective tasks.

In a definitive section of his Bampton Lectures (*The Glass of Vision*) he speaks of the human mind as 'being in the presence of God always but unable to see him until he finds a mirror in created existence which will in some measure reflect his image'.[35] He refers frequently to images, vision, reflection, shadow, looking-glass; yet in a curious way his medium is language, although the experience is visual and reflective. The human mind, he affirms, is placed between two presences, the infinite and the finite, and is capable of seeing each in the other. But the primary exercise is that of *symbolizing* the infinite in terms of the finite: the mind seizes upon some object within finite existence and sees it to be a symbol of the infinite. This symbol, to use another term, is a shadow, a reflection, and our knowledge of God comes to us by a continuous process in which the shadow imperfectly reflects the reality but in turn the reality transforms the shadow. The first operation makes possible a rational and natural theology, the second a revelational theology. The first constructs knowledge through analogies; the second through vision inspired from beyond.

In Farrer's view, humans are at all times and in all places wrestling with shadows of the infinite, seeking to see beyond them to the reality they symbolize. At the same time he is confident that there have in the history of mankind been revelations of the infinite mystery which have gained critical symbolic form and which have reformed or transformed the symbol appearing in natural theology. The revealed images he locates in certain dominant structures which are to be found in the Old Testament scriptures and which reach the fullness of their expression in the New. Every human as such is in some measure an image or symbol of the divine; the man Jesus *is* the image of the invisible God, the express image of God's very being. The teaching and the actions of Jesus as recorded in the New Testament provide the essential symbols from which all further developments in the Christian church are derived. Yet the teaching and actions of Jesus cannot be separated from the dominant images of the Old Testament which occupied so dominant a place in his own mind and imagination. Farrer's description of what he calls 'revealed images' is so central in his theology of symbols that I shall quote a section from *The Glass of Vision* in full.

The interpretative work of the Apostles must be understood as participation in the mind of Christ, through the Holy Ghost: they are the members, upon whom inflows the life of the Head. As the ministerial action of Christ is extended in the Apostolic Mission, so the expressed thought of Christ is extended in the Apostolic teaching. Now the thought of Christ Himself was expressed in certain dominant images. He spoke of the Kingdom of God, which is the image of God's enthroned majesty. In some sense, he said, the regal presence and power was planted on earth in his own presence and action; in some other sense its advent was still to be prayed for; in some sense men then alive should remain to witness its coming. Again, he spoke of the Son of Man, thereby proposing the image of the dominion of a true Adam, begotten in the similitude of God, and made God's regent over all the works of his hands. Such a dominion Christ claimed to exercise in some manner there and then; yet in another sense it was to be looked for thereafter, when the Son of Man should come with the clouds of heaven, seated at the right hand of Almightiness. He set forth the image of Israel, the human family of God, somehow mystically contained in the person of Jacob, its patriarch. He was himself Israel, and appointed twelve men to be his typical 'sons'. He applied to himself the prophecies of a redemptive suffering for mankind attributed to Israel by Isaiah and Jewish tradition. He displayed, in the action of the supper, the infinitely complex and fertile image of sacrifice and communion, of expiation and covenant.

These tremendous images, and other like them, are not the whole of Christ's teaching, but they set forth the supernatural mystery which is the heart of the teaching. Without them, the teaching would not be supernatural revelation, but instruction in piety and morals. It is because the spiritual instruction is related to the great images, that it becomes revealed truth. That God's mind towards his creatures is one of paternal love, is a truth almost of natural religion and was already a commonplace of Judaism. That God's paternal love takes action in the gift of the Kingdom through the death of the Son of Man, this is supernatural revelation.

The great images interpreted the events of Christ's ministry, death and resurrection, and the events interpreted the images; the interplay of the two is revelation.[36]

Farrer combined philosophy with poetry in a remarkable way. There can be no question about his competence as a philosopher: he argued strongly for the legitimacy of metaphysics and natural theology, for a constructive use of the method of analogy. At the same time he was convinced that inspiration from a supernatural source was a lively reality, even though such inspiration could be expressed and communicated only through 'natural' images or symbols. He used the term 'archetypal' freely, claiming that long before logical, scientific prose existed, humans communicated with one another by means of stories, parables, images and figures. The literal to him was secondary, the image or symbol primary. He was deeply concerned with that which could move the heart, though he never undervalued the importance of criticism and rational thinking especially for the creation of 'natural theology'. For natural theology the all-important symbolic form was the analogy: for revealed theology images, inspired by visions of divine activity in human affairs, which poets and prophets saw as shadows but interpreted as authentic pointers to or representations of the infinite. He was vividly aware of the place of imagery in the witness of prophets and evangelists and seers preserved in the Old and New Testaments: he magnified the place of sacramental imagery in the life of the Christian church; but so far as I am aware he wrote little about images as communicated through architecture, painting, sculpture and drama. The glass into which he constantly looked was a display of *verbal* imagery. There he found the symbols which acted as mirrors reflecting divine realities.

(g) Mircea Eliade

In contrast to the general theories of the philosopher-theologians of his time Eliade directs attention to a multitude of *particular* objects and events, considers their significance in relating humans to the divine, and lays special stress on the importance of what he calls 'hierophanies', that is, manifestations of the sacred in the context of the secular world. Such manifestations, he claims, are always represented and later recalled by means of *symbols*. The symbol participates in the sacredness and may itself come to be regarded as a sacred element in a total conception of the universe.

Eliade has established himself as perhaps the most widely informed of all twentieth-century historians of religion. He possessed an astonishing range of knowledge of religious manifestations in every part of the world and at all periods of recorded history. He was able to produce detailed examples of the way in which humans have shown, by their patterns of activity, an awareness of the *sacred* as revealed through sky and sun and moon, through water and rock, through soil and fertility, through trees and plants, through specified places and times and through consecrated persons. These activities have been formalized in patterns of ritual and accompanied by myths expressed in story or song. Is there any category which, it could be claimed, unifies and integrates this wealth of human experience? It is not, I think, an over-simplification to say that in Eliade's judgment it is *symbol* and the creation of *symbols* which most adequately comprehends the multi-faceted expressions of human experience which he describes. It is through symbolic forms that humans make response to hierophanies, not just by attempting to produce a *reflection* of what has been seen or heard but by relating themselves to that which created the manifestation by some kind of reciprocal response. In other words, symbolic activity is not simply univocal. It is multivalent, expressing variant, even seemingly contradictory aspects of the sacred object. The human, in any form of truly symbolic activity, is engaged existentially, regarding himself as in contact with the source of universal life. He is making 'a desperate effort to penetrate to the root of things, the ultimate reality'.[37]

Eliade's study of the history of religions is designed to show that a purely rationalistic or positivistic interpretation of human life cannot be sustained in view of the researches of psychoanalysts, ethnologists and philosophers of language, together with developments in modern art. He is convinced that myths and symbols are of the very substance of spiritual life and that their function as expressions of human dependence upon transcendent reality and a meta-empirical purpose can never be dismissed or destroyed.

Near the end of his survey of symbolic forms in his book *Patterns in Comparative Religion*, Eliade devotes a chapter to 'The Structure of Symbols'. He begins by showing how often objects which originally were significant through their relationship with cosmic forces can become degraded into automatically operating signs: jade and pearl, for example, had a profound symbolic significance when related to the lunar-cycle but in certain societies gradually became talismans or objects possessing magical potency. Eliade does not minimize the difficulty of preserving the life-enhancing potency of a symbol: all too easily the pearl, which could direct the imagination towards the great cosmological cycle, became simply a sign of economic affluence.

With this said, the true function of a symbol remains unchanged: 'it is to transform a thing or an action into *something other* than that thing or action appears to be in the eyes of profane experience'.[38] In Mesopotamia, for example, all manner of 'natural' objects were regarded as symbols of the activities of particular gods, as portraying hierophanies. But the important part played by symbolism in the magico-religious experience of mankind is not due to this convertibility of hierophanies into symbols. It is not only because it sustains a hierophany or takes its place that the symbol is important; rather it is primarily because of its ability to carry on the process of hierophanization and particularly, on occasion, to become *itself* a hierophany. It reveals a sacred or cosmological reality which no other manifestation is capable of revealing.[39] Eliade's fundamental distinction is between the profane and the sacred. Initially every human is immersed in the profane world, but 'symbolism effects a permanent solidarity between man and the sacred'.[40]

Thus, in Eliade's view, symbolism is a 'language' which, in any particular community, serves 'to abolish the limits of the "fragment" man is within society and the cosmos, and, by means of making clear his deepest identity and his social status and making him one with the rhythms of nature – integrating him into a larger unity: society, the universe'.[41] And finally,

> What we may call *symbolic thought* makes it possible for man to move freely from one level of reality to another. Indeed 'to move freely' is an understatement: symbols identify, assimilate and unify diverse levels and realities that are to all appearance incompatible. Further still: magico-religious experience makes it possible for man himself to be transformed into a symbol. And only in so far as man himself becomes a symbol, are all systems and all anthropo-cosmic experiences possible.
>
> Man no longer feels himself to be an 'air-tight' fragment but a living cosmos, open to all the other living cosmoses by which he is surrounded.[42]

Possibly the most succinct account of Eliade's convictions regarding religious symbolism is to be found in the essay which he contributed to the volume *The History of Religions: Essays in Methodology*.[43] In this he emphasized the multivalent and meta-empirical characteristics of symbols: they point beyond themselves to the sacred, the world of ultimate reality, a 'more profound, more mysterious life than that which is known through everyday experience'. At the same time, a symbol is never a mere pointer, unrelated to active human experience. It 'always aims at a reality or a situation in which human existence is engaged' and thereby brings *meaning* into human existence. Through an authentic religious symbol man is delivered from his isolation and subjectivity and self-interest into an 'opening toward the Spirit and, finally, access to the universal'.[44]

In defining more explicitly this expansiveness of *meaning* which humans apprehend through religious symbols, Eliade refers to two functions of symbols which I regard as of supreme importance in all discussions of religious symbolism. These are integration and conciliation. 'The religious symbol allows man to discover a certain unity of the World and at the same time to disclose to himself his proper destiny as an integrating part of the World.'[45] As an example of such integrating symbols, Eliade instances the way in which that of the moon has been able to bind together heterogeneous elements and diverse levels of human experience into a recognition of cosmic unity. Lunar symbolism has been a notable unifying factor in the experience of mankind.

Furthermore, religious symbols have also served to hold together what seem to be directly contradictory or paradoxical features of the experienced world. A favourite example in Eliade's writings is that of the Sympelgades, the 'passing between two rocks or two icebergs that bump together continuously, between two mountains in continual motion, between the jaws of a monster'.[46] This oft-recurring symbolism denotes the transcending of a seemingly impossible passage by ascending to spiritual or imaginative reality. The polarities and antinomies of experience which seem to threaten human existence are brought together in a symbol of conciliation which makes a new perspective and fresh confidence possible. It is, I believe, one of the outstanding features of the Christian religion that it provides vivid symbols both of wholeness, the integration of varied elements within a living synthesis, *and* of conciliation, a breaking down of the opposition between two antithetical forces. Human experience of the *organic world* is primarily that of encountering a multiplicity of elements which need a focus of integration: experience of *society*, of the world of inter-personal relationships, is ambiguous and ambivalent (love and hate, fellowship and rivalry, trust and distrust) and needs a bond of conciliation. The Christian believes that through the symbolism of the Christ, incarnate, crucified and risen, both these needs have been adequately met.

(h) Ernst Gombrich

The most extensive treatment known to me of the place of symbols in the history of European art is to be found in the writings of Ernst Gombrich, particularly in his book *Symbolic Images*. His major thesis is that it is possible to see in the development of art over more than 2000 years the influence of two dominant philosophical traditions, the Platonic and the Aristotelian, the mystical and the rational, the imaginative and the logical. By means of this magnificent heritage of art, the flux of life has been continuously arrested by symbolic forms and these have become objects of subsequent study and interpretation.

How far, and in what way, a particular philosophy influences artistic production, or indeed other human disciplines such as history and law, is impossible to determine. It may seem that there is no immediate effect and then, perhaps after a generation, a general change of outlook can be detected and this change can be associated with some earlier philosophical teaching. Gombrich, with his intimate knowledge of the history of art, recognizes marked changes in the vision and performance of artists in different periods but is not prepared to attribute them necessarily to philosophical influences. Yet there can be little doubt that the Platonic and Aristotelian schools of thought have been enormously influential, with now one, now the other seeming to be in the ascendant.

Here is Gombrich's own judgment.

Our attitude towards the words and images we use continuously varies. It differs according to the level of consciousness. What is rejected by wide awake reason may well be accepted by our emotions ... In the history of European thought this duality of attitudes is somehow reflected in the continuous co-existence of Neo-Platonic mysticism and Aristotelian intellectualism. The tension between these two modes of thought, their interpenetrations, conciliations and divisions make up the history of religious philosophy throughout the Middle Ages and the Renaissance.[47]

Augustine and Aquinas, Neo-Platonism and Scholasticism, Cambridge Platonism and Newtonian cosmology, these have been the dualities which have somehow constrained the creators of symbolic images. Was the symbol intended to direct attention to and even mysteriously to participate in the transcendent heavenly order? Or was it intended to focus attention on an earthly manifestation, even an incarnation of the divine, on forms which could be regarded as instruments of divine activity? In the former outlook the symbolic image was always an approximation, an initial stage on the ascent to perfection. In the latter outlook it was an efficient means to communicate the divine life or energy or wisdom, an earthly agent to reveal comparisons and correspondences, appealing primarily to the human eye though verbal symbolic forms could also reveal heavenly realities. This latter outlook could be characterized as didactic, moralistic, even practical: the symbol was regarded as the supreme means of awakening the human soul to its divine origin and destiny and of enabling it to advance towards its goal.

Gombrich illustrates the contrast between the Platonic and Neo-Platonic outlook on the one side and the Aristotelian on the other by referring to a popular mediaeval symbol, the *pelican*. In a firmly-held tradition, animals, fish and birds constituted part of the book of nature, containing symbols which could be read to confirm what was revealed in the scriptures. Thus the pelican was believed by Platonists to pre-figure Christ and his charity, it being assumed that this bird drew out its own blood to feed its young. But those who followed the Aristotelian tradition would rather have looked upon the pelican as representing the Christ *metaphorically*, its habits being seen as comparable to those of the divine Son. This would not have implied that a complete system of correspondences existed in the natural order, a system ordained by the Creator to enable mankind to perceive ultimate reality in and through its wonders. To those who embraced the Platonic tradition, it seemed clear that God had revealed himself through a multiplicity of symbolic forms, visible in nature and recorded in holy scripture, all reflecting aspects of his character and activity. By responding to these symbols in appropriate ways, humans could rise above earthly things and become mystically united to the divine unity. To those in the Aristotelian tradition, however, symbolic forms, whether in nature or in scripture, called for study and interpretation. They were to be viewed as representations of ideas or virtues or attributes. They were to be interpreted allegorically or analogically or anagogically so that a treasury of divine knowledge might be established whereby humans, through the symbols, could grow in their apprehension of divine truth.

In his interpretation of works of art Gombrich employs three key-words: representation, symbolization and expression. A picture can, most obviously, be intended to represent a landscape, a human person, a social situation or some kind of abstract configuration. Secondly, it may be intended to symbolize a reality beyond itself. Still further, in so far as it is the creation of a particular artist, it is bound in some measure to express his or her own subjective feelings, attitudes, convictions. In all works of art, it seems, each of these elements is involved though any one of them may be the dominant. For example, the obvious subject of a painting may be a solemn woman holding in her hand a finely fashioned pair of scales. This is the outward representation. But within the wide context of those who have long regarded weighing in the balance as *symbolizing* the operation of justice, the picture could not fail to awaken the sense of this wider significance. Finally the painting, being the work of an individual artist, must be regarded as the expression of his own inner experiences and feelings and values, causing him to take a subject and express it in his own individual, creative way. Through such an analysis the work of art is separated from a photographic facsimile on the one hand (though even this may need to be interpreted) and an incoherent display of miscellaneous objects on the other (though this too may be open to psychological analysis).

The combination of representation, symbolization and expression is a useful one in regard to painting and sculpture, though I should want to substitute re-enactment for representation in all forms of dramatic art. In any case symbolization is the central process and this is the secret of the power of the work of art, whether the symbolic reference is interpreted intuitively or through a more extended process of discursive reasoning.

Gombrich concludes his essay with a brief comment on the modern evidences of the Platonic-Aristotelian polarity as represented by the Romantic reaction to the overweening ambitions of the leading figures of the Enlightenment. The latter did not exclude symbols from their formulations but, following Aristotle, regarded them as valuable tools for linguistic expression. A metaphor which is a symbol could extend the learning process by bringing into prominence the likeness existing within apparent dissimilars. It was to be regarded not as irrational or anti-rational but as an extension or transference within a rational framework. In contrast, the opponents of the Enlightenment would not allow 'proud reason' unconditional sovereignty.

> Art must be allowed its link with the imagination, for the imagination sees further than 'aging reason' . . . the implication that the Great and the Beautiful provide the mind with a symbol through which we can grasp a hidden truth certainly led back to Platonism. And while German classicism had thus taken the upward path on the ladder of analogy through the image of harmonious forms to the idea of harmony, Romanticism re-discovered the Areopagite's (i.e. Dionysius the Neo-Platonist) alternative, the power of the mysterious and the shocking to rouse the mind to higher forms of thought.[48]

Thus over against the apparent invincibility of the rationalism of the eighteenth to twentieth centuries we hear and see the protests of poets and painters, of novelists and psychologists, of archaeologists and anthropologists, all regarding symbolic forms not primarily as linguistic devices but as powerful agents operating in the human subconscious, arousing the conscious to activity and pointing to the super-conscious, the mysterious, the ineffable, to that which is inexpressible in purely rational-istic terms. Thus the symbol becomes the carrier of a plenitude of meaning and the instrument of unlimited effectiveness in human affairs.

Gombrich draws upon the works of Schiller and Blake, of Creuzer and Goethe, of Hegel and Jung to illustrate the Romantic reaction. His final paragraphs, however, are devoted to an exposition of the positive contributions made by both the Platonic and the Aristotelian traditions in their understanding of the place of the symbol in human expression and communi-cation. Aristotelian logic and its representation of world categories by language, have led to spectacular results. Yet they have tended to underestimate the power of intuition and imagination and have left all too little room for flexibility and creative growth in language. In terms I have already used, the Aristotelian symbol is constantly in danger of becoming no more than a strictly defined *sign*. The Platonic symbol, at least in its development in Neo-Platonism, is ever open towards transcendent realities: its danger, an evaporation into mystical unreality. Here is an age-long polarity which will continue to influence the interpretation of symbolic images.

PART THREE

Symbolism in Social History

CHAPTER EIGHT

Symbolism in the Bible

I

Almost simultaneously two books appeared, each concerned with the forms of language used in the Bible and with the imagery represented by them. G. B. Caird in his book *The Language and Imagery of the Bible*[1] tackled the basic questions of order and meaning and how the biblical writers presented them by means of comparisons and likenesses drawn from objects and events in their own world. He listed various linguistic devices such as metaphor, metonymy, simile, irony, paradox, synechdoche and gave examples to show how biblical authors used them effectively. He concluded by chapters on the language of myth, history and eschatology, seeking to show how these particular forms were employed to convey the truths of God's relatedness to mankind.

The second book, *The Great Code*,[2] by Northrop Frye, also focussed attention on forms of language and in particular on myth, metaphor and typology and on the way the Bible uses these forms. Frye admitted that there was a marked difference between the Bible and other literary products of the ancient world, stressing the characteristics of proclamation (in the New Testament kerygma) which go beyond the informative and descriptive to the hortatory or even imperative. With a wealth of illustrations from the biblical text, both writers sought to show how symbolic forms were employed to serve the intentions of the writers and to convey their meaning.

However, in spite of my admiration for these authors' intimate acquaintance with the language and imagery of the

Bible, as well as with the varying literary forms used by its writers to convey meaning, I have wondered how far it is legitimate to apply to this literature the analysis and distinctions represented by such terms as metaphor, metonymy, synechdoche, typology, analogy, all of which have come into English from Greek literature and all of which, as originally used, represented linguistic distinctions associated with the Greek view of life. Are such distinctions to be found in *every* language system? In English we derive an immense number of words and usages from classical sources: classical distinctions are therefore readily applicable to them. But are they equally apt when surveying the literature of the Old Testament and even to a degree when analysing the rhetoric of the New Testament?

If the use of the terms I have mentioned is questioned, it might be urged that it is inappropriate to talk of *symbolism* as playing any part in the books of the Bible. Is not *symbol* a Greek term, based on a common practice in Greek society? The nearest equivalent in Latin appears to be sign (*signum*), and yet many writers on symbolism have been at pains to emphasize the distinction between symbol and sign. I do not know of any Hebrew term which represented in that culture the exact equivalent of *symbolon* in Greek. What, however, was basically represented in the Greek situation was a 'throwing together' or a 'placing together' of two separate parts. A symbol held together, either imagistically or linguistically, two apparently disparate elements, both of which really belonged to the total organism which constituted the Greek ideal of nature and society. In the Hebrew situation there were also many apparently disparate elements which needed to be thrown together or held together but this could only be done by a new creative act. The 'throwing together' was to be regarded not as the restoration of an original unity which had somehow been disrupted but as the bringing into existence of a new relationship in which the two elements were still distinguishable but were now bound dialectically the one to the other. It is perhaps allowable to call this a *symbolic* relationship so long as it is recognized that this is a different kind of symbolism from that which was commonly represented in Greek culture. Since the beginning of the nineteenth century the term symbol has been so widely used in the English language that it has come to denote little more than likeness or representativeness. But if the stronger meaning 'holding together' or 'bridging a gap' is implied, then it can be seen to stand for an exceedingly important aspect of the Hebraic interpretation of human existence.

It is significant that, when describing the Old Testament, a long-established distinction is that between the Law and the Prophets. This may be regarded simply as a convenient device for distinguishing between those books dominantly concerned with regulations for the social life of Israel and those concerned rather to recall prophetic utterances about Israel's past and future. Yet I think the distinction represents something more profound. 'The Law' has a certain static, undeviating character: God stands over against his people and these are his regulations for their social welfare. If laws are broken there are remedies, but there can be no change in the general picture of God's will and human obedience. They stand over against one another but are held together by the Law. This, so long as it is observed, is the binding agent. God and his people are held together by the observance of the Law: it is the *sign* of togetherness.

But the prophetic writings present a very different picture. There is tension, dialogue, interaction. The supreme 'symbol' of coming together is the *covenant*. This is new and creative. It is the act of God in bridging the gap between himself and a section of mankind. There is no merging or complete unification. God and his people are related within the covenant, but it is still possible for the people to be unfaithful to its requirements and to cause a temporary breakdown of the relationship. If this unfaithfulness reaches extreme limits then nothing can avail except a *new* covenant and that covenant will become the distinctive 'symbol' of a new people.

Nowhere have I found this distinctive quality of the prophetic contribution more vividly portrayed than in Robert Alter's book *The Art of Biblical Narrative*.[3] His examples and references are taken mainly from Genesis and the Books of Samuel, but the former are from the 'prophetic' documents and the latter from the 'prophetic' histories. Alter's claim is that these 'prophetic' writers developed a new kind of literature which he calls *prose fiction* or, even more significantly, *historicized fiction*. The writings themselves represent the tension or dialectic between what actually happened and the dramatic account of it. The succession of events and the prose record of those events are held together within a 'symbolic' narrative – the altogether appropriate literary expression of the dialectical relationship between God and his world, God and his people.

'What the Bible offers us is an uneven continuum and a constant interweaving of factual historical detail (especially, but by no means exclusively, for the later periods) with purely legendary "history".' This provided a 'dialectical tension between . . . antitheses of divine plan and the sundry disorders of human performance in history';[4] in other words, historicized fiction. The dialectical tension is twofold: between the divine plan and the disorder of human events on the one hand, between the divine will and human freedom (the refractory nature of man) on the other. Design and disorder, covenant-making and covenant-breaking are the subjects of the prophets' stories.

In a notable section Alter compares the work of a fiction writer at any period with that of the biblical narrators and I propose to quote two paragraphs from it:

We learn through fiction because we encounter in it the translucent images the writer has cunningly projected out of an intuitively grasped fund of experience not dissimilar to our own, only shaped, defined, ordered, probed in ways we never manage in the muddled and diffuse transactions of our own lives. The figures of fiction need not be verisimilar in an obvious way to embody such truths, for exaggeration or stylization may be a means of exposing what is ordinarily hidden, and fantasy may faithfully represent an inner or suppressed reality. What I should like to stress is that fiction is a mode of knowledge not only because it is a certain way of imagining characters and events in their shifting, elusive, revelatory interconnections but also because it possesses a certain repertoire of techniques for telling a story. The writer of fiction has the technical flexibility, for example, to invent for each character in dialogue a language that reflects, as recorded speech in ordinary discourse would not necessarily reflect, the absolute individuality of the character, his precise location at a given intersection with other characters in a particular chain of events. The writer of fiction exercises an even more spectacular freedom in his ability to shuttle rapidly between laconic summary and leisurely scenic representation, between panoramic overview and visual close-up, in his capacity to penetrate the emotions of his characters, imitate or summarize their inner speech, analyse their motives, move from the narrative present to the near or distant past and back again, and by all these means to control what we learn and what we are left to ponder about the characters and the meaning of the story. (In nearly all these regards, a more formulaic mode of storytelling like the folktale or even some kinds of epic has a more limited range of possibilities.)

In chapter 2, I contended that the biblical authors were among the pioneers of prose fiction in the Western tradition. Let me now add the suggestion that they were impelled to the creation of this new supple narrative medium at least in part because of the kind of knowledge it could make possible. The narrators of the biblical stories are of course 'omniscient', and that theological term transferred to narrative technique has special justification in their case, for the biblical narrator is presumed to know, quite literally, what God knows, as on occasion he may remind us by reporting God's assessments and intentions, or even what He says to Himself. The biblical Prophet speaks in God's name – 'thus saith the Lord' – as a highly visible human instrument for God's message, which often seems to seize him against his will. The biblical narrator, quite unlike the Prophet, divests himself of a personal history and the marks of individual identity in order to assume for the scope of his narrative a godlike comprehen-

siveness of knowledge that can encompass even God Himself. It is a dizzying epistemological trick done with narrative
mirrors: despite anthropomorphism, the whole spectrum of
biblical thought presupposes an absolute cleavage between
man and God; man cannot become God and God (in
contrast to later Christian developments) does not become
man; and yet the self-effacing figures who narrate the biblical
tales, by a tacit convention in which no attention is paid to
their limited human status, can adopt the all-knowing,
unfailing perspective of God.[5]

It is interesting that he uses the rare word 'translucent',
which appears in Coleridge's definition of a symbol. 'Translucent images' in the Alter paragraph could be replaced, I think,
by the term 'symbols', thus representing the author's contention that in prose fiction there is a continual inter-relatedness
between the characters and conversations within a story and
the reader's own feelings and uncertain wonderings. Thus in
the Old Testament the prophetic narratives present in symbolic form the words and actions of God on the one side over
against the free yet often confused and disordered events of
human life on the other. The tension and dialectic between God
and humans gains expression through a powerful symbolic
narrative which captures our interest and enables us to grasp
more fully what God is saying and doing, whatever the human
response may be.

Alter employs phrases such as 'dramatic interaction', 'con-
trastive dialogue', 'historicized fiction' to describe the character of Old Testament narratives, phrases which immediately
suggest tension and dialectic. By so doing he implicitly
distinguishes Hebraic prose fiction from the epics and dramas
of classical Greece. In these the predominant notes were those
of cyclic recurrence, of continuities between divine and human
protagonists, of the repetition of cosmic events. Symbolic forms
abound, but they are of a different kind from those appropriate
to the Israelite experience. Greek symbols express organic
rather than tensive relations, in modern terms consensus rather
than confrontation, a coming together through natural affinity

rather than through a divine act of grace. It is indeed through symbols that connections are made but the symbols are of a different kind, analogic rather than tensive, pointing to an interwoven comprehensiveness rather than to a *coincidentia oppositorum*.

The prophetic narrators looked back to critical occasions when God made specific promises to chosen agents and looked forward to the fulfilment of those promises when they had not already been realized. Their concern was with what God has done in the past and will do in the future. Some attempted to establish undeviating patterns of punishment and reward on God's part, disobedience and repentance on man's. But although these patterns provided a firm basis for the imposition of laws in social life, they failed to take account of the rich variations which cannot be impaled within a formula but which, by recalling notable events in the past, point forward to possible events in the future which will far transcend anything known hitherto.

II

The nature and function of symbols are of vital importance to all serious readers of the New Testament. Are the Gospels to be read as verbal recordings of events which happened in the first century world? Or are they to be regarded as attempts, by various gifted writers, to put together in narrative form memories of those who were actual contemporaries of Jesus of Nazareth and who transmitted those memories to all who accepted him as the promised Messiah? If the former hypothesis is adopted, then the New Testament must be regarded as unique, unlike any other book. It must have been miraculously preserved from all ambiguity and error. The events there recorded must be viewed simply as a series of divine operations, through a seemingly human agent, operations which were designed to benefit the human race but which were in no way hampered by human limitations or by the structures of the natural world.

It is clear that innumerable readers (of the Gospels in

particular) and listeners to the narratives when read, have in fact accepted them as *sui generis* and as providing a miraculous disclosure of miraculous events. No human interpretation (it is assumed) is needed. All that is required is a willingness to believe that the Son of God entered the world by miraculous generation in a virgin's womb, that he grew to maturity and then spoke divine words and performed divine actions, that he was finally arrested and crucified (this being permitted by divine providence) and that he rose from the dead and ascended to the heavens, thus returning to his true abode.

Such a view of unique divine intervention divinely recorded leaves the remainder of human history, all, that is, which was not actually involved in this intervention, still to be examined and evaluated. All humans are intimately related to the natural world, drawing in the means of survival from their natural environment. Has God no relation to this world-order? All humans are intimately related to their fellow human beings, depending on life in society to become truly human. Has God no relation to these human societies? If nature and society are independent of God and only touched as it were tangentially by a divine intervention at a particular time and in a particular place, what is the significance of the human quality which, so far as we know, is unique, the quality of being able to transcend direct and immediate reactions to the environment and to create a system of symbolic forms for reflexion, for anticipation, for aspiration and for communication? By interpreting the world and their experiences in the world symbolically, humans have risen above involuntary responses to stimuli, and have entered into conscious relationships of a dialectical kind. In other words, humans are responsible beings and any divine intervention which simply overrides this ability to respond symbolically rather than automatically can only be regarded as treating humans as mechanical robots or inanimate things.

From the earliest period of the Christian church, teachers have sought to do full justice to the humanity of Jesus. Being in the form of God, he had yet emptied himself and been made in the likeness of men. If what I have written about the distinctiveness of the human is in any way true, this means that

Jesus shared the symbol-creating capacities of humans and that both in word and deed he pressed beyond ordinary needs and drives – hunger, thirst, sex, movement of limbs, speech – to value and meaning and to a growing understanding of what life in this world signifies. That in fact he did this is unmistakably revealed by the records of his teaching. This consisted not of the mere echoing of conventional rules and the repeating of records of past experiences but of opening the way to new interpretations of familiar sights and sounds by presenting them in parabolic form. He made use indeed of suggestive analogies but it was on *stories* which awoke surprise and challenged to new thinking that his major emphasis lay. Parables and miracles were never used for self-display or to draw people's attention to himself. All were directed to the kingdom of God which he said was near, which was breaking in, which was the ultimate reality by which all human affairs were to be judged.

That Jesus walked, talked, laboured, learned, grew tired and slept like other members of the human race seems certain. But the most notable feature of his humanity was the capacity to live symbolically, to create new verbal symbols, to perform symbolic actions, to communicate with others through symbolic forms. Thus he became man, not just for a particular place Galilee, nor for a particular time early in the first century, but for all places and all times, a symbolic figure, speaking and acting symbolically, and thereby standing forth as representative man, man displaying his highest and most notable quality: that of pointing beyond the direct and immediate to the transcendent and the ultimate.

III

The Synoptic Gospels lay special emphasis on the notes of fulfilment and anticipation. Prior to Jesus' own advent, certain prophets had risen above their situations of here-and-now to see them either as manifestations of the present activity or as harbingers of the future activity of God. Their prophecies were never exact documentaries or blueprints. Rather they were pointers to a significant beyond. Moreover, the fulfilment was never to be an exact facsimile. It would still be open to further development and interpretation, even though in a striking way it would provide the answer to the questions and yearnings of earlier generations.

The stress on fulfilment by the Synoptists was natural but the greater emphasis was on the present-future. The Kingdom was nigh at hand. The Son of Man had come to seek and to save now. The process of liberation had begun. The Spirit of God was already effecting works of redemption. But whereas the Synoptic writers were concerned mainly with beginnings and potential developments, the later writers, Paul and John in particular, were concerned to interpret and draw out the symbolic significance of Jesus' own life and ministry. This they did by using a multitude of symbolic forms, forms which were structured by current associations but which pointed beyond themselves to expanding experience and richer truth.

The first challenge taken up by Peter and other early apostolic witnesses was to *name* the one who had gone about doing good, healing, preaching, exorcising, and then had been condemned to death. God had vindicated him by raising him from the dead and thereby had declared him to be Messiah (the anointed one) Son of God, Lord, Saviour, Prince of Life. Though Messiah was a term especially related to Jewish hopes and expectations, its Greek form Christos carried a far wider significance. The five titles were such as to point to the *universal* significance of Jesus. He was acclaimed as the one designated and declared by God to be His emissary to all mankind.

Other titles, symbolically relating Jesus to particular contexts, were soon coined as the Christian church became more firmly established. The initial emphasis on witness was succeeded by that on worship and pastoral care. In the sphere of worship he was acclaimed as the great high priest: in that of pastoral care as the great shepherd of the sheep and the bishop or guardian of our souls. As an institutional organization developed he was envisioned as head of the church. Still further, with the need to relate the new Christian faith to the intellectual enquiries about creation and the origins of life, he was acclaimed as firstborn of all creation and the word of life. Finally, in relation to the supreme integration of all thinking and imagining, namely, the Godhead, he was acclaimed as son, as image, as effulgence, as Logos.

In the course of history since the first century other titles have been accorded him in response to new evaluations of the human situation: king, leader, vicegerent, substitute, representative, liberator, and, (in the theology of Paul Tillich) new being. But none of these has gained general acceptance in the way that the early titles did and have continued to do. These were fresh and dynamic symbols, related to perennial features of human experience yet gaining almost startling significance through the impact upon human affairs made by the life and teaching, the death and resurrection of Jesus. No symbolic titles have emerged to replace the inspired confessions of those who saw him as saviour of the world and as reconciler of all things in heaven and earth.

IV

The titles to which I have referred related Jesus to a wide variety of human needs and experiences. But there was one aspect of the early witness which was at first sight inexplicable, and opposed to all expectations of how God would reward the altogether righteous man. Would he not be given honour amongst his fellows, prosperity in his calling and a satisfying ending to a long life? Above all, if the righteous man were one chosen and appointed by God to fulfil a special mission, would he not be protected and enabled to bring his task to its proper conclusion? Though much in Jesus' ministry had shown him to be 'approved by God' and a benefactor of mankind there was the inescapable fact that he had been betrayed, delivered up into the hands of wicked men, reviled and tortured, and finally subjected to the kind of death meted out to the worst of criminals. Where could be found symbolic forms adequate to embrace such apparent antitheses, anomalies and contradictions?

By many symbolic forms, often through daring paradoxes,

New Testament theologians sought to throw bridges over what seemed to be a yawning chasm of misunderstanding. 'A prophet mighty in deed and word before God and all the people.' 'Condemned to death and . . . crucified.' 'We trusted that it had been he which should have redeemed Israel.' The third affirmation seems to follow logically from the first. But there is the fearful gap between the two.

I have tried in my book *The Christian Understanding of Atonement*[6] to indicate ways in which early Christian writers, and some of the leading thinkers of the Christian church, have attempted to *hold together* apparent disparates or contradictories by means of metaphors, parables and even paradoxes. No single symbolic form can do justice to the immensity of the problem presented by this glaring example of unmerited suffering and unjust death. A theory which degenerates into an orthodox rationale can simply observe the wonder of the divine operation. The New Testament writers stayed close to the actualities of their traditions and their personal experiences and tried to relate them meaningfully to the actualities of the crucifixion and the resurrection.

In the Jewish tradition, the dominant motif was that of redemption and liberation. Israel had been oppressed and captivated in Egypt; had been redeemed and given a new form of communal existence under the Sovereignty of God; and this had been mysteriously associated with the killing of a passover lamb and the sprinkling of its blood. Was a similar symbolic pattern to be discerned in a new universal redemption?

Further, in this tradition, redemption was followed by the inauguration of a *covenant* which involved obedience to the injunctions of formal law. The nation had been constituted by a memorable agreement in which Moses had spoken as God's representative and the people had responded by committing themselves to a specified form of conduct. Again mysteriously, the covenant had been sealed by the slaying of animals and by the two-sided manipulation of their blood. Was a similar symbolic pattern to be discerned in the inauguration of a new universally relevant covenant?

But over against these traditions stood the realities of

subsequent experience. The law had been given, austere and unchanging in its requirements; but the story of Israel's past, corporately and individually, was stained by defections, idolatry, injustices, immorality, greed and a host of human failings. How could these be condoned or forgiven? How could reparation be made? How could the slate be wiped clean? All kinds of ritual requirements had been stipulated: sin-offerings, trespass-offerings and, above all, the dramatic slaying of animals and the application of their blood on the great annual Day of Atonement. Was a similar symbolic pattern discernible in the shedding of the blood of Christ? Was this the means of purification for the sins of the whole world?

Both in the imagination of prophets and in the interpretation of later political struggles there was support for the hope that through the selfless dedication, even to the point of suffering and martyrdom, of courageous and representative heroes, benefits would accrue to a whole community. Their merits could be celebrated (as in Isaiah 53 and in the stories of the Maccabees) not just as winning favour for themselves but as exerting a mysterious and beneficial influence on the lives and destinies of their fellows. Could a similar symbolic pattern be described in Jesus' faithful obedience unto death, even the death of a cross? Could it be that by his death the many were made righteous and by his stripes the many were healed?

Such were some of the symbolic forms to which New Testament writers appealed as they sought to grapple with what to Jews was a stumbling-block and to Greeks foolishness. They constructed no fixed dogmas; they propounded no single theory. Instead they seized upon stories and images concerned with the bringing together of the realities of death and new life in creative interaction and saw them gaining their supreme and crucial expression in the death and resurrection of Jesus.

The nearest approach to a more carefully defined rationale of atonement derivable from the New Testament is in the general context of the administration of law. There were two impressive systems of law in the social world of the first century: that of the Jews, which held the people of Israel together within its firm embrace, and that of the Romans which, supported by military power, maintained a relatively unified empire. To a Jew living within the Roman Empire, law was an overarching reality. Offences against it, in either context, were severely punished. Penalties and reparations, the supreme judge and his court, pleas for pardon or remission, were never far from the popular imagination. Was Jesus' suffering and death to be viewed within this context? Had he taken the place of sinners and suffered penalty on their behalf? Or had he offered on their behalf the fully adequate reparation for their breaches of the law?

In all lands and amongst all peoples a concern about regular relations between individuals and about recognizable patterns of social living has existed. There may be a recognition of natural law (what appear to be inexorable sequences of cause and effect) or an acceptance of imposed law (prescribed rules with appropriate penalties for breaking them). In both cases law seems to guarantee stability and reasonable order. The chief requirements of a law are readily grasped and there is a general desire that the law should be upheld and social order maintained.

Yet there are dangers. There is totalitarian law and dictatorial law. There is law which allows no appeal and no flexibility of interpretation. If God be envisaged as a maker of laws which cover every contingency and allow for no relation to the circumstances of the individual or of the social context, then humans must be prepared to live their lives within an iron cage. Symbolism, which I have defined as the peculiar glory of humans, is excluded. All are subject to laws literally and ruthlessly enforced. Humans become puppets.

Yet, it may be urged, is not this the situation which Paul describes when he speaks of all the world being guilty before God? None is righteous, no not one. In this bleak situation, God set him (Jesus) forth as the means of removing the guilt separating God from man and man from God. How? Paul does not say. The key-word is *faith*, a complete trust in Jesus and in the efficacy of what he within humanity has accomplished, a state of being united with him so completely as to gain the designation of being *in Christ*. Above all, this is a matter of being united with him in his death and resurrection through faith. The death to sin which he achieved is communicated to the believer as is the life to righteousness. How far Paul regarded the death on the cross as accepting the full penalty for the sins of mankind may be open to question. What is certain is that he regarded it as the victory over sin, as the meeting of the law's requirements, as the death which broke the iron chain of sin – death, as the death which could be appropriated by faith and then reversed in the resurrection, the source of new life to all believers.

It cannot be doubted that many have entered into new life through committing themselves in faith to Christ, believing him to have been their substitute in the divinely constructed world-order in which human sinfulness incurs God's wrathful condemnation. But is the life of humanity confined within inexorable laws of this kind? If there is grace, freedom, self-giving, self-sacrifice, how can these be contained within strict legal categories: revenge, retribution, retaliation? If we are prepared to live under complete legal discipline and to view the world-order as a macrocosm of that same legal system there is no place for *grace*: only for equivalences and deservings and an inflexible *quid pro quo*. The world-picture is devoid of all symbolism. There is strict orderliness and nothing more.

The New Testament exults in the faith that there *is* something more and the term normally employed to express it is *grace*. Through grace God gave himself in Christ to reconcile the world unto himself. The act transcended the just order which is indeed necessary for the preservation of the universe and the life of mankind. Because the act transcended this order it could not be expressed in language belonging to that order alone. The words, the images, the symbols must transcend all legal categories and all logical sequences. So a rich cluster of symbolic forms has been created down through the centuries as interpreters have sought to respond to the abounding grace of God and have seen in the death and resurrection of Christ the source of the richest symbolism that human language and human iconography can express.

In his fine book *The First Urban Christians*, Wayne Meeks has commented on the 'enormous generative power' of this 'religious symbol' which was so 'prolific and pervasive' in the discourse of

Pauline Christians. 'The node around which Pauline beliefs crystallized,' he writes, 'was the crucifixion and resurrection of God's Son, the Messiah. This was destined to prove one of the most powerful symbols that has ever appeared in the history of religions; in the earliest years of the Christian movement, no one seems to have recognized its generative potential so quickly and so comprehensively as Paul and his associates.'[7] To be sure Paul's was ever a dialectical pattern – righteousness and grace, the law and the Spirit – but there was never any question as to which of these pairs was to be regarded as symbolizing the victory of our Lord Jesus Christ. The law of the Spirit of life in Christ Jesus has set me free from the law of sin and of death. Thanks be to God who giveth us the victory.

V

In letters of the New Testament grappling with problems of faith and practice which arose in the life of the Christian communities, there are countless examples of the use of vivid symbolic language to stir the imagination and so lead to active response. In what is perhaps the earliest of Paul's Epistles (I Thessalonians) we find verbal images of a thief in the night, a woman in travail, soldiers armed and marching, and a succession of contrasts between light and darkness, wakefulness and sleep, sobriety and drunkenness, putting on clothes and taking them off. In the Epistle of James the images are particularly vivid – the sea whipped up by the wind, a drunken man staggering in his walk, horses controlled by the bridle and ships by the rudder, the experience of looking in a mirror and then forgetting the likeness, a spark kindling a stack of timber – all symbols with some deeper meaning.

But it is the Fourth Gospel which is pre-eminently the source of those symbolic forms that have proved of untold value in the history of Christianity, pointing to and participating in ultimate realities with such power that Christian interpreters have drawn fresh insights from its chapters from the first day until now. It has been called 'the Gospel of Signs', but this hardly does it justice if sign (a term regularly used in the King James translation) is regarded as denoting formal correspondence rather than expansive suggestiveness. The constant aim of the writer is to lead his readers onwards beyond the obvious external word or event to the richer truth, the divine reality to which it points and in which it may actually participate.

The most challenging of the symbolic utterances are Jesus' seven 'I ams'. In the Gospel they are associated quite naturally with situations or incidents (except in the case of the vine) belonging to Jesus' own ministry, but they have proved to be applicable in far wider contexts and without limitation to a particular period. The same is true of his *actions* called 'signs'. These, however, constitute only a minor part of the extensive symbolism of the Gospel. Words, events, titles, parables, even polemics point beyond themselves to the reality which Jesus came to reveal.

The poet-author lays hold of memorable images and stories from Israel's past and reinterprets them within the context of the revelation in Christ. The lamb of God taking away the sin of the world; the brazen serpent lifted up to provide healing from a deadly plague; the temple still in process of being built; the supply of manna in the wilderness; the blaze of light in the city at the time of the feast of tabernacles; all were used as symbols of richer meaning and indeed as pointing to ultimate mystery through the person and work of Christ.

It would need a full commentary on the Gospel to cover the wealth of suggestive symbolism contained in it. I have counted more than thirty objects (well, dove, cup, etc.) which seem to point beyond themselves and half as many verbs (lifting up, washing, anointing, etc.) which do the same. There are certain distinctive symbolisms in this Gospel associated with the natural order – farming, sheep-tending, vine-growing – which suggests interpretations somewhat different from those of writers more familiar with city-life and trading communities.

There are obvious examples. The Baptist's cry: 'Behold the *Lamb* of God'. What are the symbolic associations? The long discourse on sheep and the sheepfold with its reiterated reference to *life*. What is the nature of this more abundant life? The apparently simple conversation with the woman by the

Samaritan well and its profound implications. In the whole history of mankind no element has carried more varied and more powerful symbolisms than *water*. The story of the blind man and the coming of sight. Beside water, *light* has been a constant source of symbolic suggestiveness.

In addition, the sufferings and death of Christ are interpreted by means of symbols taken from the order of nature and the process of food production, comparisons which do not appear in other books of the New Testament. There is the famous sixth chapter principally concerned with the human need for bread: there is the fifteenth chapter with its concentration on vine culture. In each case the process of production is seen as involving cost: pruning, harvesting, consuming. The symbolism drawn from the regular processes of the natural world is expressed most forcibly, however, in chapter 12. How will the Son of Man enter into his glory? 'Except a corn of wheat fall into the ground and die it abideth by itself alone; but if it die it bringeth forth much fruit.' Through death to life, through darkness to light, through confinement to fruitfulness. The same profound principle is symbolized by a woman travailing in childbirth, by a man laying down his life in some worthy cause. Such sacrifices exercise a compelling power: 'I, if I be lifted up from the earth, will draw all men unto me.'

The symbolic pointers of this Gospel have been seized and employed literally, materialistically and often questionably. Yet they have proved a source of endless fascination and of spiritual illumination. They point to transcendence ('The glory which I had with thee before the world was'); they point also to immanence ('We beheld his glory, the glory of an only-begotten Son of the Father, full of grace and truth'). They point to past experiences (manna in the wilderness, the uplifted serpent); they point to future experiences (the coming of the Comforter). They point to sacramental means of grace, they point to communion through spiritual meditation. The Gospel constantly challenges the reader to go beyond that which appears in the bare record, to transpose the scenes into our contemporary world, to apply the words to our present needs. The book of 'signs' is, in our terminology, an inexhaustible treasure-house of symbols.

VI

Much might be written about the symbolism of the Epistle to the Hebrews and the Apocalypse of John. Leaving them aside, however, I want to raise a leading question about the use of symbolic language in the effort to interpret the meaning of the mission of Jesus. Is it helpful to describe the incarnation as symbolic? Or to speak of Jesus himself as a symbol? Or his work as symbolic?

These issues received considerable public attention through the publication of a book with the title *The Myth of God Incarnate*.[8] Unfortunately the real issues were immediately clouded by the use of the term myth, a word which over the past two centuries has so frequently been used to denote falsehood. In my judgment a far better title would have been *The Symbol of God Incarnate*, though even that presents difficulties because of the term 'incarnate'. Does 'God Incarnate' truly represent the significance of *ho logos sarx egeneto* of John 1.14? In any case I would prefer to speak of the total *mission* of Jesus (the words 'send' and 'sent' are constantly used in the New Testament) and to ask whether it is legitimate to refer to Jesus or to the mission of Jesus as a symbol. Or alternatively, may we rightly speak of Jesus as a metaphor (or metaphorical symbol) of God?

Probably most would agree that it is valuable and helpful to speak of his mission in symbolic terms. It points beyond itself to the nature and purpose of God in his relations with mankind. It stirs the imagination to conceive of God in his self-giving, even to the point of self-sacrifice. But the question which has been almost fiercely debated is whether to speak symbolically is enough. Must not symbol be based upon historic factuality? Could there be a symbolic interpretation unless there had been an event on which it could be firmly grounded? And further, in the case of Christianity, what was the nature of the event and how was it recorded?

These questions have led to the use of another term: core. If it is once allowed that the New Testament records cannot be regarded as inerrant in every detail and cannot therefore themselves be the unshakable foundation on which interpretation has to be built, a search is bound to be set in motion to discover what portions of these records *can* be regarded as historical in the sense of documenting what actually happened. This search has been carried on with immense assiduity, using all the best methods of modern historical research, sifting texts, comparing documents, analysing language, referring to writings and conditions in the contemporary ancient world and thereby trying to reach behind all uncertainties and possible misinformation or misunderstandings on the part of witnesses to a *core* either of historical factuality, or of testimony to what actually happened.

Making a wide generalization, it would, I think, be fair to say that British and Continental scholars in the more Catholic tradition have focussed attention on a core of *historic factuality*, German and to a degree American Protestant scholars on a core of *verbal testimony*. There is a deeply ingrained feeling amongst Catholics for the sanctity of the created order, for the earth itself, for the processes of the natural world, for *bodily* existence and for things pertaining to the body, for dramatic events occurring in a particular place, at a particular time. Newman once expressed this feeling when he said that there is no such thing as abstract religion. Worship is at the heart of Catholic religion and you cannot worship an abstraction. Therefore the actuality, at a particular place on earth, of the virgin birth at Bethlehem, the Galilean miracles, the death on Golgotha and the empty tomb of the resurrection are vitally important matters. They are foci for worship. They can be represented dramatically at any period of time. Above all, the sacrifice of Calvary can be re-enacted and its effects appropriated by overt physical acts in any age.

Thus worshippers cling to the actual happening which can be presented visually to the imagination. As Dom Gregory Dix well put it: 'It is not myth or allegory which is at the heart of (the mystery of the Christian faith) but something rooted in a solid temporal event, wrought out grimly and murderously in one Man's flesh and blood on a few particular square yards of hillock outside a gate, *epi Pontiou Pilatou*.'[9]

'Rooted in a solid temporal event.' Rooted: a horticultural

term. Has the Christian faith grown like a plant from a root, directly, impersonally, physically? Solid: a material term; is it applicable to an event? Temporal: by what means can it be dated *exactly*? Does it matter whether the event was in AD 30 or AD 33? And 'a few particular square yards'. Does the *exact* location matter? The only real approach to firm historical dating is in the reference to Pontius Pilate, whose governorship has been attested by other records. Even so, he is a shadowy figure and his part in the crucifixion drama was simply the final condemning to death.

It is surely a yearning for *certainty* (which seems to exist in the quest for that which is *solid* and *temporal*) which causes authors such as Dix and Louth to affirm that the mystery of the Christian faith is *rooted* in them. Can faith, and the expansion of faith, be derived from and quickened by that which is solid and temporal? Faith as used in the New Testament is inconceivable outside and apart from *personal relationship*. It is not the square yard of ground and the precise date in the first century which are of crucial importance. It is the person who was tried, condemned and crucified to whom faith must be related. And that person can be identified today only by the testimonies of persons who companied with him and were witnesses of his resurrection. We may scrutinize their testimonies and decide that there is a consensus, a convergence on certain events which together constitute the Christ-event and give it a notable place in all efforts to reconstruct the 'history' of the first century. But there is no certainty regarding the person or his work. There is no solid *core* of unassailable *fact*. There are personal testimonies to a personal career and faith regards these as symbolic forms capable of pointing to unlimited splendours of thought and imagination.

In contrast to the Catholic tradition, which has always had special associations with the natural world and the processes of human life within it, the Protestant tradition, which has always had associations with formal bonds of social relationships and with the primacy of language for the establishment and maintenance of those bonds, has focussed attention on what can be *known* about God and his ordering of human society and what in particular can be *known* about Jesus and his ministry. The primary emphasis, as I have suggested, has been upon *language* as the essential key to the understanding of the revelation through Christ. At the Reformation there was a remarkable upsurge of new interest in Hebrew and Greek and Latin as well as in the vernaculars. To *know* the linguistic background of the New Testament records and to translate them accurately into the language of people at large was regarded as the major way of making true Christianity known to all classes and, later, to all nations.

Thus within the Protestant tradition the study of languages has been consistently encouraged, Aramaic and Syriac and other ancient languages being added in course of time with a comparable attempt to bring knowledge of the true God to other nations by translating the Bible into their respective tongues. It was a natural consequence of this interest in language that the study of history should also have been promoted. The essential equipment for the construction of an accurate historical record is facility in the language or languages belonging to the period under surveillance. Writings from that period are invaluable as sources. Monuments and artifacts are also valuable but only as accessories and checks. The written documents must be translated and as far as possible interpreted.

With the advance of the knowledge of human history, reinforced by new knowledge of geological and biological developments, there came a growing scepticism both about the reports of earlier writers and about how much, in fact, could be *known* about earlier civilizations. In particular, what could be *known* about events in Palestine 1900 years ago? And would what might be known increase our knowledge of God? What is the essence, the core of Christian testimony? Does it depend on the results of historical research or can it be deduced from the gospel, the *kerygma* which the early witnesses proclaimed? Is there in fact a central *word* or group of words in the New Testament which did in fact communicate to mankind that knowledge of God which is necessary for salvation unto life eternal?

Early in this century Albert Schweitzer, after surveying the
historical research of a large part of the nineteenth century,
came to the conclusion that Jesus had committed himself
wholly to God in the expectation that a new divine order would
thereby be inaugurated: the essential word in the Christian
faith was 'Follow me'. Knowledge could only come by launch-
ing out in faith in the One who believed that in serving
humanity he was setting forward the purpose of God. In the
later years of the century, however, Schweitzer has been
overshadowed by Rudolf Bultmann, whose concentration on
the Word, and faith in response to the Word, has been
unswerving.

The preaching of the Word and the response of faith have
been twin foci in Lutheran churches since the time of Luther
himself. For him all was to be subordinated to hearing the word
of justification and forgiveness and to making the consequent
response of faith. Since his time there have been varying
interpretations of what it means to be justified or to be in
communion with God, but the emphasis on the Word of
proclamation has remained undiminished and the necessity of
the human response in faith unqualified. Bultmann has gone to
the limit in separating the Word from its first-century historical
context. Although the term which has come to be applied to his
method is 'demythologization', a more apt term, it has been
suggested, might be 'desymbolization'. He does not call us to
look upon the cross of Golgotha and the resurrection appear-
ances as symbols, pointing us to the wider activity of God
in nature and in history and thereby leading us to a fuller
knowledge of God himself. Rather, he sees the cross and
resurrection as constituting an eschatological event which has
to be constantly re-enacted as the *word* of the cross is
proclaimed and as hearers respond in faith. Death, to which all
are subject and which represents the one sure part of human
knowledge, is reversed as response is made to the word which
proclaims that the death and resurrection of Jesus was God's
act. Thus we cannot discover the meaning of Jesus' cross and
resurrection by any symbolic interpretation. It can only be
discovered as the event is re-enacted in the moment when the

Word makes its impact on our minds and imaginations. Bultmann states this forthrightly when he declares that 'the incarnation is continually being re-enacted in the event of the proclamation'. It is in that moment that the Word pierces to the depth of humanity's death-in-life and transforms it into life-in-death.

Catholicism, in its extreme forms, conceives God as acting constantly in the natural world to transform bread and wine into the body and blood of Christ. This happens as an authorized priest re-enacts the offering of the eucharistic sacrifice and worshippers receive the sacred elements: all this is irrespective of any symbolic activity on the part of priest or worshippers (symbolic in the sense of acknowledging the bread and wine to be symbols of the body and blood of Christ and consequently to be received symbolically through the acts of eating and drinking). Protestantism, in its extreme forms, conceives God as acting constantly in the mental world to communicate the word which proclaims Jesus' death and resurrection. This happens simply as an authorized preacher re-enacts the proclamation and hearers respond in faith: all this is irrespective of any symbolic activity on the part of preacher or hearers (symbolic in the sense of acknowledging the words proclaimed to be symbols of the crucifixion and resurrection of Christ and consequently to be received symbolically through the discernment of meaning and wider relevance). From each side comes a striking affirmation that God is continually acting towards humanity, at moments of intense solemnity, through chosen human vessels, in ways related directly to the actual nature of human existence. The crucial question is whether this diagnosis of the nature of human existence is adequate or inadequate. Is the human being rightly described as *animal symbolicum*? Is the creation and interpretation of symbols the most distinctive, the most creative, the most god-like characteristic of the creature who is called human? Is the highest form of achievement known to us the creation of symbolic forms – in poetry, in music, in science, in history, in literature – and the highest form of responsive activity the interpretation of symbols through some mysterious quality which we call imagination or empathy or insight or understanding?

It will be evident from what I have already written that my own answers to these three questions would in each case be affirmative. But I believe that I am not alone in regarding symbolic activities as supremely important in all human relations. I have already looked at the place which symbolism occupies in the systematic writings of certain contemporary writers.

In my view it is both fitting and true to the witness of New Testament writers to confess Jesus as the central *symbol* of God. 'Centre' is a category which has played a dual role in human affairs. Both in a circle and in a straight line the centre is a point of major significance: society is normally ordered from a central place: a covenant or agreement between two parties also finds its guarantee through joint assent and signature at a central place. Jesus, as symbol, becomes the centre in both ways.

In confessing him by means of the numerous titles to which I have referred, early Christians declared that he is the symbol through whom humans can pierce beyond the temporal to the eternal, beyond the contingent to the permanent, beyond the partial to the total. 'He that hath seen me hath seen the Father (son as image of the father, a favourite New Testament symbol). 'Thou art the Christ' (the anointed one points to the anointer). The Logos embodies the word of the God who speaks and thereby directs attention to the speaker. As saviour, leader, high priest, he performs God's work and brings humans into relationship with God. As image, effulgence, glory he acts as medium through whom humans may ascend to communion with God himself. A symbol occupies a central position but radiates outwards to ever wider horizons, even to the limits of human imagination. Moreover the New Testament affirms that this expanding vision is effected not by means of human endeavour but through the continuing operation of the Holy Spirit. All growth towards wholeness, all movements towards conciliation are through the mediation of Jesus (the name which encompasses the totality of his earthly career) by the energy of the Holy Spirit.

A *human* symbol is the highest in potential of all symbols. A central human symbol, which always points beyond itself to God, is the highest in potential of all human symbols. It is the confession of Christians of all ages that Jesus himself, revealed through the words and life-patterns of his followers and interpreted to successive generations by the inspiration of the Holy Spirit, was the central symbol, potentially uniting the whole of humanity to God Himself.

CHAPTER NINE

The Letter and the Spirit

I

Few Pauline statements have exercised such an influence on later doctrinal developments as has the memorable contrast contained in II Corinthians 3.6: 'The letter killeth but the Spirit giveth life.' The original context of the aphorism seems clear. Paul is contrasting the giving of law under the old covenant (law which issued in condemnation and death) with the gift of the Spirit under the new covenant, a gift which issued in creation and renewed life. Law, written on stones, killed; the Spirit, inspiring the heart, brought life. That the work of the Messiah inaugurated a new covenant is one of the central themes of the New Testament. The conviction followed that the coming of the Spirit was a dramatic manifestation of the dawning of a new age.

The whole conception of covenant institution, however, was unfamiliar to the Hellenistic world and it was not long before the Pauline statement was being interpreted in a way corresponding to the general Greek outlook. The method of interpretation which had already attained wide acceptance amongst intellectuals was that of *allegorical* exegesis: words which seemed to bear a plain meaning actually concealed a far deeper significance. This needed to be drawn out. Such a view seemed to be directly in line with Paul's own statement. The letter, that is, any outward and literal interpretation, reached its end immediately: it had no continuing life. But the inner treasure, which it was intended to enclose, was life-giving, was capable of leading readers or hearers into ever expanding ranges of meaning.

Amongst patristic writers it was Origen in particular who took the Pauline phrase to imply that it was the duty of every Christian to pierce through the obvious and visible to the inner and spiritual: the way was now open, justified apparently by New Testament authority, to use the method of allegory to interpret what was proving to be the difficult book of the Christian faith, namely the Old Testament. 'This interpretation of II Cor. 3.6 by Origen had a decisive effect on the history of exegesis, since it seemed to draw a legitimization of allegory from the very heart of Pauline theology.'[1]

To a degree Augustine held on to the contrast between the condemnation of sin and the bestowal of grace but even he was prepared to regard the letter as hiding some deeper spiritual reality. In general the distinction between letter and spirit was linked with that between visible and invisible, between symbol and reality, which dominated the mediaeval outlook. With the ordinary senses it was possible to see the world of nature and to hear the words of scripture. With spiritual insight it was possible to penetrate beyond them to the reality of which they were only outward manifestations. In the words of Maximus the Confessor, this insight was 'the ability to apprehend within the objects of sense perception the invisible reality of the intelligible world that lies beyond them'.

Thus, in the Middle Ages, to interpret symbols, whether in the Bible or in the order of nature, was to decipher God's code. This conviction led to the establishment of the fourfold method – literal, allegorical, tropological and anagogical (though the last three could all have been classed as allegorical) – and to the proliferation of allegorical fancies which were held in check only by the authority of the church with its teaching of official doctrine. It was in many respects a magnificent system of symbolism which has been exhaustively investigated by H. F. Dunbar in her fine book *Symbolism in Mediaeval Thought*. In the objective universe the sun was the central symbol, source of light and life and warmth; in the inner consciousness of humans the sexual urge promoted life and love. Between the two there was, it was held, an intimate correspondence and thereby the whole process of fertility and regeneration was sustained. The supreme task entrusted to humans was that of interpreting God's self-expression through nature and through scripture. 'The whole development of thought to which the thirteenth century fell heir had been progress through symbol to more adequate symbol.'[2] And this comprehensive symbolism provided a framework within which people could live confidently, believing that their lives were secure within the continuing process of creation, providence and regeneration, a process symbolic of the eternal life of God himself.

This process attained its symbolic focus in the regular, daily celebration of the Mass. Just as each morning the sun rose and shed its life-giving rays on the fields and on humans who laboured in the fields, so the priest rose to perform his divinely given office of re-enacting the drama of life-through-death and providing heavenly sustenance for the faithful.

There was no educative factor in the life of the Middle Ages more powerful than the Mass, attended daily by the leisured class while the poorest laborer was fined if he failed to be present on Sunday . . . The pictures, images, curtains and ornaments were the lessons and scripture of the laity . . . the symbolism of the Mass, . . . ubiquitous and omnipresent, formed the atmosphere of the Middle Ages.[3]

'Letter' had been vastly extended to include the outward shape of church buildings, the material of their construction, the vestments of the clergy, festivals and processions, stained glass and above all the eucharistic elements: these were outward signs. In, with and under them all, it was believed, was the ultimate spiritual reality: by contemplation and by participation in the sacramental actions humans could be incorporated into and sustained within eternal life.

II

The dramatic change between the atmosphere of the Middle Ages and that of the fifteenth to seventeenth centuries could be described in many ways. One way is that of noting the change concerning language and language is one form of symbolism.

Whereas in mediaeval Europe Latin (often of an inferior kind) was dominant, by the sixteenth century eager attention was being paid to Greek and to some extent to Hebrew, while the long-standing desire for vernacular editions of the Bible suddenly became practicable through the invention of printing. By 1522 fourteen German versions of the New Testament had appeared.

Attention to the Greek of the New Testament and to its background in the Old Testament narrative made it possible to interpret II Cor. 3.6 in quite a new way. Instead of the Platonic framework of visible and invisible, of material and spiritual, of earthly and heavenly, there began to be a sense of two dispensations, an old and a new covenant, an age of law and an age of spirit. Such a revelation was at first a source of terror. Sinful men and women were not just sickly, needing the Church's ministrations. They were guilty, standing under the wrath and condemnation of a holy God. The letter, the law was the instrument of killing, of death. Where and how could life be found?

For Luther, scripture as a whole answered this urgent question (not the world of nature) by its revelation of salvation from the law's demands through the work of Christ. In the Old Testament God's revelation was through figure and promise; in the New Testament through entering humanity and accepting the penalty of death on a cross. Thus the contrast between letter and spirit was for him constantly re-enacted through the encounter between death and life, between judgment and salvation, between condemnation and justification. The proliferation of allegories and synechdoches and analogies – language-forms all expressing continuity – seemed to him trivial and powerless to deal with the great discontinuity between the moral law of God and the sinful nature of mankind. Letter and spirit were to be interpreted as law and gospel: the plain, straightforward condemnation of all that was man made and self-sufficient and lifeless so that the spirit of life in Christ Jesus might be freely displayed.

In a somewhat unexpected way Luther extended his interpretation of letter-spirit beyond the primary experience of law-gospel in the life of the individual to the danger of resting on some particular understanding of a verbal statement as being final and definitive.

What was a sufficient understanding in times past, has now become the letter to us. Thus at the present time . . . the letter itself is more subtle in nature than before. And this is because of the progress of time. For everyone who travels, what he has left behind and forgotten is the letter, and what he is reaching forward to is the Spirit. For what one already possesses is always the letter, by comparison with what has to be achieved . . . We must always pray for understanding, in order not to be frozen by the letter that kills.[4]

So Luther came to the text of scripture and to the task of understanding it in two ways, each of which was different from the accepted method of the Middle Ages. Most urgently he saw the text as pointing him to Christ and to his salvation. The law was always there, telling of condemnation. Still more the gospel was there telling of salvation. Not allegory but paradox and dialectic and translation. Through the text he found not simply a higher level of life but a personal acceptance by Christ himself. In the second place, however, he interpreted the letter-spirit contrast as symbolizing the necessity of constantly going on, of never resting in some well-rounded 'letter' expression but rather of ever reaching forward at the call of the Spirit. He was astonishingly modern in recognizing how easy it is for a doctrine or a formula to become *frozen* by the letter that kills (thus becoming a static sign, useful at a particular period but ever needing to be reinvigorated). With all his defects Luther was deeply sensitive to the character of his own time. The people of God were on the move and new symbols were needed. He recaptured the Pauline dialectic between law and spirit and made it a dynamic means of reformation. Simultaneously he turned away from the hitherto dominant framework of lower and higher, visible and invisible, to a framework of old and new covenant, of preparatory law and existential grace, leading towards a future in which the life-giving Spirit would ever be dominant.

III

John Calvin, like Luther, was a master of language. Luther wanted the gospel to be *heard*. Through his magnificent translation of the Bible into German he enabled people of all kinds to hear the good news in their own tongue and, with his notable gift for musical expression, he enabled them to sing out what they had received. Calvin's gift for language was different, his aims being clarity and simplicity. His influence on the development of the French language was immense and his own four-volumed *Institutes of the Christian Religion* has become a classic, not only by reason of its content, but also because of its splendid organization. He had less concern for visual aids than had Luther, but his logical precision made a profound appeal to the new urban populations who were seeking to organize their social life in ways conformable to the divine intention.

Calvin also focussed attention on II Cor. 3.6 and linked it closely with Jeremiah's notable prophecy that a new covenant would in course of time be established. Calvin quoted the prophecy at length and commented: 'the former (i.e. the law) is the preaching of death, the latter of life; the former of condemnation, the latter of righteousness; the former to be made void, the latter to abide.' He then concentrated attention on the New Testament passage.

> The Old Testament is of the letter, for it was published without the working of the Spirit. The New is spiritual because the Lord has engraved it spiritually upon men's hearts . . . The Old brings death, for it can but envelop the whole human race in a curse. The New is the instrument of life, for it frees men from the curse and restores them to God's favour. The Old is the ministry of condemnation, for it accuses all the sons of Adam of unrighteousness. The New is the ministry of righteousness because it reveals God's mercy through which we are justified.[5]

By so stark a contrast Calvin laid himself open to the charge of teaching that the Old was simply an instrument of death and needed to be replaced by the New, the instrument of life.

Against such a charge he made much of Paul's description (in the Epistle to the Galatians) of the Law as a tutor guiding children to the true school of Christ; further he used the language of figures and types pointing forward to the true substance. But it seemed doubtful whether these comparisons which suggest a gradual, continuing process do justice to the radical *discontinuity* suggested by unrighteousness – righteousness, killing – giving of life. He was deeply conscious of the inexorability of the *moral* law: all had sinned and so all were under its unquestioned condemnation. Yet there were promises in the Old Testament, ceremonies pointing to spiritual fulfilment, and temporary ordinances for the welfare of God's people. Were these not the work of the Spirit?

Moreover in II, 9.7 he claimed that Word and Spirit belong inseparably together. He criticized those who seek God's favour simply by obeying the written law. 'The letter . . . is dead and the law of the Lord slays its readers where it both is cut off from Christ's grace and, leaving the heart untouched, sounds in the ears alone. But if through the Spirit it is really branded upon hearts, if it shows forth Christ, it is the word of life.' Proper 'reverence and dignity' must be given to the Word; then the Holy Spirit will show forth his power by confirming the testimony of the Word in the heart.

Thus Calvin combined two doctrinal inferences from his consideration of II Cor. 3.6. On the one hand he aligned himself with Paul in contrasting the death-dealing function of the Mosaic Law with the life-giving function of the revelation through Christ. On the other hand he tried to hold together letter and spirit, Word and Spirit in an intimate relationship. The Word which merely sounds in the ears is deadly; only the Spirit applies it livingly in the heart. Correspondingly, the Spirit alone without the Word may engender empty speculations. The 'wood, hay, stubble' of false verbal doctrines are purged by the fire of the Spirit. Only through the constant relationship of Word and Spirit can the truth be preserved.

Calvin's profound regard for the majesty of law led him to interpret the human condition as hopeless and inexcusable. Only the New Covenant, the new revelation of Christ through the Spirit, could bring salvation. The Law kills: the Spirit gives life. Yet such a conviction left him with the problem of what to say about the Old Covenant. The contrast between letter and spirit seemed in a measure applicable. But this left unexplained the promises, the figures, the faith of the patriarchs, the testimony of the prophets. Calvin wrestled with these; he saw them as pointing forward to the full manifestation of the Spirit in Christ, but in the end he seems to have fallen back upon the claim that the Word was given in and through the Old Testament but that only through the mysterious operation of the Spirit was that Word sometimes received and thereby made effective. And such a conviction has held sway amongst the later followers of Calvin. The Word must be preached, but only the Spirit, operating in the hearts of hearers, can make it effective to their justification and sanctification.

The same is true of the dominically ordained sacraments. These serve as visual seals, signs, guarantees, tokens to confirm the Word. But not automatically. Only by the working of the Spirit can they become efficacious. Ironically, no one did more than Calvin to express the Christian religion in *words*. The *Institutes*, the *Commentaries*, and, in the Reformed Churches, the *Confessions* set forth the faith in comprehensive, definitive, *verbal* form. This, it was believed, was necessary and the invention of printing made these forms available to hosts of readers. Yet the fundamental danger became ever more acute. Would the letter, the written or printed word kill? Would it confine and imprison? Or would there be a readiness to listen to the Spirit, to allow the Spirit to create that liberty which Paul claimed at the end of II Cor. 3 was the very essence of his manifestation? The new enthusiasm for the Word in Reformation and post-Reformation theology could all too easily lead to the jealous preservation of orthodox statements and inflexible signs and so to the death of symbols.

IV

The late Middle Ages, at least amongst those exercising authority in church and state, became almost obsessed with the

notion of *order*. 'Take but degree away' and anything might
happen. In matters spiritual the church had seemed to be the
guardian of order, but defects in the papacy had turned men's
hopes to the calling of a general council while abuses in the
ranks of the clergy had led to the search for some more reliable
guidance. Out of this atmosphere of religious uncertainty and
disillusionment came new hope through the re-discovery of the
divine *Word*. Here was the authority needed for the true
ordering of individual and social life. Moreover this authority
was no longer to be encased in poor Latin, understood only by
relatively few, but rather to be first translated out of the original
languages into vernaculars understood by the many and then
to be circulated widely in printed form. The Word of God
would stand supreme over church and nation. By obedience to
its injunctions a stable order could be maintained.

Enthusiasm for the power of the Word was for a while
unbounded. Orders of worship were constructed by reliance on
the Word: orders of ministry could now serve to proclaim the
Word; ideally orders within society could be made conformable
to the Word. Articles, confessions, catechisms could be drawn
up to express in words that which must be believed and
practised if all things were to be in accordance with the Word of
God. At least amongst the peoples of the Reformation it seemed
that the all-important authority, directing orders, had been
found. Through preaching, common praying, hymn-singing,
reading printed homilies and commentaries, the Word of God
could become the governor of community life.

But one major problem remained and it has continued to be a
major problem within Protestantism ever since. It was the
problem of *interpretation*. Every translation involved interpretation, however great the effort to give an exact, literal rendering
of the orginal. Sermons, and literature bearing on moral issues,
all involved interpretation. However competent grammatical
and philological skill might be the relation of the original to the
contemporary scene was bound to involve interpretation. As I
have indicated, Calvin was in a measure aware of the problem
and appealed to the power of the Spirit to test doctrines and to
guide expositors. But the *manner* of the Spirit's working was left

undefined. Appeals might be made to the principle that any particular part must be interpreted in the light of the whole. But there might still be very different estimates concerning some parts included within the whole.

Yet over a considerable period, while nations and societies continued to be relatively self-enclosed, the Word of God as final authority remained unchallenged and interpretation followed the guide-lines set forth in the various confessions. As knowledge of the universe and of world-history (not included within the biblical narrative) began to grow, however, problems of interpretation became more acute. The scientific revolution was directing attention to signs capable of representing movements of heavenly bodies and of their earthly counterparts. Extensions of trade and commerce were opening minds to the existence of patterns of life quite different from those of the biblical tradition. Could the Bible include the whole of the universe and of mankind within its terms of reference? And could a uniform method of interpretation be imposed upon every part of scripture?

At a time when it began to be necessary to come to terms with the phenomena of change and expansion and movement, Christian leaders began to look more closely at the doctrine of the Spirit. According to the New Testament, the Spirit inspired men to bear witness to the Word, to do so in new areas and in unfamiliar circumstances, and to draw out the inner significance of the recorded events of the gospel story. Both Luther and Calvin had recognized the need of the Spirit's assistance for the true understanding of holy scripture, but this was largely a matter of praying for guidance and of searching the scriptures as a whole.

Yet there were sectaries within Reformed Christendom also claiming the guidance of the Spirit for their own particular interpretations of biblical passages. Some of those most devoted to the Bible and to its commands insisted on breaking with what was regarded as official doctrine or established order because they were acting, they believed, under the guidance of the Spirit. The distinction between letter and spirit was beginning to be drawn in a new way. Could letter, that is language, whether used to represent structure and energy in the natural order or used to record the characters and activities of humans living in earlier periods of history, become lifeless, formal, stereotyped, frozen, 'icily regular, splendidly null' and thereby devoid of spirit? Could dogmas and confessions and formulae, all carefully structured verbal forms, become like prisons preventing all freedom of expression and movement. 'Where the Spirit of the Lord is, there is liberty.' 'The law of the Spirit of life in Christ Jesus has set me free.'

There is a revealing passage in Hans Frei's magisterial history of hermeneutics in the eighteenth and nineteenth centuries. He is describing the work of Bengel, a famous biblical interpreter.

> Bengel was self-consciously orthodox and proudly acknowledged the close connection between his literal and his theological reading of the Bible . . . The doctrine of emphasis which endowed the words of the Bible with as much force, overtone and hidden spiritual meaning as they could bear was for him a bridge from the isolated and purely grammatical or philological reading of single passages to an understanding of the Bible as a unitary whole . . . 'Most learned men', he wrote, 'shun the spirit and, consequently, do not treat even the letter rightly.'
>
> It was a reciprocal relation. There is an inner word or meaning given with the outer word, and appropriate to this state of affairs there is a grammatical reading, open to all who have the training and native ability, and a spiritual reading restricted to those who are awakened to it by the Holy Spirit . . . The most striking impact of this position was to come when historical criticism had loosened the tight connection that prevailed in Bengel's, as in Spener's and Francke's day, between grammatical and inner or mystical sense and between literal and spiritual understanding. Once the common biblical world in its apparently common outward meaning started to break up, a kind of reading became all important, which stressed the self's distinctive perspective upon the text. The view came to persist that such

a distinctive perspective alone allows a living connection with the Bible.[6]

The contrast between letter and spirit takes the form, from this period onwards, of the tension between language which is formal, technical, literal, factual and that which is poetic, metaphorical, mystical, spiritual. If the former emphasis prevails, then language tends towards the cipher, the sign, the formal correspondent. If the latter, then language tends towards the fanciful, the grotesque, the private code. Complete restriction to literal correspondence produces a series of mechanical signals: uncontrolled flights of spiritual inflation produces a series of meaningless abstractions. To hold letter and spirit together, in vital symbolic relationship, has been one of the major tasks of the past two centuries.

The dominance of the *word* in religion, celebrated by the Reformers, was followed by its dominance in the outlook of the Rationalists. It seemed that divine-human relations could be expressed verbally in dogmas and formulae and constitutions. But humans refused to make a final obeisance to any such tyranny of the word. So the struggles for liberty of the Spirit in Evangelicalism, for evolving and continuously adapting life in Darwinism, for rights of self-expression in democratization. Most comprehensively, the Romantic movement sought to preserve the human values of beauty and mystery from being eclipsed within a rigid, mechanically organized world. In all this, however, questions of the meaning of spiritual and of the role of the Spirit received no clear answers. There was no slackening of effort in scientists' examination and interrogation of the physical world, nor in historians' study and reconstruction of the development of mankind. The result was a vast expansion of reports and recordings and data files. Language was geared to correspond to objects and events as closely as possible. But did it represent life and change in nature, feelings and relationships in humans? The Spirit, so the Christian tradition has claimed, is the lord and giver of *life*; the Spirit has spoken by *prophets*, that is, by those not content to submit to conventional patterns of existence. Could there be forms of language other than the positivist and the technical and the so-called factual which would not only be true to aspects of human experience but which would also inspire to new visions and new possibilities?

Leaders of thought in the seventeenth and eighteenth centuries were in danger of starving the human imagination. Their emphasis lay on logic, clarity, precision, permanence. The favourite image was the clock. God had set the great universal machine in motion and it moved, it was thought, in regular cycles, with only occasional interventions by the deity when things were out of joint. Reason and intellect were regarded as prime factors in culture and these ensured a relatively stable society.

Both in church and nation such an outlook led ultimately to reaction, to a new emphasis on feeling and imagination and the place of the subjective in all commerce with ultimate reality. In this reaction no concept proved to be more important than that of the symbol. In logical or legal discourse there is constant need for definite meaning, for *signs* which correspond in unitary fashion to external reality. But in artistic expression and inter-personal discourse the need is rather for *symbols* which are flexible and open in their immediate significance and which point beyond themselves to transcendent realities.

Immense changes have taken place in the twentieth century: the theory of relativity, quantum mechanics, the notion of indeterminacy, the discovery of the genetic code, the recognition of the personal equation in all forms of scientific observation. So far as language is concerned, the great division seems to me still to be between that which can be expressed mathematically and logically and that which can be expressed analogically and complementarily. That a vast amount of our knowledge of the operations of the universe can be expressed through signs or equations which have a uniform meaning and represent an ordered system must surely be allowed. But can *everything*, the totality, be thus represented? It is a well-substantiated claim that many phenomena can be expressed only by models or analogies or paradigms or by complementary statements. The analogue model has proved to be an exceedingly useful instrument in the task of interpreting and manipulating material phenomena. If the attempt is made to include *everything* within a single unambiguous formula, that formula proves to be the letter that kills. It is by means of the symbol that humans confess that it is the Spirit who both gives life and enables humans to bear witness to the nature of that life in symbolic language.

V

However, although symbolic forms of language have been employed in the onward march of science over the past two centuries, it has been within the representation of human relationships through history and art that the idea of the symbol has proved to be of exceptional importance. As I have suggested, in the reaction from verbal uniformity in corporate worship (from what Edwin Muir called Calvin's iron pen in dogmatic formulation), as well as from the increasing mechanization through industrial development, a new emphasis began to be laid on human feeling and the possibilities of creative imagination. So far as personal religion was concerned, the Pietistic movement in Germany, supported by Zinzendorf's hymns, and the Methodist movement in Britain, with Charles Wesley as its hymn-writer, brought a new quality of life to multitudes, a quality which consisted in emotional release, in symbolic celebration of the formative events of the Christian faith, and in an outreach to those bewildered by changing social conditions. The concern for evangelism and the redemption of society continued in the Evangelical Revival. A bare orthodoxy no longer satisfied. There was a yearning for the bestowal of the Spirit of life.

This new emphasis found its expression not only in the enthusiasm of popular religion but also in music, literature and philosophy. Goethe, Schleiermacher, and Hegel in Germany together with Coleridge and Wordsworth in England represented a new concern for the place of the *imagination* in the commerce of humans with Nature and with God, for the importance of feelings as well as reason in interpreting the human situation. Humans had profound experiences when contemplating nature or listening to great music or reading creative poetry. How were such experiences to be evaluated and interpreted? How were they created and by what means were they to be sustained? Speaking very generally the answer was: by the use of symbolic forms rather than by logical, abstract or propositional statements. Symbolism in art, in literature, in theology was to be the concern of one large area of humanistic studies in the nineteenth century. An ambiguous discipline, though an increasingly popular one, was to be the study of history. Was the main concern of history to be the establishment of dates, annals, causes and sequences of events and the reliability of texts or was it to be the *significance* of recorded actions and sayings, the relation between individuals and their social contexts? That the former quest was highly important could hardly be doubted. But was it to gain so dominant a position that the exploration of human relationships, the attempt to identify mental attitudes and personal intentions, and the *significance* of works of art in past ages, would be overshadowed or even ignored?

The rise of the novel, the towering achievements of the philosophers of idealism, the wondering response to nature by poets and painters, the dramas of Ibsen and the operas of Wagner, all bore witness to the urge to pierce beyond the obvious and the commonplace and to point, by means of symbolic forms, to higher or deeper realities. Life could indeed be lived in a sign-cage where a primrose by the river's brim was a yellow primrose and nothing more; or it could expand by attention to symbolic forms towards beauty, towards mystery and finally towards God.

Coleridge's famous term in his definition of symbol was *translucence*.

Symbol is characterized by a translucence of the Special in the Individual or of the General in the Especial or of the Universal in the General. Above all by the translucence of the Eternal through and in the Temporal. It always partakes of the Reality which it renders intelligible; and while it enunciates the whole, abides itself as a living part in that Unity of which it is the representative.[7]

It is, I think, the prefix *trans* which is of particular interest. It occurs in other significant words – translation, transference, transfiguration, transcendence – and is the Latin equivalent of *meta* occurring in metaphor, metamorphosis, metaphysics. The basic process represented by these terms is that of carrying over, of bridging a gap, of taking a word (or phrase or theme) from one context and using it in a quite different context, or of taking a word from one language and supplying as nearly as possible an equivalent in another language. Coleridge believed that a symbol can transluce, that is, bring into vivid light the eternal in and through that which is temporal. A person, an action, a saying, an object can by this definition shed light on the eternal not simply by way of illustration but by being a living part of that unity of which it is the representative. This is a large claim, for it means that certain words or objects may actually become living parts of that which they symbolize.

Within the specifically Christian context, Coleridge saw the reality of God suffering as vividly symbolized first in the whole life of Christ in the flesh and then in the words and images which bore witness to that life. This is how he expresses this central conviction:

> The crucifixion, resurrection and ascension of Christ himself in the flesh, were the epiphanies, the sacramental acts, and phenomena of the Deus Patiens, the visible words of the invisible Word that was in the beginning, symbols in time and historic fact of the redemptive functions, passions and procedures of the Lamb crucified from the foundation of the world; the incarnation, cross and passion – in short, the whole life of Christ in flesh, dwelling as man among men, being essential and substantive parts of the process, the total of which they represented; and on this account proper symbols of the acts and passions of the Christ dwelling in man as the Spirit of truth.[8]

Coleridge refers to the 'sublime idea of the Deus Patiens'; to the inadequacy of abstractions or mere illustrations to represent the idea; to the need for feeling and imagination to bring the idea into present-day experience. So comes the need for the *symbol* to 'compress' eternal truth, to be 'consubstantial' with the truth, to 'conduct' the truth into the imagination of those who come after. His concern (as indeed it was that of the Romantics generally) was to escape from 'the general contagion of . . . mechanic philosophy' and the rigid barriers of confessional orthodoxy. It is true that some amongst the Romantics sought this escape by retreating into some imagined golden age of the past – the patristic period or the Middle Ages. But such a policy was not that desired by Coleridge or others of the nineteenth-century advocates of Symbolism. Their desire was rather to discover symbols which would create in hearer or viewer or reader a sense of *tension – in – relationship* between visible and invisible, between past and future, between nature and humanity, between God and his creation. Such a tension in words and images would always be threatened by the same process of entropy as operates in the natural order. The symbol would be in danger of becoming a lifeless sign, a dead letter. It is the Spirit that giveth life. Bergson's concept of *élan vital* is applicable to language as well as to natural life. The fresh and creative metaphor is the most powerful of all symbolic forms in human experience.

It has been pointed out, especially since the rise of a new interest in narrative theology, that a story can be in a real sense an extended metaphor. Since the eighteenth century the story has assumed new forms – in the novel, in opera, in history, in drama, in journalism. No feature is more important within a story than *suspense* or (to use the term employed above) *tension*. There is the tension between author or composer and reader or hearer; between the time and place of the story and the time and place of the audience; between the theme of the story and the wider understanding of the world as a whole. So long as the story remains open to continuous reinterpretation and to extended application within contemporary life, it continues to be the instrument of the Spirit leading into ever fuller truth. Only when an exclusive emphasis is laid on grammatical and philological and archaeological and sociological aspects of religion or art does the symbol gradually lose its power and become simply a constituent relic of world-history, without any relevance to the problems and crises of contemporary life.

There is, I think, no more pregnant sentence in the New Testament on the work of the Spirit than Paul's in II Cor. 3.17. 'Where the Spirit of the Lord is, there is liberty.' I suggest that this applies to language as well as to personal life. In an essay on another author, Frank Sargeson has written: 'What fascinates him about words is their enormous suggestive power, and he uses them to liberate the imagination not, as some writers do, to restrict and pin it down.'⁹ No contrast could more aptly describe the dintinction between symbol and sign. The sign pins down: the symbol liberates the imagination 'even as by the Spirit of the Lord'.

CHAPTER TEN

Symbols and Culture

I

Culture, in the sense of the life-style of a particular society, becomes describable and definable because of its association with the whole concept of order. Where there are divisions and conflicts and a clash of ideologies there can be no communal culture. But the need to live in an ordered environment appears to be an imperative constituent of human nature. Indeed Simone Weil once declared that 'order' is the first need of the soul (in a time of severe social disturbance through war, she had been asked by the Free French in London to report on the possibilities of bringing about the regeneration of France).

'The first of the soul's needs,' she replied, 'the one which touches most nearly its eternal destiny is order; that is to say, a texture of social relationships such that no one is compelled to violate imperative obligations in order to carry out other ones.'[1]

This definition of order raises at once the question of how such an order can be established. By force? By inflexible law? By exact definition of obligations? Such questions lead at once to the problem of the place and functions of symbols in any society. Can they assist to the establishing of order? Can they help to prevent that conflict between obligations to which Simone Weil referred?

If sheer force is employed to establish a completely uniform pattern, as for example under the régimes of Stalin and Hitler, then there is no question of a variety of symbols being employed. The one unchanging and inflexible visual device is either the hammer and sickle or the swastika. The colours red or black may be added, but such signs are irrelevant whenever there are deviations from the official order. Then the imposition of appropriate punishment is regarded as the only way of preserving the deadly uniformity.

However, even when no such repressive force is exercised, there is still the possibility of establishing an imposing symbol of order by constructing an edifice of *signs* within which members of a society are expected to frame their own lives. These signs consist either of what wise men reckon to be the undeviating regularities of the natural order or of what powerful legislators consider to be absolute necessities for social order. The former are integrated into a structure of duties in relation to nature (the care and preservation of life and the means of subsistence), the latter into a structure of rights and responsibilities necessary for harmonious social living (respect of the person, property rights etc.) The signs forming this framework may be visual, they may be verbal. As soon as they are crystallized into static forms, inscribed or written on some kind of plastic material, they gain clarity and definiteness but lose flexibility and the possibility of adjustment to changing conditions.

Undoubtedly the attractiveness of living within a stable framework of *signs* is very great. Life then seems entirely secure. The future seems predictable. Relations with fellow human beings are under control. A completely isolated culture, with its own structure of traditional signs incorporated in oral or written laws, seems eminently desirable. If minorities within the society are dissatisfied with the accepted structure, let them depart. If those from outside wish to live within the accepted structure, let them conform entirely to its rules. The rise of nations, the dissolution of empires, the ambitions of sects, the tensions within societies, are all connected in some way with the fundamental problem of the maintenance of order within a world which can never stand still, not even when the rhythm of the natural order seems to be invariable.

Nowhere, it seems, has the tension between living under a dependable order and freedom to express the self in non-conforming ways been felt more acutely and persistently than in Russia. It was almost a century ago that Dostoyevsky wrote the searching fable of the Grand Inquisitor in which the Christ seems to stand alone in a commitment to freedom over against the masses who choose rather to live within the securities of assured food for the body, miraculous interventions in times of crisis and a cosmic organization of social relations. More recently a Russian writer Alexander Yanov has confessed to the acute tension in his own culture.

In me, as in every offspring of Russian culture, two souls co-exist exactly as two cultural traditions contend in the consciousness of the nation. Each of these has its own hierarchy of values. The highest value of the one is order (and correspondingly the lowest is anarchy and chaos). The highest value of the other is freedom (and correspondingly the lowest is slavery). I fear chaos and hate slavery. I feel the temptation to believe in a 'strong regime', able to . . . dry all tears and console all griefs. And I am ashamed of the temptation. Sometimes it seems to me that freedom gives birth to chaos . . . that slavery gives birth to order.[2]

But Russia does not stand alone. Every nation, every organized social group has experienced the same tension in varying degrees of intensity. In natural science, rules and laws are constructed by observing and experimenting with natural phenomena. Are they signs of an unchanging orderliness? Or are they symbols of connections which make ordered living possible but which are open to reconstruction and readjust-ment as the search for significant patterns continues? Again constitutions and laws are indispensable if interrelationships within any society are to be preserved from sheer arbitrariness with each individual seeking his or her own advantage. Are those to be regarded as inflexible signs, essential for the preservation of ordered living? Or can they function as symbols, pointing beyond themselves to that justice which can never be fully achieved or guaranteed but which is a goal, in striving toward which a worthy order can be maintained? While a pyramid, a temple, a cathedral is being built it is a source of inspiration, of challenge and of hope. What happens when the structure is complete? It continues to be a sign of what has been accomplished by human dedication, by corporate endeavour. But only if it remains a focus of creative, pulsating, responsive activities, only if constantly, through the use made of it, it is seen to point beyond itself to widening horizons and richer experiences does it constitute a vital and meaningful symbol.

> No building is objectively a temple. No space is objectively sacred. No object (or, I might add, event or person) is objectively a symbol in and of itself: an object becomes a symbol in the consciousness of certain persons . . . I do not contend that we must know what a given symbol 'means' in general: rather what it has in fact meant to particular persons or groups at particular times.[3]

Later, the author of this quotation returns to his insistence that the link between the objective and subjective is of crucial importance. It is this relation which is vital in all symbolic activity. Yet such a conviction still leaves open the double question of priority and universality. Does a symbol actually create a group-consciousness? And are there certain symbols which have the capacity to create a group consciousness at any place and at any time?

This question has assumed special urgency in the enterprise of Christian missions. From the very first, according to the Acts of the Apostles, Christians were expected to be witnesses to the risen Christ in Jerusalem and in all Judaea, and in Samaria and unto the uttermost parts of the earth. The final commission of Jesus according to Matthew was to go into all the world and proclaim the gospel to all people. This gospel certainly included the symbol of cross – resurrection. Could this become a symbol for all people? Could it awaken such a response in the consciousness of those exposed to the witness that they, sharing in the symbol, could become sharers in the fellowship of the Christian community?

II

The first major test as to whether Christian symbols could awaken responses in the consciousness of those belonging to a different culture arose when the Christian witnesses endeavoured to establish the church firmly in *agrarian* contexts. The faith originated in the midst of a culture which to a degree depended on the land but which was primarily concerned to maintain the strict purity of personal and social life in the tradition of the Mosaic law. It was a quite different culture from that of the great Mediterranean world, and although there had been numerous rapprochements and attempts to build bridges between Hebraic and Hellenistic culture (the Septuagint, for example and the method of allegory), in general the symbolisms belonging to the two were radically different from one another.

In particular, there was the interpretation of the central event of cross – resurrection. Within the Jewish milieu appeal could be made to patterns of imagery contained in the Old Testament scriptures, patterns which were dominantly those of a nomadic, pastoral, trading, fending culture. How could this symbolism grip the consciousness of a settled society, attached to land and crops, concerned for fertility and the preservation of life, ordered by the seasonal regularities of the Mediterranean region?

So far as I can judge, the transposition was effected mainly through the agency of two symbolic forms, the first dramatic and visual, the second verbal with dramatic consequences. These two forms were sacrifice and law. Each culture, Hebraic and Hellenistic, possessed a tradition of dramatic sacrificial ritual; each culture was held together within a system of law. Sacrifice and law were familiar categories. But their actual structural forms and their meanings within the two cultures were vastly different. Yet although they were very different, it still was the case that if the crucifixion – resurrection event could be proclaimed either in terms of the offering of sacrifice or in terms of the repairing of a broken law, it could appeal to the consciousness of those within the agrarian as well as of those within the wilderness and pastoral cultural tradition. Thus the great transition in Christian symbolism was made from an interpretation based on Hebraic sacrificial and legal practices to that based on Graeco-Roman agricultural traditions of sacrifice and law.

Was this a falsification or an enrichment? This question has prompted and sustained one of the most persistent debates in Christian history. If the object of true religion is to provide *signs*, signs which can take either visual or verbal shape and remain virtually unchanged both in form and in interpretation throughout the centuries, then it can be claimed that the expressions of crucifixion-resurrection in the Mediterranean world and later in mediaeval Europe obscured and perverted the given originals. This to a considerable degree, though not absolutely, was the complaint of the Reformers. They considered that the concept of sacrifice had been funnelled into a single narrow channel of theory and practice, had become an essential sign of orthodoxy and so had perverted the biblical interpretation. With the *concept* of law they were less confident. There was, Calvin declared, the moral law, applicable to the lives of all peoples at all times; there were judicial and ceremonial laws, applying only to particular societies in particular periods. Could the moral law be expressed in language which could be displayed (as it was on church walls) as a completely unambiguous and unchanging *sign*? Or, even in the realm of law, was there a tension of dialectical interaction between the original and the changing, between the primordial conception and the existential experience, between law and gospel? There were differences even amongst the Reformers as well as between the Reformers and the Catholic church.

Nevertheless, a new culture came into being in northern Europe during the fifteenth to sixteenth centuries and this culture sought to recover the original symbolic forms of the Hebraic tradition. Concurrently it promoted faith-response (with its ingredient of personal freedom) in relation to these forms in place of an unquestioning assent to a system of signs and their authorized interpretation. The application of the original Christian symbols in life in an agrarian culture was not immediately regarded as having been a huge mistake. Rather, in the light of the challenge from the new culture, it had to be asked how far that application had congealed into narrow and rigid forms which were throttling the range and expansiveness of the crucifixion-resurrection symbol.

Unhappily, it soon became clear that many in the Reformation camp were all too eager to erect a new edifice of verbal signs – confessions, articles, formulae – which might be of value for establishing orderly communities but which could all too readily become obstacles to freedom, whether of thought or of practice. Yet the very tension between the two dominant cultures (those of the Mediterranean and of Northern Europe and their religious expressions) prevented stagnation and complacency. Meanwhile the opening out of new worlds in East and West began to present a challenge of a new kind. Could the Christian religion, whether in its Catholic or Protestant form, become established in these new lands? So far the only cultures known in Europe, distinct from those of Catholic and Protestant Christianity, had been the Jewish and the Muslim. Attempts had been made to present the Christian faith to members of these two cultures but with little success. Frustrated by resistance to their appeals, Christians had turned to brute force. By their savage persecutions of Jews and by their militaristic campaigns against Muslims they built up such a wall of resentment and even hatred as has been virtually impossible for later generations to break down.

Jews and Muslims shared much in common by reason of their origins in the arid regions of the Middle East. But Jews had no land of their own, their language was different from that of the Muslims and, most important of all, their law was that of Moses rather than of Muhammad. In each tradition law, fixed and unchangeable in its written form, was a *sign* holding the community together in its powerful embrace. There might be breaches, delinquencies and shortcomings. But the law itself remained intact: an eternal sign of divine relationship to a chosen people. In the desert and in the ghetto life is hard, often dangerous, either black or white, with little scope for compromise or differences of interpretation. Symbolism, except amongst a minority of mystics, is virtually unknown.

The great expansions of European nations, however, have been in territories either hitherto unoccupied or occupied by peoples living off the land. Where lands have been unoccupied, colonies have been established with forms of government and of religion imported almost without change from their places of origin. Where cultures related to the land have already been in existence the task of relating the forms of the explorers – colonizers – traders – rulers to those of the indigenous peoples has been far more complex.

III

I shall not attempt to deal with countries such as Canada, the United States, Australia, New Zealand and South Africa, all of which have largely been occupied by those belonging either to Catholic or Protestant traditions. The real collision of cultural traditions (and symbols) has come to pass in territories where for centuries peoples, living on the land and off the land, have built up their own distinctive cultures and expressed them through linguistic, through artistic and through religious forms. As merchants and traders and soldiers came to these areas, how would they deal with members of these unfamiliar cultures? In particular, how would chaplains and missionaries deal with ancient religious forms and practices?

The ruthless method, unfortunately practised by early adventurers, was to use force, either exterminating or enslaving or compelling to a formal Christian allegiance. In time better counsels prevailed and two strategies emerged. On the one hand Catholic missionaries, perhaps recognizing their own affinity with the symbolic forms of peoples living off the land, sought to purify them and direct them to the true focus of devotion – the Son of God through whom we have access by one Spirit to the Father. Sacred buildings, purification ceremonies, sacrificial offerings, festal occasions, all had a place in native religion and through them a bridge could be constructed from one symbol-system to another. Crucial questions, however, were still to come. Were there *limits* to what could be accepted into Catholic Christianity? Could what had become permanent *signs* in ancient religions be converted into *symbols*, pointing the worshippers to the living God and his revelation in Christ? And would converts be willing to abandon practices which had seemed to provide stability for their whole social life?

A notable example of the complexity of this problem has recently occurred in Zambia. From there, the Roman Catholic archbishop was summoned to Rome while careful investigation was taking place concerning the patterns of his ministry. I quote from *The Times* account:

> Apart from his faith healing (which has caused him to be likened to a witch-doctor) the archbishop is deeply convinced of the need for Christianity in Africa to be expressed in an African way and not according to European models. If God can only be explained and taught about properly by the white races, the archbishop argues, he must be a small god indeed, while he himself as an African feels that he knows God intimately and so cannot accept a European monopoly.
>
> There are colourful reports of Mgr Milingo's handling of the liturgy. The priest sits with his concelebrants, 'like a chief with his elders around him', as drums open the Mass. Traditional dancing accompanies the Gloria and at the Offertory not only the bread and wine are offered, but also fruit and vegetables. 'They carry branches heavy with bananas on their heads.'

It appears that disquiet in Rome had been caused chiefly by the archbishop's methods of healing: exorcism and rituals were comparable to those of native healers. Disquiet in the diocese had come about because older Christians, (like many in the West who have been critical of liturgical changes since Vatican II) have resented being deprived of the ordered forms through which they have found solace and security. The tension between order and freedom erupts in many different ways.

The problem of healing and exorcism has been endemic in the church since New Testament times and it seems impossible to lay down hard and fast rules governing the exercise of what is called 'spiritual healing'. I do not know what has been the outcome of the enquiry concerning this part of the archbishop's ministry. But that he has been justified in encouraging freedom in liturgical expression seems to be plain. The interplay of two cultural traditions, each correcting and complementing the other, is, I believe, a wonderful means of keeping symbols alive and preventing them from degenerating into obligatory signs. The earlier undeviating regulation that Mass must be recited in Latin sustained an impressive orderliness but at too great a cost. Uniformity, in the Church of England through the Book of Common Prayer, is subject to the same criticism. But is the new flexibility in liturgical language applicable to other parts of the Christian liturgy and to doctrine also? Certainly there have been radical changes in shapes of buildings. Few things have been more striking in Catholic circles than the virtual abandonment of concentration on the high altar, with now the priest facing the people over a simple table. Decoration has become more austere, less sentimental. The traditional time of saying Mass has been extended to later hours of the day and fasting regulations have been modified. Vestments and frontals (where used) have either become plainer or more related to the daily lives of the congregation.

The symbols which those in authority have been most reluctant to alter in any respect have been the bread and wine of the eucharist. In Roman Catholic circles, as in the case cited in Zambia, additional offerings have been allowed, just as in Anglican circles it has been customary to add alms. But any substitution for actual bread and fermented wine has been strongly resisted, even though bread used may be in the form of a thin wafer or a small square or a section of an ordinary loaf.

Not many years after the first Christian mission had begun in Uganda, the leading missionaries wished to authorize for use in Holy Communion the simple food and drink of the Ugandans, stiff plantain meal and banana beer. But the Archbishop of Canterbury, to whom the matter was referred, demurred. He ordered the traditional elements to be retained as symbols of the continuity and universality of the church. The missionaries on their part urged that bread and wine were utterly strange importations which would stamp Christianity as a foreign religion at its very heart. The dilemma is a real one, affecting many symbolic forms. Tradition and continuity (which can so easily lead to rigidity and formality) or existing bonds of community (which can be a barrier to the consciousness of *new creation* in Christ). Can a symbol, representing food and drink so characteristic of Mediterranean culture, be transferred into the worship of all other cultures? Or does an unchangeable transfer reduce it to no more than a sign, useful in its way but unable to touch the depths of human feeling?

IV

Missions originating from Britain have been particularly exposed to this dilemma of how to deal wisely with the collision of cultures. The Church of England has retained many symbolic forms of the Catholic tradition – episcopacy, mediaeval buildings, its parish structure (linking it to the life of the land), its emphasis on the two major sacraments and its attachment to many legacies from ancient liturgies. Yet in the sixteenth century it embraced the Reformation emphasis on the Word of God, the reading of scripture, the appeal to the Bible as the criterion of doctrine and practice and the recital of passages of scripture in its worship manual, the Book of Common Prayer. In Reformed churches, whether in England or Wales or Scotland, there was little concern for man's relation to nature (which often seemed harsh and inhospitable) or to liturgical patterns of worship. Rather, the attempt was made to subjugate everything – doctrine, worship, conduct – to the revealed Word of God and to establish communities whose bonds would be not those of a particular place but of election and covenant and common destiny.

The initial aim of Anglicans, who began to organize colonies overseas, was to regard them as outposts of the Church of England, completely retaining her structure of faith and worship. Clergy could go out as chaplains or pastors and the Book of Common Prayer could provide the authorized pattern for teaching and worship. The major difficulty arose in regard to bishops. Without them there could be no ordination or confirmation overseas. Yet there was stubborn reluctance to establish what might appear to be independent dioceses overseas, far removed from direct allegiance to the Crown.

However, a combination of circumstances, the Evangelical Revival under the Wesleys, the Declaration of Independence of the United States of America and the rapid growth of trading and colonization both by British and by continental powers in outlying parts of the world, brought about the great expansion of Christianity from the late eighteenth to the early twentieth century. This resulted in an unprecedented interaction of Western culture with cultures of other lands, the respective symbol systems coming almost violently into collision. Whereas Roman Catholics and those upholding the more Catholic emphasis in the Church of England sought to transplant their own symbolic forms and promote their growth in other lands, the Reformed Churches and the Evangelical wing of the Church of England threw themselves into the task of making the gospel known throughout the pagan world by translating the scriptures into other languages and by giving personal testimony to the saving work of Christ.

Begun with enthusiasm and maintained by heroic devotion, the missionary task has become increasingly difficult. Roman Catholics were cultured not only by Christianity but by the myths and rituals of the Mediterranean world. Anglicans were cultured not only by Christian creeds and sacraments but by centuries of English national history. Moreover, if the task was difficult for those rooted in more Catholic traditions, it was often more difficult for those seeking to be faithful to their Reformed convictions. Their confidence was in the Word of God but they found themselves amongst peoples who were illiterate and whose culture was certainly not simply a culture of the written word: it was a culture whose dominant symbols had been songs, stories, dances, dramas, votive offerings, ascetic practices. Were these all to be swept away and replaced by a strange book, the only allowable additions to it being preaching and hymnody?

Nearly thirty years ago, the distinguished Sri Lankan Bishop, Lakdasa de Mel, wrote ironically, yet with sad frustration, about the clash of symbols which has characterized the life of so many Christian communities in so many parts of the world but perhaps especially in India and Sri Lanka, both inheritors of ancient and distinguished cultural traditions. He wrote in the *Ecumenical Review* of October 1955:

They (i.e. Ceylonese Christians) looked on many things in their national heritage with suspicion, as incompatible with their newly-embraced faith. They loyally settled down to worship the Trinity in small churches with pointed arches and insufficient ventilation, wherein most of the pictures and ornaments were dutifully imported.

Gathering together at an hour sufficiently remote from the freshness of the tropical morning to give chronological unity with the 11 a.m. gatherings which had found favour with their brethren of the West, they attended services of a Western type, listening patiently to translations of the Holy Scriptures and to the preaching of the Word in language which would have been, on occasion, quite excruciating had they known more of their own literature; and with a self-denial that turned their backs on the music of their own land, they proceeded in doubtful consonance with a well-intentioned harmonium to raise hymnal offerings to heaven, consisting of the combined mutilation of a native language which could not survive the metrical structures therein demanded and of a Western tune rendered at a tempo which doomed it to slow extinction.

This complaint may seem exaggerated, but there is no escape from the fact that Christian cathedrals and churches exist in India and Sri Lanka which were built entirely according to English models, that for a long time a literally translated Book of Common Prayer served as the liturgy of congregations within the Anglican Communion and that nineteenth-century hymns in translation, with English tunes, were regarded as a necessary part of a regular service. There have been major attempts to change all this in the past fifty years, though church buildings remain, and, as in other parts of the world, those accustomed to forms which had become signs of security amidst the turmoil of changing political and economic conditions have clung tenaciously to those symbols which were in use when first they became Christians. Some words of Shirley Williams in a somewhat different context are applicable to the plight of countless souls today. 'As we observe chaos lapping around the edges of our own industrial civilization, to what truth will we cling?' It is to seemingly changeless *signs* that people tend to cling. If these are removed or superseded, what refuge remains? (Hong Kong is facing the prospect of political and social change. The Dean of the Anglican Cathedral has commented: 'Many look to the Christian church as a symbol of the solid, unchanging values of yesterday.' But no true symbol can be bound by yesterday.)

Yet the word which has dominated missionary strategy since World War II has been *dialogue*. No real translation, no creative transformation is possible without dialogue or interrelationship. Earlier efforts to translate the scriptures or Christian doctrines into vernaculars, to transplant ritual practices and musical forms into other cultural contexts, demanded not one-to-one correspondences (which is merely a sucking of other individual words and practices into own's own pattern) but dialogue, dialectic, twoness, and (an even more comprehensive term) *reciprocity*. The existing symbols of the other culture must be respected and (a lengthy process) learned. Only so can a creative interaction begin and new symbolic forms emerge.

It may indeed be claimed that this is one of the ways in which new symbols have always sprung to life. Just as there is a bridge over which a transmission of 'information' takes place to create the human embryo, so there may be a bridge over which a transmission of 'imagination' takes place to form a cultural symbol. Signs or codes are part of the *biological* process which directs human growth and development. Symbols or ciphers (Jaspers' term) are part at least of the *cultural* process which brings humanity to the fullness of its potential. And symbols are the product of *relatedness and reciprocity*, just as truly as new biological life is the product of the union of male and female in sexual intercourse.

Humans are unwilling to live for long without order (though I prefer the term orderliness) and this necessarily involves the construction of a system of *signs*. Yet the paradox and the peril is that such a system seems inevitably to deteriorate into fixity, he single vision, automation, equilibrium. Only through dialogue, dialectic, meeting, interchange, interaction, reciprocity can the creative process of *symbolization* be maintained.

CHAPTER ELEVEN

The Life and Death of Symbols

I

Why do some symbols illuminate a situation and stimulate human responses to it while others fail to awaken echoes in the hearts or resolutions in the minds of those who encounter them? Why do symbols prominently displayed in a place of worship, which were obviously powerful agents at some time in the past, become merely antique reminders of that past, having no clear relevance to the life of the present? Erich Heller has described this kind of situation vividly so far as the world of poetry is concerned:

> The notorious obscurity of modern poetry is due to the absence from our lives of commonly accepted symbols to represent and house our deepest feelings. And so they invade the empty shells of fragmentary memories, hermit-crabs in a sea of uncertain meaning.[1]

Symbols, formerly powerful, too easily become 'empty shells of fragmentary memories'.

Once upon a time a church spire was an eminent symbol of uplift for a community, raising the vision and aspiration of its members heavenwards: it might be surmounted by a cross, the symbol of Christian salvation. But today the high-soaring building is either the skyscraper or the cooling-tower or the nuclear reactor or the block of flats; the surmounting symbol is the plume of smoke rising from the energy-producing furnace far below. Preaching in Salford a century ago, Cardinal Wiseman could refer to 'the union of those two symbols which are here: on the one side those vast and darkened piles of building which fill your city with their tall columns above which the banner of industry ever streams in the wind; and, on the other, the vast magnificent church of God, with its spire bearing the symbol of peace and salvation'.[2] The banner of industry may still be a symbol of earthly prosperity: it is questionable how far the spire moves city-dwellers to thoughts of heaven.

One of Robert Lowell's finest poems is entitled 'Waking Early on Sunday Morning'. It begins with images from the natural world – the chinook salmon, the fieldmouse in its dark nook, the termite in the woodwork. Then the poet's thoughts go to yachtsmen busy down in the harbour, to tasks he might himself engage in outside the house. Suddenly he hears the new electric bells playing *Faith of our Fathers* and he reflects on the 'vanishing emblems' in the small town. The white spire and flag pole rising above the fog: now 'useless things to calm the mad'. The Bible has been 'chopped and crucified' to provide hymns with stiff quatrains which 'sing of peace and preach despair'. What remains is old lumber 'cast for the kingdom, banned in Israel, the wordless sign, the tinkling symbol'.

It is a sad poem. The great symbols – the sabbath, the Bible, the tree of life, the noble church spire – have lost their power and their meaning. A few of the faithful cling to weak substitutes. But joy has disappeared from the planet. War follows on the heels of war and the earth remains 'a ghost . . . forever lost in our monotonous sublime'. With the decay and virtual death of traditional religious symbols, where are the upward – pointing and forward – looking creations to take their place?

II

More than twenty-five years ago Anthony Bridge wrote a seminal article entitled 'The Life and Death of Symbols'. Having once been a professional painter, he was well qualified to write about the arts; having been ordained into the Christian ministry he was equipped to speak of theology. As far as the arts were concerned he claimed that the Renaissance in Europe marked a great divide: then the close relation which had

hitherto existed between religion and painting was severed and
a dominantly secular school emerged. For a long time naturalism became the accepted 'style'. 'Now, however, this post-
Renaissance European naturalism and its traditional style of
symbolism is dead. Why?'[3]

Bridge answered his question by enunciating what he
regarded as a fundamental principle concerning symbolization. 'In the arts (and I would urge that the same is true for
theology) a style lives for just so long as the symbols continue to
be used as symbols pointing to something beyond themselves.
Once a symbol is used for its own sake and is treated as a *fact* –
that is to say, as a self-sufficient reality – it dies.' Applied to
theology this principle has been illustrated by the rise both of
naturalistic humanism, which accorded no place to any
transcendental reality, and by fundamentalism which regarded
the recorded fact *as* the reality. In each case symbolism had no
part to play: it was dead.

Bridge went on to suggest a twofold remedy. On the one
hand he urged that new symbols should be created, though the
task is difficult and public response is invariably slow. On the
other hand (and this is the more practicable course) every effort
should be made to show the relation between old symbols and
the reality to which they pointed. Symbols only continue to live
in so far as they strengthen our apprehension of that divine
reality which they were originally designed to represent or
make present. How far these remedies are achieving positive
success may be open to question. What is certain, Bridge
affirms, is that once a symbol is used for its own sake to express
unquestionable *fact* its usefulness is finished: it becomes a
lifeless cipher.

A second important article dealing with the life and death of
symbols appeared in the same periodical some sixteen years
later. Discussing present-day eucharistic spirituality John
Riches focussed attention on the symbols employed and on
their subjection to processes of change. His thesis, he wrote,

is this: religious symbols are relative to particular societies;
within certain societies certain symbols express effectively a

general view of reality, of God, the world and men; *but* conditions, economic, social and political may change in such a way that these symbols no longer express such an overall view and then either the religious symbolism must be altered or the religion will cease to be related to the life of the society. There will be in Christian terms a tension between love of God and love of neighbour; in other terms, the survival of a religion as a dominant force within a society may well depend on its ability to adapt and change its symbolism to the new pattern of society, otherwise it will have a distorted view both of God and of the world and society.[4]

Later, referring to 'kingship' symbols, he urged that they now speak to fewer and fewer people. 'That is to say, that although the words themselves are perfectly intelligible they no longer stand as symbols for ultimate reality because they are in their concrete representation no longer of central importance in our lives.' Even more importantly, such symbols may become instruments of distortion when divorced from the actual structures of peoples' social existence.

Riches' thesis is consonant with my own contrast already made between the life-structure of more settled societies and those of societies on the move. The symbolism of the former has been dominated by words and images drawn from an intimate relationship with the land: sowing and reaping, springtime and harvest, birth and death in humans and in nature, hierarchical structures needed for production and distribution. And just because humans, wherever cultivation is possible, have continued to depend on the 'fruits of the earth in due season', this symbolism has retained an extraordinary hold on peoples' hearts and minds.

In the case of more mobile societies in Christendom it is the imagery of the Old Testament which has proved to be the all important source of symbolism. For early Christians, for mediaeval sects, for Protestant communities in the sixteenth and seventeenth centuries, for Mormons in the nineteenth century and for liberation groups in the twentieth, the Old

Testament symbols of oppression and deliverance, of law and liberty, of tribulation and triumph, of promise and fulfilment have stimulated the imagination and strengthened the resolve. A major question, however, still remains unanswered: what religious (or artistic) symbols are appropriate for a society increasingly dominated by machines and computers?

III

The question of the use of ancient and traditional symbols in Christian worship – paintings and windows and wall-inscriptions in churches and chapels, hymns and anthems and canticles in their services – is a thorny one. Strength and encouragement comes through expressing continuity with past generations who created powerful symbolic forms; yet there is the constant danger that these forms may become stereotyped, decorative, pastiche, meaningless. I have sat in a once famous nineteenth-century Church of England church and gazed at symbols painted or inscribed on the east wall and concluded that scarcely one of them would evoke the slightest response from modern worshippers. I have admired a fine modern chapel in the United States as a building but found it festooned with all kinds of ancient symbolic forms whose significance could be learned only by the aid of a handbook providing the necessary clues. I have looked at Graham Sutherland's massive tapestry in Coventry Cathedral and wondered about the four living creatures of the Apocalypse so dramatically recon-structed. As artistic creations they are wonderfully impressive. The colours, the vitality, the grouping all testify to the genius of the creator. But do they point beyond themselves? To what? Do they stir the imagination and the religious feeling of the modern beholder? The Quakers adopted the policy of plain walls, plain windows and plain meeting-houses. Is this the only solution for today?

A strategy which neither abandoned past symbols altogether nor employs them in a merely conventional and imitative way is intensively difficult to devise and maintain. Arthur Koestler was well aware of the problem in the realm of the arts.

As conventions crystallize the audience becomes conditioned to accept, without recreative effort, one particular set of relevant stimuli as representing the thing or process for which they stand and the particular type of illusion conveyed in the conventional manner becomes smooth and automatic. The 'consumer' reads the conventional novel, looks at the conventional picture, and watches the conventional proceedings on the stage at his ease; there is no need for him to strain his imagination. People prefer the conventional to the unconventional because its acceptance requires no creative effort. Art then becomes a pastime and loses its impact, its appeal to self-transcendence, its integrative effect.[5]

Koestler feared convention and saturation in artistic performance. A comparable danger within the Christian tradition is the constant repetition of some treasured symbolic form until it loses its power and becomes trivialized. No symbol combination has occupied so central and dominant a position in Christianity as cross-resurrection. At first, though both were celebrated in words and dramatic actions, it was the resurrection which captivated the artists' imagination and expression. Later the cross, the tree, the crucifix were depicted again and again: the cross became easier to portray and repeat visibly than the resurrection and the risen Christ. The result was that miniature crosses multiplied and with the constant repetition (and this has been true of hymns as well as of fabricated emblems) there came a loss of creative power.

We are surrounded today by the remains of dead symbolism. It can be seen most clearly in the ritual and art of the Church and perhaps we may quote as an example the Christian use of the Cross today. Clearly this is the prime symbol of Christianity and hence it finds a place at the focal point of most modern churches, on the altar or close to it. But little by little the Cross has come to be used elsewhere as well and present-day artists and carpenters with the best motives in the world, are apt to mark all the sacred objects of the church with a cross. So there are crosses on the hymn-books, crosses on the hangings, crosses carved on the pew-ends and crosses all over the parish magazine. What had been useful when it appeared in its context in one, or perhaps two places, loses its meaning when it is vainly repeated.[6]

One further cause of the death of a symbol is the attempt to impose upon it a completely fixed, restricted, confined *interpretation*. Literalism, rigid one-to-one correspondence between symbol and reality, removes all the overtones and intimations and imaginative suggestions which a true symbol always possesses. Perhaps the outstanding example in the recent history of Christianity of a sustained campaign to impose literal correspondences on a symbolic narrative has been the treatment of the creation stories in the first two chapters of Genesis. The bringing-together of God and his universe through the symbols of spirit and word and light and life and water was transformed into a detailed recording of stages in the creative process. That which bore witness to the primacy and creative activity of God became a fixed blueprint whose sequential stages were supposed to correspond exactly to what had actually happened.

Symbolism cannot live with literalism. Yet it can also be claimed that humans, without symbolism, cannot truly live. If a symbol is to retain its vitality it must be constantly re-adapted and re-interpreted within fresh contexts. Even so, the invention of and appearance of quite new symbols remains something of a mystery. A particular 'form' – verbal, visual, musical – 'catches on', stirs to action, binds together a social group. The consequences may be beneficent or destructive. It is relatively easy to give reasons for the decline and death of a particular symbolic form: it is far from easy to explain how a new or reconstituted symbol captures the imagination and inspires to action often in a quite dramatic way.

CHAPTER TWELVE

Conclusion:
The Double Paradox of Symbolism

I

More than fifty years ago Nicholas Berdyaev wrote an article entitled 'Man, the Machine and the New Heroism'.[1] It began dramatically:

> It is no exaggeration to say that the question of technique has now become that of the destiny of man and of culture in general . . . Technique is man's last love, for the sake of which he is prepared to change his very image . . . A technical epoch demands from man the making of things in great quantities with the least expenditure of power, and man becomes an instrument of production: the thing is placed above the man.

Then, contrasting the age of technique dominance with the earlier dependence of man on the earth and organic life, he declared:

> Culture was full of symbols: in shapes of earth it reflected Heaven, prefigured another world. Technique knows no symbols, it is realistic, reflects nothing, only creates new actualities; it is plainly visible in its entirety, and divorces man from nature and from other worlds.

The domination of techniques: the disappearance of symbols! This, in Berdyaev's view, summarizes the stark *contrast* of the modern situation. In his article, however, he described it rather in terms of *paradox*:

We are confronted by a fundamental paradox: without technique culture is impossible, its very growth is dependent upon technique, yet on the other hand final victory of technique, the advent of a technical age, brings on the destruction of culture. The technical and the natural-organic elements are ever present in culture, and the definite victory of the former over the latter signifies the transformation of culture into something which no more bears any likeness to it . . . A return to nature is a perennial feature in the history of culture, it expresses the fear of the destruction of culture by technique, its destruction of the integrity of human nature . . . The longing after a return to nature is but a reminiscence of the lost Paradise, a craving to return to it, though man's return to paradise is always obstructed. French theorists like to distinguish between *agir* and *faire*, which is an old scholastic distinction. *Agir* means a free play of human forces, whereas *faire* is the making of things, their fabrication. In the former case the centre of gravity lies in man himself, the maker: in the second – in the thing made.

Berdyaev's fundamental distinction is between the organic world, of which man himself is a part and in which there is the possibility of the free interplay of natural forces, and the technical world, in which man stands apart, alienated from things and using techniques to construct fabrications serving his own purposes. Yet he admits that without technique culture is impossible. If man exists simply as a part of nature, he is no different from plants and animals. If on the other hand he completely dominates nature, he destroys his unique cultural potentialities. It is by holding the extremes together by means of *symbols*, the organic and the technical, the natural and the organizational, that man creates and goes on re-creating his culture. What seems to be a final paradox becomes creative through the instrumentality of the symbol.

Berdyaev's paradox vividly illustrates the function of the symbol in preserving the connection between organic wholeness and instrumental particularities. By technique man's powers are extended; by the *vision* of organic wholeness, value and integrity are preserved. Complete surrender to nature or complete mastery of nature are equally destructive of the distinctive quality of man (at the moment the latter is by far the greater danger). It is by the construction of *symbols* that man can live and develop within what appears to be a totally paradoxical situation.

Although Berdyaev provides a striking comment on the nature and destiny of man, my contention is that by itself it is inadequate. It needs to be complemented by a second paradox concerned with the function of social *law*. I state it in this way. Without law, culture is impossible; its very survival depends upon the framing of rules. On the other hand a final victory of law, the advent of a total, inflexible system of law, results in the destruction of culture. In other words, man is for ever involved in the tension or dialectic between order and freedom. That the systems of Mosaic, Roman, Muslim law have promoted the advance of culture few would doubt. That each has tended towards a totalitarian domination of social life is equally clear. The attractiveness of a social order in which every one knows his or her place and role and responsibility is all too evident as can be seen, for example, in Russia and China today. To live by law is to be relieved of all anxious decisions. To live in freedom is to be the prey of uncertainties arising both from one's own activities and those of neighbours. It is the *symbol* which can hold law and liberty together as was evinced at the time of the Reformation, even though the term symbol was rarely used. Law and grace, justice and redemption, obedience and faith were the constantly reiterated cries, and the symbol holding them together was the Christ-figure in whom and through whom the paradox could be welcomed. To resolve it prematurely by surrendering to one side or the other was tempting but disastrous. To live by the power of the symbol was to advance towards the fullness of creative human experience.

II

I have drawn attention to two paradoxes within the development of human culture. Yet the history of mankind reveals how strong in the human heart is the yearning for *the one*, for uniformity, for a well-rounded system in which there are no threats of ambiguity or uncertainty. On the one side there is the search for a *logical* system, a unitary definition of constants, a compact scientific formula to represent the origin and subsequent evolution of the universe. On the other side the search is for a *legal* system, an unchanging constitution, a single control of all the myriad inter-relationships within the life of society. Hensley Henson once referred to the human 'lust for uniformity'. More delicately one might refer to the lure of the single vision, of the grand theory, of undifferentiated unity. Few prefixes are more sinister than *mono*. Monotony, monochrome, monopoly, monocracy: few adjectives are more inhibiting than inerrant, infallible, inflexible; few regimes are more oppressive than the one-party state or the totalitarian system. In all attempts to direct human beings to the absolute and unchangeable One, the symbol has no place.

The supreme examples of an undifferentiated unity in contemporary life are the single-function machine and the single-purpose military unit. In the first, technique allows no deviation, in the second, discipline allows no feedback. Of the former none is more representative than the *clock*. Its single function is to record the mathematical passage of time. It has proved to be of immense importance, especially in the development of Western nations. It may perhaps be called a *symbol* of man's dependence upon an agreed schedule of the measurement of time. But it is in fact a machine, subject to no deviation or variation either in its manner of working or in the interpretation of the information it provides. And the nearer any machine comes to clock-like precision, automation, and uniform interpretation the less does it possess any *symbolic* significance. This is not to deny its value. It is simply to underline Berdyaev's paradox. We are dependent on clocks. At the same time precision and automation are forces which threaten to destroy culture.

The military situation I find described with profound insight in Thomas Mann's *The Confessions of Felix Krull*. Felix manages to deceive the army medical corps:

Although martial severity, self-discipline and danger had been the conspicuous characteristics of my strange life, its primary prerequisite and basis has been freedom, a necessity completely irreconcilable with any kind of commitment to a grossly factual situation. Accordingly, if I lived *like* a soldier, it would have been a silly misapprehension to believe that I should therefore live *as* a soldier; yes, if it is permissible to describe and define intellectually an emotional treasure as noble as freedom, then it may be said that to live like a soldier but not as a soldier, figuratively, but not literally, to be allowed in short *to live symbolically* (my italics) spells true freedom.[2]

Martial likenesses have exercised a peculiar attraction (on men in particular) even in religious circles: the Salvation Army, Orange Parades, defeated miners returning to work with banners flying and brass bands playing. To live *like* a soldier can be powerfully symbolic. To live *as* a soldier, especially in the front line of battle, may be a regrettable necessity but it is the antithesis of freedom. Mann's dictim holds: 'To live symbolically spells true freedom'.

There is a more subtle way of seeking some kind of ultimate uniformity and certainty. It is expressed in such terms as the search for the core, the essence, the foundation, the basis, the substance, the facts. For example, the late Bishop John Robinson once said that he never doubted the *fundamental truth* of the Christian religion but queried its expression in symbols. Yet how can this *fundamental truth* be expressed? Any expression which is not symbolic is either an unchangeable form or an inflexible rule (corresponding to technique and law). Yet it is of the genius of Christianity to be open to new scientific discovery and to be adaptable to new social conditions, this being possible through the continuous reinterpretation of symbols. Bultmann is surely right in claiming that the world-view of people living in the first century cannot be regarded as an absolute for today. Equally he is surely wrong in imagining that we can by-pass the world-view of our contemporary situation. Similarly, no set of social rules prescribed in New Testament situations can be regarded as absolutes for all time. They must be related *symbolically* to the changed conditions of societies today.

The core, the essence, the substance, once defined, may be regarded as final. (Usually ignoring the problem of how such a definition is to be *translated* into another language and culture.) But such a past finality is of no use unless it can be related to the present, and this can only be done *symbolically*, i.e. by throwing the two together. Past events can indeed be preserved, fossilized, frozen, crystallized and as such can be treasured and admired. But their influence on the present then becomes minimal. Techniques, validated in the modern age, can and must be used to examine the authenticity of earlier reports of natural events: laws, validated in contemporary social experience, must be compared with those which governed early societies. But such enquiries cannot lead to *absolute* claims. The dialogue, the interaction must continue through openness to symbolic encounters and relationships. There are some people, a character affirms in a modern novel, who 'keep moving forward and making new trysts with life and the motion of it keeps them young. In my opinion they are the only people who are still alive. You must be constantly on your guard, Justin, against congealing'.[3]

The crystalline, the fossilized, is static, held fast by physical determinants. The congealed, the closed, is static, held fast by social experiences stored in the brain. That there are hard, physical constraints in the world cannot be denied: that there are social laws to which everyone living in a particular society must conform is equally true. But where there is life, biological or psychological, there is inter-relationship and interaction, inter-animation and interpretation. This is the world of symbolic intercourse and, returning to Thomas Mann: 'To live symbolically spells true freedom'.

III

In his book *A History of Religious Ideas* Mircea Eliade stresses what seems to me a most significant element in the whole development of symbolic forms. He writes:

In addition to agriculture, other inventions took place during the Mesolithic, the most important being the bow and the manufacture of cords, nets, hooks, and boats able to make fairly long voyages. Like the other earlier inventions (stone tools, various objects made from bones and antlers, clothes and tents made from skin, etc.) and like those that will be achieved during the Neolithic (first and foremost, pottery) all these gave rise to mythologies and paramythological fictions and sometimes became the basis for various ritual behaviours. The empirical value of these inventions is evident. What is less so is *the importance of the imaginative activity inspired by familiarity with the different modalities of matter.*

In working with a piece of flint or a primitive needle, in joining together animal hides or wooden planks, in preparing a fish hook or an arrowhead, in shaping a clay statuette, the imagination discovers unsuspected *analogies* (my italics) among the different levels of the real: tools and objects are laden with countless symbolisms, the world of work, – the microuniverse that absorbs the artisan's attention for long hours – becomes a mysterious and sacred center, rich in meaning.[4]

Symbols *connect*. Eliade affirms that artefacts have proved to be vital influences on the human imagination as it seeks to connect ordinary daily experiences with some transcendent, other-worldly, spirit-realm of existences. 'Familiarity with the different modalities of matter' inspires the human imagination to employ terms denoting familiar tools or weapons when referring to activities of divine beings. For example, in the Old Testament, Yahweh is freely spoken of as a man of war, using sword and shield and riding in a chariot. Even more strikingly, the invention of pottery (to which Eliade refers) provides appropriate imagery to describe Yahweh's dealing with his people. Where humans have settled on the land and are engaging in agricultural processes, the experiences of sowing and harvesting seem peculiarly apt when speaking of Yahweh's care of those who depend on his bounty.

Tools and weapons, Eliade claims, are laden with countless

symbolisms. But these are not the only components of the human context. What is constantly *seen* also influences the human imagination and it is fair to say that the agriculturalist is peculiarly dependent on what he *sees* – the state of the soil, the appearance of the seedlings, the manner of their growth, the depredations of weeds, the process of ripening, the quality of the harvest. He is ceaselessly on the watch. He draws upon visions stored in the memory. He projects upon the world of supernatural reality images drawn from life in the fields. Analogies so constructed appeal to all who share the same dependence on a plot of land.

On the other hand, those whose lives are surrounded by great tracts of desert or who sail the wide open sea acquire a very different set of visual images. What is seen can be utterly drab and monotonous: arid flatness or unbroken stretches of water. The chief assailants of the imagination are the wind (which can be *felt*), whose effects are obvious even though it remains unseen, and atmospheric temperature (which again can be felt). Wind and fire and their opposites, calm and biting cold, are outstanding symbols connecting human experience with divine operations. Further, as Edwyn Bevan has shown, height and depth, light and darkness provide vivid symbolic forms for all, whatever their daily occupations may be.

Over thousands of years of human existence, familiarity with a bounded environment, and with a limited range of the modalities of matter within it, remained virtually unchanged. There were indeed many surprising events which could be seen or heard and whose effects could be felt. Yet to describe them required neither an entirely new vocabulary nor completely new symbolic forms. Through extension of or combination of already existing symbolic forms, a satisfying interpretation of the universe could be developed.

All this was to be drastically changed by new inventions which not only increased human ability to manipulate the environment but also expanded the imaginative interpretation of the invisible world. The lens extended the ability to *see*; the compass and sail the ability to *travel*; the clock the ability to *plan*; the printing press the ability to *communicate*; gunpowder the ability to *kill*. In some cases, the expansion was spatial, in some cases temporal. In all cases, symbolic forms were affected. There were new symbolic interpretations both of the natural and of the social order. Man began to construct imaginative world-views on the one hand, imaginative social constitutions on the other. And these inevitably influenced attempts to give symbolic expression to the belief that the physical world owed its existence to divine creation, the cultural world (that is the system of ordered relationships between human beings) to divine government. How could the knowledge and powers gained through the new inventions be applied to the imaginative interpretations of the relationship between human apprehension and divine reality?

This, I think, has been the clamant recurring question during the past five centuries as invention after invention, experiment after experiment, observation after observation, experience after experience has changed the whole picture of the physical universe and the pattern of social organization. Basically the question has depended for its answer on what can be achieved by human initiative and sustained effort as far as the physical universe is concerned, on what can be worked out by human planning and communication so far as the cultural universe is concerned. Technique and organization seem to have achieved wonders. They can be given external and public expression by means of diagrams, statistics, codes, neologisms, mathematical formulae, charters, agreements; they can be communicated with ever increasing rapidity by telex, satellite, photography, computers. In this way a scientific and cultural world of corresponding technical and organizational *signs* is being established. Is there place any longer for a world of *symbols*, for the uncertain, the indirect, the tentative, the personal? Can symbols be created which draw upon the language and imagery of technological and organizational experiences and at the same time are not encircled and enclosed by them? Scholars have pleaded for *openness* of being, for *openness* of society, and in so doing have magnified the function of symbolic forms for the survival of the distinctively human. Yet great is the lure of technical efficiency and ordered uniformity.

Reductionism and 'nothing-more'-ism have many powerful advocates. The personal and its expression through symbols are under constant attack.

If the whole universe is simply a set of techniques and nothing more; if the history of mankind is the record of increasingly efficient social organization and nothing more; then symbolism is now a relic of the past, a means perhaps of arousing mass-emotion or revolutionary fervour but of no significance in the interpretation of ultimate reality. Logical positivism and dialectical materialism, biological determinism and scientific psycho-analysis have no place for *symbolic* forms. All seek to reduce the universe and humanity to some single operative principle and to exclude the continuing effects of personal relationships either between humans and their world or between humans and their neighbours. The eclipse of the personal involves the eclipse of the symbol. Returning to Thomas Mann: 'To live symbolically spells true freedom'.

IV

It is time to attempt to summarize my enquiry into the nature and function of *symbols*. A distinction which has constantly emerged, but which is by no means clear-cut, is that between *sign* and *symbol*. Sign in English is derived from the Latin *signum* and preserves something of its Roman flavour. Romans have been famous for their practicality, their organizational skill, their efficient handling of raw materials. Signs need to be unambiguous, definitive, corresponding as closely as possible to a particular object or event. In this context words and images are *signs*, used in the process of human communication to represent as precisely as possible elements belonging to common experience. There may be shades of variation in the way any two people experience the object or event. But these are regarded as negligible when using *signs*. The ideal is one-to-one correspondence and this ideal has become increasingly realized by means of such devices as photocopying, tape-recordings, mirror-images, and computers. The nearer we approach to that which is strictly mechanical and automatic, the closer we are to a world of *signs* in which everything is repeatable and predictable.

A major problem arises when there are two or more systems of signs. Not only are different names given to objects and events, but that which in one culture may be regarded as unchanging (and therefore capable of being named by a *sign*) may in another culture be regarded as open to variations and adaptations. Moreover, there is always the possibility of the emergence of a secret society, trying deliberately to construct a system of signs in the form of a *code*; each word or image stands for an objective reality whose existence is known to members of the secret circle but to no one else. A famous example can be found in records of the Second World War when opposing nations devised secret codes to communicate commands which the enemy could not decipher. In such a case, the sign is not the product of tradition and common experience but rather of deliberate manipulation and control. Signs may be the instrument of a correspondence common to all societies or of a limited correspondence whose secret is known only to a select few. In all such cases *signs* are being used to promote the efficient ordering of a society either for constructive or destructive purposes.

Symbol in English is derived from the Greek word *symbolon* and preserves something of the Greek flavour. Greek civilization was famous for its promotion of dialectic, dialogue and debate. The coming together of distinguishable elements need not be confusing or deleterious but could rather be creative and constructive and this in two ways. The elements may be distinguishable but may yet bear many marks of similarity; or they may seem to be in most respects dissimilar. In consequence a symbol may serve to bind together and build up into an organic whole (comparable to the way in which innumerable members constitute a single body). Or it may serve to bind together in a surprising way elements of experience which had seemed to be incompatible and even contradictory. Terms such as *coincidentia oppositorum* or *conjunctio* have become famous. A symbol of this kind is not just an isolated rarity. It initiates a new sequence in which the *conjunctio* can gain further application and create new bisociations.

Thus the symbol is essentially concerned both with steady growth in knowledge and with creative leaps of the imagination. To observe living processes, to compare elements of similarity, to construct 'chains of being' and genetic sequences representing the constant thrust towards organic wholeness; this is one part of the symbolic task. To observe the conjunction of the living person with the social environment, to portray surprising connections issuing in new relations; this is the second part of the symbolic task. This second part is less easy to describe for it is essentially innovative, surprising, seemingly opposed to accepted traditions and even destructive of that wholeness which it is the aim of the organic symbol to reproduce. To concentrate on a symbol of this kind and then to make it the mark of a separatist, power-seeking group is to turn it into a death-dealing *sign* of a fearsome kind. (The swastika and apartheid are glaring examples.) *Corruptio optimi pessima.* Yet that daring correlations of apparent dissimilars initiate new eras in human history seems to me abundantly clear.

The most powerful of all symbols is a living person. The person may be an outstanding representative of the first category of symbols that I have tried to delineate. Absorbing in a phenomenal way the accumulated scientific knowledge of the universe, of its elements and their integration into ever-expanding wholeness, such a person may observe and experiment and hypothesize and ultimately propound some new symbolic representation of the whole movement of the natural order towards a more comprehensive integration. The great figures in the progress of modern science have themselves become symbols of that openness of vision and patience of investigation which promotes the advancement of knowledge and the well-being of the social whole.

In addition, however, there have been the revolutionaries, primarily perhaps in the world of the arts but active also in the world of science. They have seen visions and dreamed dreams and expressed them in symbolic forms which have seemed to contravene all the accepted standards and structures of their time. Such forms may indeed prove to have been the product of hubris or fantasy or sheer ignorance. Yet sooner or later the 'genius' gains recognition. The person creating the symbolic form becomes the symbol of a new epoch.

What then is the function of the symbol in the task of describing the development of human history, the emergence of the distinctively human and the progress of civilization? Again there have been two aspects of this task. On the one hand there has been the search for regular patterns and recurrences which can be represented by symbolic forms derived from our knowledge of processes in the organic world: growth and decline, adaptation and resistance to change, survival and extinction. In nature these are seen as *physical* regularities, in society as *moral*. A symbolic connection is made between the ordered pattern of organic growth (observable in field and farmstead, in plants and trees, in animals and humans) and the orderly development of human societies, the disciplines, the cultivation, the feeding, the propagating, the pruning, the cleansing (in moral terms rather than physical), linked by symbolic connections. Famous attempts have been made to interpret human history by means of symbols derived from processes observed in the natural world, and these have proved to be illuminating and capable of promoting confidence. There *are* likenesses and recurrences in the social order which can be represented symbolically by making connections with processes in the natural order. Prescriptions for moral health *can* be symbolically expressed by referring to known requirements for physical health. Interpretations of human history by the use of organic symbols are impressive and often to a degree convincing.

But they are not sufficient to embrace the complexity of advancing knowledge of the particularities and surprising developments in human history or the outcomes of encounters between social groups held together by differing traditions. Symbols must be found to represent unexpected, even catastrophic happenings. No longer are myths, inspired by the experience of regularly recurring patterns in nature, adequate. Instead symbolic stories represent dramatic changes, the overthrow of one situation and the establishment of another, the turns and twists brought about by sudden and unexpected events. This symbolic connection between upheavals in nature and moral revolutions in society is powerfully represented for example in the biblical story of Jonah. A violent storm, a sea-monster, scorching heat, become the symbolic elements in a parabolic story of a social revolution. It is assumed that some dramatic change came about in the moral behaviour of the citizens of Nineveh. This was no matter of growth or adaptation or gradual enlightenment. Instead it is depicted as revolutionary, instigated by storm and tempest, by an unwilling and bruised emissary. Dissimilars abound. History, it is inferred, consists of deliverances and catastrophes, of judgment and mercy, of the coming together of apparent opposites and so of change in social direction.

Once again it is the *person* who becomes the most powerful and the most memorable symbol sometimes by words, sometimes by deeds. On the one side a person can embody and exercise naked power, based upon laws either of his own devising or selected from some inherited written code and interpreted literally. Such a framework of law, though providing a certain stability, allows no qualification or adaptation to changing conditions. On the other side, a person can embody and exercise naked opposition to reigning authority, based upon anti-laws, either of his own devising or selected from some known revolutionary system already in existence. Such a framework provides a temporary legitimation for his followers' activities but again allows for no qualifications. Records of past history and reports of contemporary political struggles reveal innumerable examples of tyrants, despots, dictators on the one side, revolutionaries, terrorists, anarchists on the other side. All seek to enforce laws of their own choosing, applied literally. They have no place for symbols. Either – Or is the absolute demand.

Such persons, however, appear and disappear, leaving behind them little except their names and the records of their destructiveness. But there are more lasting influences exercised by those who may justly be termed *symbolic* figures, those who have been prepared to qualify and modify rigid law by means of continuing dialogue, debate, question-and-answer, transformation of situations by patient symbolic interaction and discourse. Disavowing violence, either in word or action, they construct parables pointing the way to growing together or perform dramatic representations of meeting together. Thereby the leaders themselves become symbols of integration (building up parts into organic wholes) or of conciliation (forming bridges whereby apparent opposites can unite).

Each of the great religions or religious philosophers has a central symbolic figure: Moses, Muhammad, Confucius, Buddha, Socrates. Each gained followers but never dominated them to the extent of transforming them into replicas of himself. Laws, though necessary, could never be limited to single inflexible interpretations. The very existence of transcendent reality implied that no earthly symbolic form could be absolute.

The Christian religion centres upon one symbolic figure, Jesus, who lived in Nazareth, was crucified outside Jerusalem and appeared in visible form after his burial to many who had known him in the flesh. He became to them and to successive generations of disciples the symbol of God's purpose for all creation ('That in the dispensation of the fullness of times he might gather together in one all things in Christ, both which are in heaven and which are on earth, even in him: in whom also we have obtained an inheritance, being predestinated according to the purpose of him who worketh all things after the counsel of his own will,' Eph. 1.10–11) and of his reconciling activity within all human relationships ('For he is our peace, who hath made both one and hath broken down the middle wall of partition between us; having abolished in his flesh the emnity, even the law of commandments contained in ordinances; for to make in himself of twain one new man, so making peace,' Eph. 2.14–15).

Christ, God's symbol of integration; Christ, God's symbol of conciliation. The double process continues. It operates within successive human formulations of *signs* which act as frameworks or guidelines or safeguards against chaos but which become deadly if viewed as final definitions of the nature of the universe or as final prescriptions for the conduct of human life. To live symbolically, through our growing understanding of the natural order and through our imaginative interpretation of human history spells freedom. And in Paul's witness to what has come and is still coming to mankind through Christ there is perhaps no finer affirmation than that in which he declares that where the Spirit of the Lord is there is freedom. If the Christ is God's symbol, it is the Spirit who interprets the gospel of Christ to humans, and thereby inspires them to become in turn symbolic figures within the never-ceasing activity of the living God.

Notes

Chapter Two What is a Symbol?

1. R. M. MacIver, *Society*, Macmillan 1950, p. 340.
2. Edmund Leach, *Culture and Communication*, Cambridge University Press 1976.
3. A. N. Whitehead, *Symbolism*, Cambridge University Press 1928, p. 9.
4. Louis Macneice, *Varieties of Parable*, Cambridge University Press 1965, pp. 94, 97.
5. Arnold Toynbee, *A Study of History* (one-volume edition), Thames and Hudson 1976, p. 53.
6. Erwin Goodenough, *Jewish Symbols in the Graeco-Roman Period*, Vol. 4, Pantheon Press, New York 1953, pp. 28f.
7. S. T. Achen, *Symbols Around Us*, Van Nostrand Reinhold, New York 1978, pp. 8f.

Chapter Three Literal and Symbolic

1. Edwyn Bevan, *Symbolism and Belief*, Allen and Unwin 1938, pp. 252f.
2. Bevan, op. cit., p. 272.
3. *Metaphor and Symbol*, ed. L. C. Knights and Basil Cottle, Butterworth Scientific Publications 1960.
4. Kenneth Cragg, in *Christological Perspectives*, ed. Sarah Roberts and Edward Berkey, Pilgrim Press, New York 1982, p. 27.
5. C. L. Stevenson, *Ethics and Language*, AMS Press, New York 1944, p. 74.

Chapter Four Visual and Dramatic

1. Arthur Peacocke, in *Thinking about the Eucharist*, SCM Press 1972, pp. 14ff.
2. Jadwiga Swiatecka, *The Idea of the Symbol*, Cambridge University Press 1980, p. 86, quoting *Sartor Resartus* I, xi, p. 58.
3. Swiatecka, op. cit., p. 90.
4. C. H. Dodd, *The Interpretation of the Fourth Gospel*, Cambridge University Press 1953, pp. 201f.
5. F. W. Dillistone, *Christianity and Symbolism*, reissued SCM Press and Crossroad Publishing Company, New York 1985.

6. Cf. Jean Daniélou, *From Shadows to Reality*, Burns and Oates 1960, passim: baptism as covered under varying OT types.

7. Mircea Eliade, *Patterns in Comparative Religion*, Sheed and Ward 1979, p.188.

8. Hyam Maccoby, *The Sacred Executioner*, Thames and Hudson 1982.

9. Walter Burkert, *Homo Necans*, University of Califonia Press, Berkeley 1983, p. 2.

10. Cyril Bailey, *The Religion of Ancient Rome*, Constable 1921.

11. Bailey, op. cit, p. 49.

Chapter Five Spoken and Written

1. David Tracy, *The Analogical Imagination*, SCM Press and Crossroad Publishing Company, New York 1981.

2. J. Z. Young, *Doubt and Certainty in Science*, Clarendon Press 1951, p. 50.

3. David Burrell, *Analogy and Philosophical Language*, Yale University Press 1973, p. 266.

4. Grace Jantzen, *God's World: God's Body*, Darton, Longman and Todd 1984, p. 150.

5. Jantzen, op. cit., pp. ix-x.

6. Andrew Louth, *Discerning the Mystery*, Clarendon Press 1983, p. 120.

7. Seamus Heaney, *Death of a Naturalist*, Faber 1966.

8. Jacob Bronowski, *The Visionary Eye*, MIT Press, Cambridge, Mass 1978, p. 108.

9. Richard Rorty, *Philosophy and the Mirror of Nature*, Blackwell 1980, p. 359n.

Chapter Six Social Anthropologists

1. Raymond Firth, *Symbols: Public and Private*, Allen and Unwin 1973.

2. Firth, op. cit., pp. 15f.

3. Ibid., p. 26.

4. Ibid., p. 20.

5. Ibid., p. 132.

6. Ibid., p. 408.

7. Ibid., p. 428.

8. Mary Douglas, *Natural Symbols*, Penguin Books 1970.

9. Mary Douglas, *Purity and Danger*, Routledge and Kegan Paul 1966.

10. Douglas, *Natural Symbols*, p. 112.

11. Ibid., p. 72.

12. Ibid., p. 73.

13. Ibid.

14. Victor Turner, *The Ritual Process*, Routledge and Kegan Paul 1969, p. 15.

15. Quoted in *Theology Today*, January 1986, p. 402.

16. Victor Turner and Edith Turner, *Image and Pilgrimage in Christian Culture: Anthropological Perspectives*, Columbia University Press, New York 1978.

17. V. & E. Turner, op. cit., p. 245.
18. Ibid., p. 246.
19. Turner, *The Ritual Process*, p. 203.
20. *Anthropological Approaches to the Study of Religion*, ed. Michael Banton, Methuen 1968.
21. Banton (ed.), op. cit., p. 3.
22. Ibid.
23. Ibid., p. 5.
24. Ibid., p. 28.

Chapter Seven Philosophers, Theologians and Historians of Religious Forms

1. Ernst Cassirer, *An Essay on Man*, Yale University Press 1944.
2. Cassirer, op. cit., p. 22.
3. Ibid., p. 24.
4. Ibid., p. 25.
5. Ibid., p. 224.
6. Ibid., p. 62.
7. Paul Tillich, *Systematic Theology* 3, University of Chicago Press 1964, reissued SCM Press 1978, pp. 130f.
8. *Religious Experience and Truth*, ed. Sidney Hook, Oliver and Boyd, Edinburgh 1962, p. 5.
9. Paul Tillich, *Ultimate Concern*, SCM Press 1965, p. 149.
10. Hook (ed.), op. cit., p. 301.
11. Ibid., p. 302.
12. Ibid.
13. Ibid., p. 303.
14. Tillich, *Ultimate Concern*, pp. 88f.
15. Paul Ricoeur, *The Conflict of Interpretations*, Northwestern University Press, Evanston 1974, pp. 12f.
16. Paul Ricoeur, *The Symbolism of Evil*, Beacon Press, Boston 1970.
17. *The Philosophy of Karl Jaspers*, ed. P. A. Schlipp, New York 1957, p. 615.
18. Ibid.
19. Ibid., p. 622.
20. Ibid., p. 789.
21. F. W. Dillistone, *Religious Experience and Christian Faith*, SCM Press 1983.
22. Schlipp (ed.), op. cit., p. 689.
23. Ricoeur, *Symbolism of Evil*, p. 15.
24. Ibid.
25. Karl Rahner, *Theological Investigations* 4, Darton, Longman and Todd 1966, p. 235.
26. Rahner, op. cit., p. 239.
27. Rahner, op. cit., p. 251.
28. Rahner, op. cit., p. 252.
29. *A Rahner Reader*, ed. Gerald A. McCool, Seabury Press, New York and

Darton, Longman and Todd 1975, p. 278.

30. McCool, op. cit., p. 243.
31. Bernard Lonergan, *Method in Theology*, Darton, Longman and Todd 1972, p. 64.
32. *Myth, Symbol and Reality*, ed. Alan M. Olson, University of Notre Dame Press 1980, pp. 34, 37.
33. Lonergan, op. cit., 67.
34. Ibid.
35. Austin Farrer, *The Glass of Vision*, Dacre Press 1958, p. 92.
36. Farrer, op. cit., p. 42.
37. Mircea Eliade, *The Two and the One*, Harvill Press 1965, pp. 191f.
38. Mircea Eliade, *Patterns in Comparative Religion*, p. 445.
39. Eliade, *Patterns in Comparative Religion*, pp. 446f.
40. Ibid., p. 41.
41. Ibid., p. 45.
42. Ibid., p. 455.
43. *The History of Religions: Essays in Methodology*, ed. M. Eliade and J. M. Kitagawa, Chicago University Press 1959.
44. Eliade and Kitagawa, op. cit., p. 103.
45. Ibid., p. 100.
46. Ibid., p. 101.
47. Ernst Gombrich, *Symbolic Images*, Phaidon Press 1972, p. 179.
48. Gombrich, op. cit., p. 186.

Chapter Eight Symbolism and the Bible

1. G. B. Caird, *The Language and Imagery of the Bible*, Duckworth 1980.
2. Northrop Frye, *The Great Code*, Harcourt Brace Jovanovich, New York and Routledge & Kegan Paul 1982.
3. Robert Alter, *The Art of Biblical Narrative*, Allen and Unwin 1981.
4. Alter, op. cit., p. 34.
5. Ibid., pp. 156f.
6. F. W. Dillistone, *The Christian Understanding of Atonement*, Westminster Press 1968, reissued SCM Press 1984.
7. Wayne Meeks, *The First Urban Christians*, Yale University Press 1983, p. 93.
8. John Hick (ed.), *The Myth of God Incarnate*, SCM Press and Westminster Press 1977.
9. Dom Gregory Dix, *The Shape of the Liturgy*, Dacre Press 1945, p. 748.

Chapter Nine The Letter and the Spirit

1. G. Ebeling, *Luther*, Collins 1970, p. 101.
2. H. F. Dunbar, *Symbolism in Mediaeval Thought*, Yale University Press 1929, p.113.
3. Dunbar, op. cit., p. 402.
4. Ebeling, op. cit., p. 100.
5. Calvin, *Institutes* II, 11, 7–8.

6. Hans Frei, *The Eclipse of Biblical Narrative*, Yale University Press 1974, pp. 177f.

7. Coleridge, *The Statesman's Manual*, p. 30.

8. Coleridge, *Literary Remains*, Vol. 5, pp. 83f.

9. Frank Sargerson, *The Times Literary Supplement*, 12 April 1985, p. 403.

Chapter Ten Symbols and Culture

1. Simone Weil, *The Need for Roots*, Routledge 1962, p. 9.

2. Alexander Yanov, *The Origins of Autocracy. Ivan the Terrible in Russian History*, quoted in the *New York Times Review of Books*, 17 February 1983.

3. Wilfred Cantwell Smith, *Towards a World Theology*, Macmillan 1981, p. 63.

Chapter Eleven The Life and Death of Symbols

1. Erich Heller, *The Disinherited Mind*, Penguin Books 1961, p. 243.

2. Quoted by E. R. Norman in *The English Catholic Church in the Nineteenth Century*, Clarendon Press 1984, p. 151.

3. Anthony Bridge, 'The Life and Death of Symbols', *Theology*, January 1958, pp. 8f.

4. John Riches, 'Eucharistic Spirituality', *Theology*, April 1974, pp. 176f.

5. Arthur Koestler, *Insight and Outlook*, Macmillan 1949, p. 509.

6. J. W. Wilkinson, *Interpretation and Community*, Macmillan 1963, p. xix.

Chapter Twelve Conclusion: The Double Paradox of Symbolism

1. Nicholas Berdyaev, *Putj*, 1933, translated *Hibbert Journal*, October 1934, pp. 76f.

2. Thomas Mann, *The Confessions of Felix Krull*, Secker and Warburg 1955, p. 115.

3. Gail Godwin, *From the Finishing School*, quoted in *Time Magazine*, 11 February 1985.

4. Mircea Eliade, *A History of Religious Ideas*, Collins 1979, p. 1.

Index